open

open

open

editorial

JORINDE SEIJDEL

<u>AUTONOMY</u>
NEW FORMS OF FREEDOM AND
INDEPENDENCE IN ART AND CULTURE

In many Western states, not lastly
in the former subsidy paradise of
the Netherlands, huge cutbacks are
taking place in governmental budgets
for the arts and culture, in addi-
tion to equally drastic financial
measures in the public sector and
social services, in health care,
education, the environment and
developmental aid. Not only is there
a question of national economic,
social and political crises, which
here and there are coupled with a
rise of populism, but there is also
a euro crisis and a global free market crisis. What's more, a wave of
revolution is going on in the Arab
world which is bringing about new
local and global relationships. All
of this compels a drastic revision
of national and international positions and the interests of nations,
parties, institutions and citizens
in relation to one another, to
authority and also to the communal
and the shared.
That a concept like autonomy comes
into this, and that it would be put
forward in an issue of *Open* as a
topic of thought and investigation,
would seem both obvious and surprising, or even dubious: it seems inevitable that this notion would be
reconsidered and probablematized at
a time when people and things are
being thrown more upon their own
resources; but at the same time, a
number of its connotations evidently
run directly counter to the urgent
call for new forms of involvement
and participation that is resounding
everywhere – witness the rise of the
Occupy movement. In the arts, certainly, the term is often directly
related to Clement Greenberg's sterile notion of autonomy, in which the
art object must in the first place
refer to itself and its own formal
characteristics. According to
Greenberg, a work of art must try to
avoid dependence on every order of
experience that is not inherent to
the most essentially construed
nature of its medium.

This modernist art theory is
miles apart from the political
thinking of the Italian Autonomia
movement in the 1970s, which was
about the autonomy of the working
class, of immaterial labour, biopolitics, precarity, the 'multitude'
and the 'commons'; topics that tell-
ingly enough are currently in the
spotlight again. Where does the call
for engagement and performativity,
which in the arts in particular has
been frequently made over the last
few years, converge with the desire
for autonomy, broadly seen as the
urge to take the helm oneself and

have a significance that is separate from old structures? Doesn't engagement actually spring from a desire for autonomy?

Open 23 was made in collaboration with art historian and publicist Sven Lütticken, author of *Secret Publicity* (NAi Publishers, 2006) and *Idols of the Market* (Sternberg Press, 2009). This issue picks up the thread of The Autonomy Project, which Lütticken participates in and which is a collaboration between the Van Abbemuseum in Eindhoven and a number of art history and art study programmes in the Netherlands and abroad (see http://theautonomyproject.org/). From 7 to 9 October 2011, a several-day symposium took place in the Van Abbemuseum within the framework of The Autonomy Project, where the ideas of Jacques Rancière on politics and aesthetics and the intertwining of autonomy and heteronomy played an important role. During the symposium, the Occupy movement manifested itself at various places in the world; this became an important topic of debate in the Van Abbemuseum, and is also reflected in this issue.

The symposium was organized by an editorial team comprised of Jeroen Boomgaard, John Byrne, Clare Butcher, Charles Esche, Annie Fletcher, Thomas Lange, Sven Lütticken, Nikos Papastergiadis, Gabriëlle Schleijpen and Steven ten Thije, with assistance from Laurie Cluitmans and Arnisa Zeqo. Furthermore, in Eindhoven there were contributions by, among others, Peter Osborne, Gerald Raunig, Franco Berardi, Hito Steyerl, Thomas Hirschhorn and Joost de Bloois, each of whom also has a voice in *Open 23* with either a new contribution or an adapted or extended version of their lecture. Willem van Weelden interviewed Franco Berardi on Autonomia, the Occupy movement and the educational system for *Open*. Steven ten Thije investigates the underlying motivation for The Autonomy Project. The issue includes an e-mail exchange between Rancière and Hirschhorn on presence and production and new, in-depth articles by John Byrne, Andrea Fraser and Johan Hartle as well as a column on autonomy and Anonymous by the undersigned and an essay titled 'Autonomy After the Fact', on 'autonomy as praxis' in the intervals between disciplines and structures, by Sven Lütticken.

In *Open* 23, autonomy is regarded from the viewpoints of art, art history, philosophy, political theory and cultural criticism, a variety of artillery that is necessary in order to break open the concept and give it new meaning. The friction between these different discourses and disciplines and between theory and practice is precisely what allows perspectives to emerge for an 'engaged autonomy', a compound term that Charles Esche, director of the Van Abbemuseum, coined in order to escape the limitations of thinking in terms of engagement on the one hand and autonomy on the other.

Steven ten Thije

Autonomous Art as Process
Reflections on the Autonomy Project

From 7 to 9 October 2011, the Van Abbemuseum in Eindhoven held a symposium on autonomy. Steven ten Thije, one of the symposium's initiators and organizers, reports on the urgency of this project. Particularly during this period of drastic cutbacks that are being borne by a majority of the population, it is necessary to reformulate the position held by autonomous art and its associated activities in our society.

*Politics occurs when those who 'have no' time take the time
necessary to front up as inhabitants of a common space and
demonstrate that their mouths really do emit speech capable
of making pronouncements on the common which cannot be
reduced to voices signalling pain.*
— Jacques Rancière, 'Aesthetics as Politics', p. 24

The Autonomy Project took place at a turning point, in
which a roughly ten-year-period of fluorescence, characterized by internationalization and a tight interweaving of
theory and practice, was being fundamentally reconsidered.
A period of fluorescence that to a large extent was the result
of the inspired policy of the Mondriaan Foundation and of
the Foundation for Visual Arts, Design and Architecture
(Fonds BKVB). The subsequent merging of the Mondriaan
Foundation and the Fonds BKVB into the Mondriaan Fund,
the withdrawal of financing for international showpieces
like postgraduate schools, and the stopping of the subsidy
for SKOR| Foundation for Art and Public Domain – and con-
sequently for art magazines like Open – are the bitter signs
of a chapter that is coming to an end. Until the cutbacks,
it seemed as if there was social support for the activities
developed by the art sector. Now, with a one-seat majority,
it is clear that that support is no longer there – to which it
must be added that general support for the cutbacks in art
and culture is greater than the majority in the chamber that
advocates them. It confronts professionals active in the Dutch
art sector with the question of why there is so little support
for art and culture in the public domain. And following upon
that, what is the legitimization of (autonomous) art in a
democratic society? The Autonomy Project's urgency lay in
the contribution it made to answering these questions.

These questions were not explicitly posed as such
when the Autonomy Project had its informal kickoff in
March of 2010. For the group of people involved in the
project, the autonomy of art was sooner a kind of 'past
imperfect', which despite many objections kept popping
up again in the practice of making, mediating and thinking
about visual art. Autonomy had turned into a 'dumpster'
concept, an all-purpose label for the necessary, yet

frustrating, distance between the art world and society. This dumpster concept was both friend and foe. On the one hand, autonomy stood for a formalistic approach to art that stuck it in its own playing corner, where it could do nothing but harmlessly conduct an endless and often boundless discussion about 'quality'. Notwithstanding all noble intentions, 'autonomy' functioned as a shield to hide behind in this discussion. On the other hand, it was clear that socially involved art also needed a certain freedom in order to be able to exist. However delicate, art was still a domain of its own that must not be entirely absorbed by the general political discussion. Autonomy remained the shield, but for protecting something else. But what and how?

Initially, the manner in which the members of the Autonomy Project went about answering this question was fairly abstract, more of a specialist discussion between a number of professionals than a general public debate. But because we were posing it in a society which a year later so radically questioned the importance of this space, we were in a very short time forced to bring the answer back to the concrete political reality of the Netherlands in the year 2011. (To give an example of the turnabout that has taken place: The conservative-liberal party VVD, which only five years ago had published a liberal manifesto in which 1 per cent of the GNP was relegated to art and culture – back then this meant an increase of more than 40 per cent in the cultural budget – took the standpoint during the deliberations on the latest cultural budget that, in an ideal world, art doesn't need subsidizing at all!) In this tense political climate, our research on autonomy turned into an investigation into the very same question that is so painfully urgent now: What is the significance for society of an 'autonomous art', and how do we realize that significance?

Ideological Position

The symposium at the beginning of October 2011 ultimately became the place to seek an answer to the question of art's social significance. Within the context of this paper, it is useful to spend a moment on two of those contributions. The first is cultural philosopher Kees Vuyk's description of the historical development of the Dutch arts and cultural policy; the second is Rancière's analysis of the relation between art and society. In his contribution, Vuyk gave a small tour d'horizon of the development of art and cultural policy in the Netherlands since the Second World War. The crux of his argument was that Dutch cultural policy during the Cold War took an ideological position within the larger political-ideological conflict between the 'free' West and the communistic East. For the West, free, autonomous art was the perfect counterpart to the applied, social-realist art promoted by the Soviet Union. All states in the West were thus ideologically obligated to accommodate a free art. While this did not lead to a complete absence of debate on art, the approach to that debate was not the question of whether an autonomous art deserved a place in the public domain, but was mainly directed at the question of how to interpret that place. For indeed, political support for autonomous art did not stem from a debate on art itself, but was a paragraph, as it were, in the broader ideological contract to which the Western states had committed themselves. When this contract lost its validity in the 1990s, art's place in the public domain initially remained unaffected, seeing as there was neither a lot of money nor a lot of votes to be gained politically by tinkering with it, until the situation changed with the rise of an ultra rightwing political party, the PVV. What the PVV stirred up is not only an awareness that the majority of the electorate is indifferent to art and culture at this point in time, but also that all other parties now suddenly have had to rethink their motives for considering art socially important in the first place. The present situation therefore not only shows that a conservative, popular, neoliberal politics can make relatively heartless cuts in the cultural sector, but also that there is no solid political counter argument affording broad insight into why an autonomous art is a great social good.

Finding a political argument for an autonomous art is therefore of vital importance. One of those who have made a start at this is Jacques Rancière, whose work was pivotal for the entire symposium.[1] The value of Rancière's work is that he describes art not as an entity in itself, nor as a part of a more universal quest for knowledge, but as a structural component in a

1. Jacques Rancière, 'Aesthetics as Politics', in: Jacques Rancière, *Aesthetics and Its Discontents*, trans. Steven Corcoran (Cambridge: Polity Press, 2009), 19-44.

The Autonomy Project, symposium at the Van Abbemuseum, Eindhoven.
Photos by Emilio Moreno

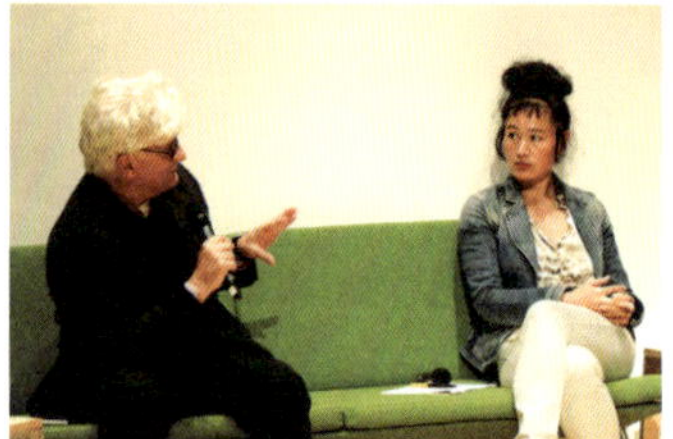

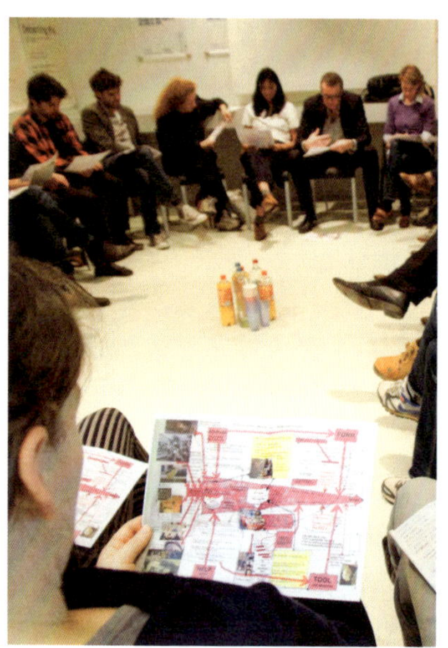

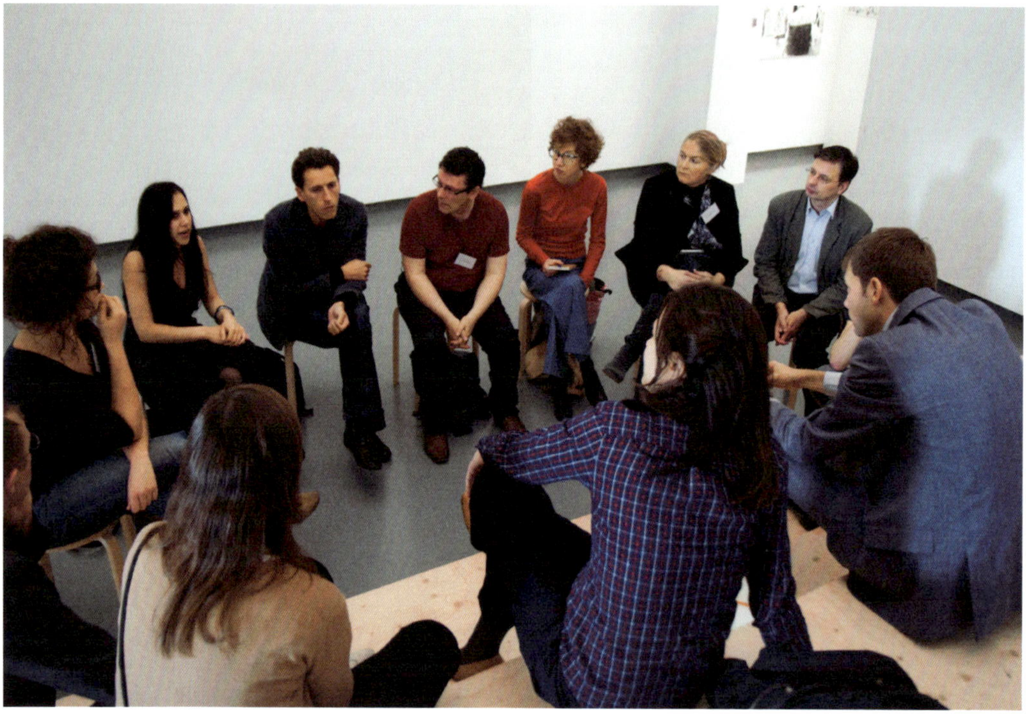

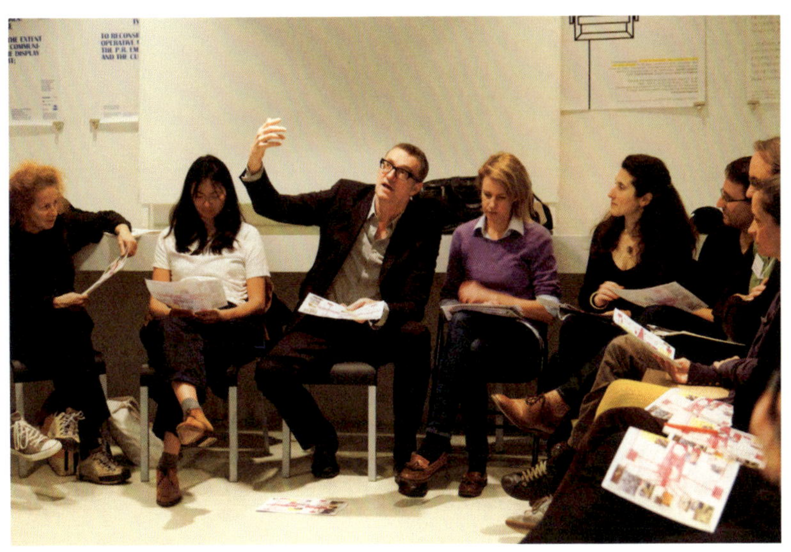

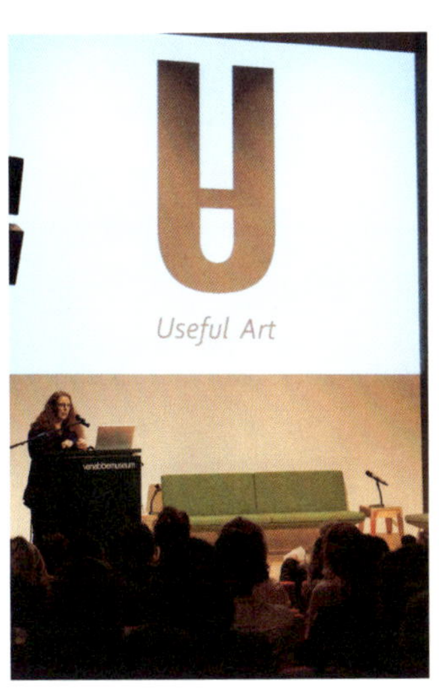
Useful Art

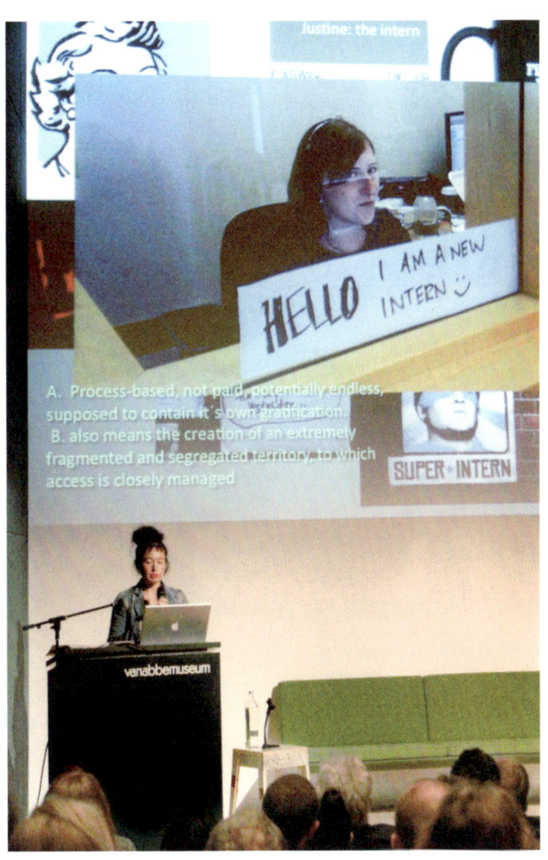
Justine: the intern
HELLO I AM A NEW INTERN :)
A. Process-based, not paid, potentially endless, supposed to contain it's own gratification.
B. also means the creation of an extremely fragmented and segregated territory to which access is closely managed
SUPER INTERN
vanabbemuseum

The Autonomy Project, symposium at the Van Abbemuseum, Eindhoven.
Photo by Emilio Moreno

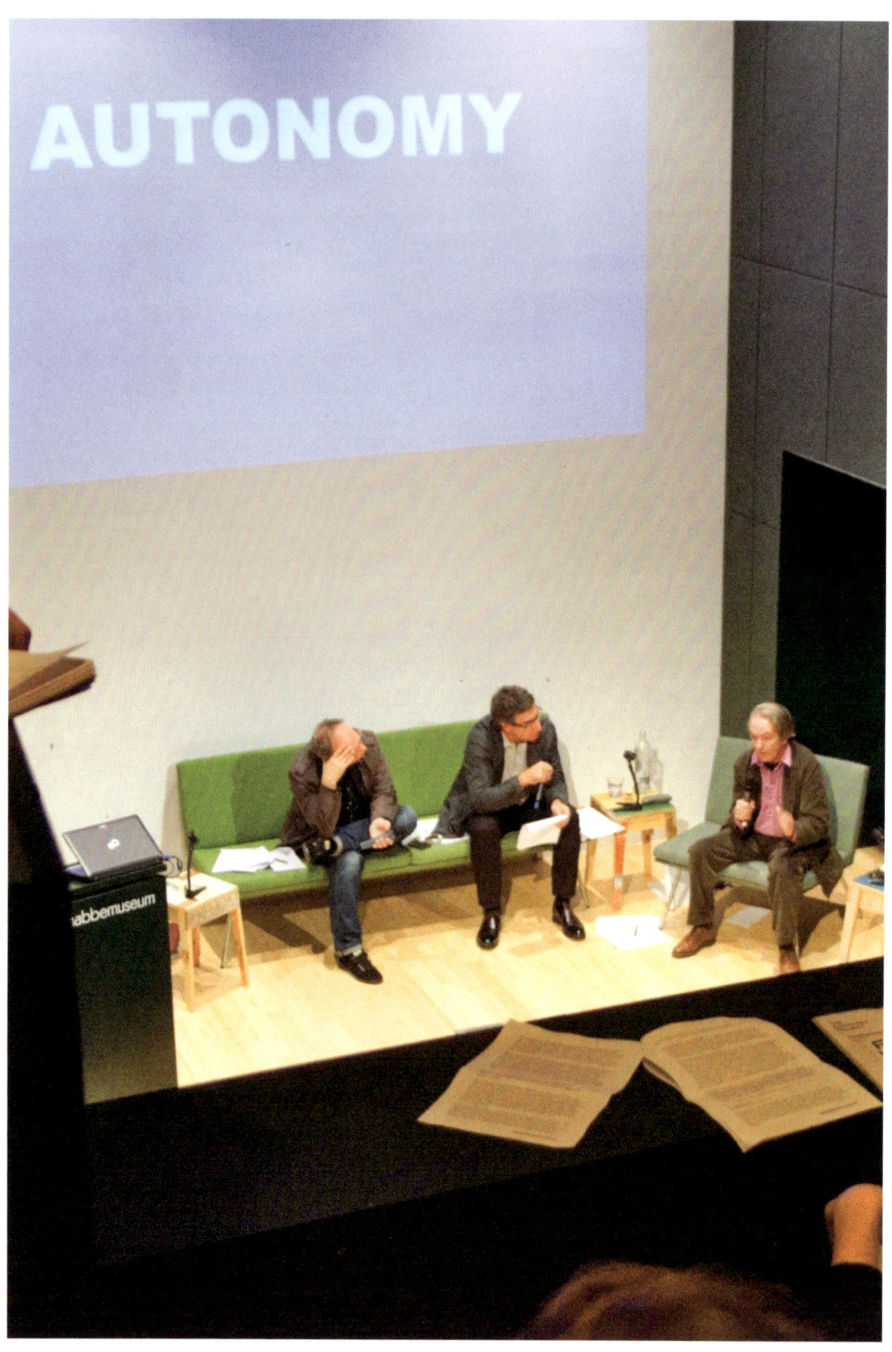

democratic political process. Rancière observes that politics does not so much consist of a struggle for power, but rather is about the struggle to be 'heard'. He gets this notion from Aristotle and his description of man as a 'political animal'. What makes man political is his gift of speech, which Aristotle describes as 'the capacity of placing the just and the unjust in common, whereas all the animal has is a voice to signal pleasure and pain'. In Rancière's definition, politics is the process in which voices that at first only seem to be a personal, 'animalistic' expression of pleasure or pain turn into an expostulation that makes a pronouncement on justness or unjustness. The misconception about politics that Rancière addresses here is that the discussion about what is good or bad does not only take place in the domain of reason. Politics is not a rational discussion about standards and values, but a process in which emotions and experiences must be translated into a sensible argument that says something about the whole.

In the political process, the private becomes public, which means that something that initially was not rational translates itself into something that is rational. And that is essentially an aesthetic process in which 'autonomy' plays a determining role. In order to explain this, Rancière turns to Schiller and his letters on the aesthetic education of mankind. In a fictitious gallery, Schiller describes a meeting with a Greek statue and remarks that the statue 'rests in itself' and therefore radiates a certain passivity. The statue expects nothing of the viewer and is indifferent, autonomous. The viewer is thus capable of reflecting on this passivity, because he or she does not have to look at the statue from a pre-defined agenda (the statue wants this or that) and gains the space to freely speculate on the meaning of the statue. It is this open space that is necessary in order to hear someone whose voice initially was not understood as being politically significant. The political aspect of autonomous art, according to Rancière, therefore does not so much lie in a work's political content, but in the space that the work creates through its passivity so that people can be open for arguments that at first were irrational and invisible. Autonomous art's creation of a space for this process makes it an indispensable component of the political process.

If we go along with Rancière, it seems as if the art sector in the past ten or 20 years sooner has moved in the opposite direction, and that theorization about the public aspect has gradually entered the almost closed and private context of the art world. Even when there is much talk about the public domain in a certain segment of the art world, the language and manner in which it is discussed maintains the gap between art and society. The severity of this reproach must be put in perspective, however, for the neoliberal 1990s produced a technocratic politics in which hardly any traces of the political process described by Rancière were left to be found. That also made the free space of autonomous art one of the last places where many people felt they could still truly speak about public aspects. Although this is very understandable, it does not take away the fact that, as Vuyk argues, this space had been maintained by an obsolete ideological construct from the Cold War that perished for good in the populist first decade of this century. The sudden (for that's what it has felt like to many people) vanishing of support for practices developed over the years has forced those who are involved, in which I include myself, to reformulate the place that autonomous art, and the activities we now associate with it, has in society. In doing so, we must critically examine whether the present method really does justice to this place.

The Autonomy Project has been a step in this direction – perhaps a small one, but purposeful. It has shown that we should not treat autonomy as a 'given' or as a self-evident privilege, but should realize that it describes a process that is necessary for our form of politics. From Rancière's analysis, it is understandable that this process consists of a combination of experience and language: politics is literally the translation of the private into the public. And the fact that the discussion on art and society is characterized by a certain degree of abstraction and specialism is also not insurmountable. The material is often complex, and there must be space in order to investigate this complexity in all of its subtleties; the free speculating done by the visitor in Schiller's gallery does not come about just like that, but requires effort and dedication. This doesn't take away the fact that the search for subtlety and complexity must not become set in a methodical shutting out of the rest of the world. There must be places where the translation to society at large is the central focus and where non-professionals can learn from the discussions in art or can participate in them in a constructive and meaningful manner. If the existing system has to be consigned to the rubbish heap, let's try to set up the new system in such a way that political parties can clearly see how the social significance of an autonomous art finds its way back into society by investing more in the areas where the translation can take place. In order to do that, the art sector will not only have to look critically at society, but also at itself – which will not be easy, but if it does this, it might emerge from the storm stronger than before.

John Byrne

Use Value and the Contemporary Work of Art

Freeing Art from the Present Technocratic Framework

According to John Byrne, works at the School of Art and Design in Liverpool, autonomy in art is by no means a given any more, but a socially constructed and produced possibility that constantly must be fought for. Using Marx's distinctions between 'work' and 'labour', and 'use value' and 'exchange value', he investigates the role and significance that art could have in the 'smooth, mirror-like surface of global capital'.

Since the world was gripped by the banking crisis of 2007, the internal logic that underpinned the globalized neoliberal economy has continued to implode under the weight of its own contradiction. The inability of a deregulated multinational economy to look after itself is plain for all to see – as is the lie that economic deregulation would guarantee a fairer distribution of wealth. Yet no viable alternative to this system has been allowed to emerge – the rich get richer, the debt gets bigger, the middle classes continue to lose their influence and the poor foot the bill. In November 2011, new 'technocratic' governments were imposed on Greece and Italy by a European Union in financial crisis. The hope seems to be that 'sensible' and 'apolitical' solutions can be found before the collapse of the single European currency finally pushes the global economy over the brink of the abyss. All of this drama has, of course, caused a series of systemic shifts and ruptures within the once comfortable world of contemporary art. Furthermore, these shifts and ruptures have not simply been caused by the substantial withdrawal of public funding over recent years in countries such as the UK and the Netherlands. As the Dutch situation shows, there is a change in the public's conception of contemporary art. What was once generally accepted as a necessary and functioning component of a progressive and self-reflexive society is now treated with distrust and disdain.

Furthermore, within a newly emerging form of populist politics, parties of both left and right have shown a willingness to use the suspicion now surrounding contemporary art as a tool for political gain.[1]

At the crux of these debates remains the complex issue of art's alleged autonomy. While the European tradition of art's self-referential and self-contained aesthetic autonomy has long since been debunked as an ideological fantasy, its legacy still haunts the production, distribution and consumption of contemporary art. Perhaps more importantly, art's alleged autonomy is now often confused with more general uses of the term to describe a type of economic freedom, or more accurately agency, which is held to be the ideological cornerstone of globalized neoliberal economics. An example of this can be found in the 'Big Society' election pledge that the current UK Prime Minister David Cameron made in 2010. The idea of the Big Society was to give further autonomy to citizens in the governance of their own lives – by encouraging the breakdown of government offices and councils into independent small businesses and by allowing communities to establish their own 'self-

1. This shift in opinion has been recently illustrated by the difficulties engulfing the Van Abbemuseum. In October 2011 the local Social Democratic Party in Eindhoven effectively put the Director of the Van Abbemuseum, Charles Esche, on trial. The charge was that hospitality, progressive thinking, commissioning new works, the production of engaging contemporary art shows and, finally, a dialogical and inclusive curatorial process were both un-Dutch and unprofitable.

help' charities. In reality, such rhetoric provides little more than a gloss over new forms of centralized capital deregulation which continue to erode the power and rights of under-represented and vulnerable individuals. And yet the proximity of such rhetoric to the emancipatory dreams of the historical avant-gardes is striking; it is this proximity of language, between the utopianism of avant-garde rhetoric and the systematic instrumentalization of neoliberal discourse, that is the key problem that we must all now confront. Artists, critics, theorists, curators, gallerists and museologists alike are faced with the task of pinpointing 'just what it is that makes art special' in a world where contemporary art has long since become indistinguishable from all other forms of popular culture and mass media.

However, due to the legacy of the high art/low life divide, by which art in the bourgeois epoch was defined by its alleged superiority to kitsch, many critical, curatorial and evaluative methodologies still depend upon the a priori assumption that art somehow occupies a different kind of critical space. Artists, we are still too often told, just see things differently from the rest of us. While this lingering anachronism may still sell blockbuster shows and coffee-table biographies, its danger is twofold. On the one hand it denies the critical proximity and interdependence of contemporary art practice to the production of meaning within society. On the other, it also propagates and popularizes another key habitual assumption – that art's autonomy is something of a given. When these two key assumptions begin to get mixed up in the call for art's autonomy to be financially protected by the state, the neoliberal response is clear – what better way is there to prove art's autonomy than by its financial survival within the cut and thrust of the open market? However, the current situation facing the production and distribution of meaningful contemporary art is much more complex than this. Art's autonomy is not simply a given, it is a condition that has to be continually fought over and struggled for in an era of globalized neoliberalism – and this struggle is the precondition for the production of contemporary art if its meaning is still to have any political consequence.

Complicity

Contemporary art, if it is to be of any use at all, has to do more than simply contribute financially to the emergent tourism and leisure industries – it has to help us identify the cracks, fissures and ambiguities within the rhetoric of similarity and certitude that are currently provided for us by transnational capital in decline. The use value of contemporary art in this sense would seem to remain at least partially utilitarian; in the best traditions of the late nineteenth- and early twentieth-century avant-gardes we need art and artists to help us re-think ourselves in a moment of crisis. The problem with this, of course, is that neither art, nor the self-proclaimed job of the artist, is anything special any more. Ever since Warhol replaced the self-referentiality of the painterly surface with the self-referential celebration of his own image, the job of art changed. If art's 'artness' had previously resided in a functionless preoccupation with its own separate and remote world, it is now firmly situated within the functional operations of commercial culture. Warhol's work in film and early video, the grooming of his superstars, his work with the Velvet Undergound and the Exploding Plastic Inevitable, the founding of Interview magazine, his MTV series and, perhaps most of all, his constant longing for the glitz and glamour of Hollywood, provide a Rosetta Stone for analysing the shifting role of art within an all-encompassing society of image. In the age of self-image and self-aestheticization, a world in which the continual manicure of appearance has become interchangeable with the search for self-identity, the qualitative evaluation of art has become interchangeable with the quantitative evaluation of popularity, celebrity, visitor figures and auction-house sales.

This new proximity of art to everyday life, once the messianic dream of the historical avant-gardes, has made it increasingly difficult for artists and art institutions alike to distinguish their output from more instrumentalized forms of corporate entertainment, advertising and leisure service. To make matters more complicated, the working methods of artists are now shared and understood by the majority of people who go to look at art in galleries or assist artists in the production of their work. The issue is not that art has become a philosophical question, as Danto argued, simply because it is impossible to tell art apart from other everyday objects on a purely visual basis.[2] Nor is it, as Claire Bishop has argued, that a division is opening up between the ethical and aesthetic role and function of art in our society – where ethics, seen as little more than the artists imperative to do good, is pitted against an aesthetic that offers imaginary asylum for political dissent.[3] Instead, the problem for contemporary art is that artists have become implicated within and complicit with the very regimes of capitalization they try to resist – like everybody else. Art now shares the very procedures that neoliberal economies have deployed to produce the false freedoms of the creative economies. As the artist Liam

2. Arthur C. Danto's famous adage 'Art After the End of Art' refers not to the end of art as such, but to a Hegelian notion that art has entered a new phase in which it has become a philosophical question. See for Example Arthur C. Danto, Art After the End of Art: Contemporary Art and the Pale of History (Princeton: Princeton University Press, 1996).

3. See Claire Bishop's article 'The Social Turn: Collaboration and Its Discontents', Artforum, February 2006, 179-185.

Gillick has put it: 'The accusation . . . is that artists are at best the ultimate freelance knowledge workers and at worst barely capable of distinguishing themselves from the consuming desire to work at all times, neurotic people who deploy a series of practices that coincide quite neatly with the requirements of neoliberal, predatory, continually mutating capitalism of the every moment. Artists are people who behave, communicate and innovate in the same manner as those who spend their days trying to capitalize every moment and exchange of daily life. They offer no alternative to this.'[4]

4. Liam Gillick, 'The Good of Work', e-flux Journal 16, 05 2010, www.e-flux.com/journal/view/142.

Use Value and Exchange Value

This proximity of contemporary artistic work to the labour patterns of audiences for art has quite explicit consequences for any possible theorizations of artistic autonomy. At the most basic level, the action of deciding to become an artist doesn't make that much of a difference now in terms of how one might live out a lifestyle or construct a livelihood. The idea of the free, self-determining Bohemian – most succinctly characterized by the image of the artist with a folding easel strapped to his back who is greeting a collector in Bonjour, Monsieur Courbet – has long since given way to the image of the artist attached to her laptop, mobile phone in hand, inquiring about a recent residency or funding application while waiting for the latest video edit to render. On a more sophisticated level, the post-structuralist shift away from a relatively fixed Enlightenment concept of the historical subject in the 1960s and 1970s, and its subsequent conceptual replacement by more fluid theories of a social body contingent upon process, has long since allowed for a radical re-think of the possible terms and conditions of autonomy within capitalist culture. According to Franco Berardi, autonomy can now be seen as 'the self-regulation of the social body in its independence and in its interaction with the disciplinary norm'.[5] However, the corollary to this less idiosyncratic and personalized notion of autonomy in the social sphere has been the concomitant processes of industrialized deregulation that has spread across the globe since the Regan/Thatcher era.

5. Franco Berardi, 'What is the Meaning of Autonomy Today', http://eipcp.net/transversal/1203/bifo/en.

For Berardi, the historical demand of workers for freedom from industrial constraints has been answered by the 'flexibilisation and the fractalisation of labour'.[6] This has taken the shape of the freeing up of enterprise from the juridical role of the state, cutbacks in social spending, the dismantling of social protections, detaxation, industrial downsizing and the outsourcing of production. The

6. All other quotations in this paragraph: ibid.

result of this process, Berardi argues, has been a growth in recombinant labour (flexible forms of labour that are no longer closely connected to particular industrial processes and can be easily moved from one place to the other) and the 'fragmentation of time-activity'. The labourer has become an 'interchangeable producer of micro-fragments', and for Berardi, it is now the cell phone that 'is the tool that best defines the relationship between the fractal worker and recombinant capital'. In this scenario the self-organization of cognitive labour seems to offer the only plausible form of resistance in a world in which the utopia of Enlightenment reason has failed. It is 'the dissemination of self-organized knowledge', Berardi argues, that 'can create a social framework containing infinite autonomous and self-reliant worlds'.

The dominance of neoliberal capitalism over the last decades has eroded our sense of community though the continual promotion of competition and individual needs, but the recent mobilization of resistance against power (from the protests of the Arab Spring, the anti-capital occupations of financial zones such as Wall Street, and even the inchoate and 'politically incorrect' commodity riots in the UK) all point towards the re-emergence of a social body that has been lost. In the light of this, the job of artists or poets for Berardi is to free words, language and concepts from their daily form, to release their meaning from an increasingly instrumentalized, technocratic and abstract chain of conformity – a chain of conformity that has torn language away from its roots in the social production of identity – and to re-imagine a place 'where we can again be lovers'.7

7. I refer here to Berardi's contribution to the Autonomy Symposium, 9 October 2011.

To posit the work or job of the artist or poet firmly within the reconstruction and reconstitution of a living common socius in this way – and to pit this against the reduction and abstraction of language into a technocratic framework for the propagation of commodified individuals – is a manoeuvre that traces its roots back to the separation that Marx attempted to make in Das Kapital between use value and commodity or exchange value. As Fredric Jameson has recently reminded us, Marx was keen to bracket use value off from exchange value in any consideration of the commodity form. Marx argued that use value did not matter one jot to the capitalist who wished to sell commodities – that the capitalist would only ever consider use value in so far as it could assist the profitable sale of units. This argument belied a more fundamental and metaphysical distinction, which underpinned much of Marx's thought, between Quality and Quantity on one hand and Body and Mind (or Soul) on the other. As James points out, Marx tended to equate Quality with the

Body and physicality – as a positive term in the materialist sense – and Quantity with the vagaries of the Mind or Soul – in a negative and idealist sense. For Jameson: 'Use value is therefore quality; it is the life of the body, of existential or phenomenological experience, of the consumption of physical products, but also the very texture of physical work and physical time . . . Quality is human time itself, whether in labor or in the life outside of labor; and it is this deep existential constant that justifies that Utopian strain in Marxism which anticipates the transformation of work into aesthetic activity (from Ruskin to Morris, from Marcuse to Paulo Virno's notion of virtuosity), a tradition somewhat different from the Hegelian delight in activity and the more orthodox celebration of work or productivity as a central human drive.'[8]

8. Frederic Jameson, Representing Capital: A Reading of Volume One (London/New York: Verso, 2011), 19-20.

In this sense, it is also interesting to remember that this distinction frequently underpinned Marx's use of the term work – as the form of labour that creates use value and therefore quality – and his use of the term labour – as an indication of a commodifiable capacity that can be bought by the capitalist and used to produce exchange value and quantity. In this sense, the use value of art is intimately linked with the kind of work that the work of art has now become; it is the work of Berardi's poets, the work of those who try to rescue the vagaries and uncertainties of socially produced meaning from the rigid frameworks of consensus and conformity, the struggle to exploit and make sense of minute cracks and fissures that currently seem to be opening up in the smooth, mirror-like surface of global capital.

The Constant Search for Meaningful Art

But what kind of role can art really play in the reconstitution of a socially autonomous body? How can artists, curators, critics and intellectuals usefully contribute to the development of a constantly shifting network of micro self-reliance and resistance? How can we even begin to consider opening up the cracks and fissures that are emerging in the surface of globalized neoliberal capital? And what, if any, are the meaningful strategies for releasing the vagaries of language from the straightjacket of capital? Perhaps one way to begin thinking these questions though was recently offered by Tania Bruguera when, in January 2011, she initiated the 'Useful Art Association'. For Bruguera, the production of Useful Art is an activity that attempts to confront the hierarchies that have developed between different kinds of audiences. This activity also necessitates an exploration of the divisions that have opened up between the languages of art and the historical avant-garde on one hand, and the more immanent languages of politics, science and other disciplines on the other. As such, Bruguera tends to associate Useful Art with projects that are capable of generating and sustaining a range of critical relationships over an extended period of time. For Bruguera 'Useful Art aims to transform some aspects of society through the implementation of art, transcending symbolic representation or metaphor and proposing with their activity some solutions for deficits in reality'.9 An example of this approach can be found in Bruguera's own project The Immigrant Movement International, which is a one-year-long artist initiated social movement. The project consists of operating 'a flexible community space in the multinational and transnational neighborhood of Corona, Queens'.10 Bruguera is working alongside residents, activits, policymakers, politicians, artists and international communities to tackle issues around the representation of immigrants in our society and culture. In this way, The Immigrant Workers International uses art to re-address the social production and discourses of identification that tell us who is or what it means to be an immigrant, and what it may mean to be a citizen of the world.

If artistic autonomy is no longer a given but rather a socially constructed and produced possibility, then it is something that has to be continually struggled over and worked for. This struggle, this work to open up spaces of critical autonomy within the instrumentalizing constraints of a neoliberal economy, then becomes both the kind of work that is now the work of art and also the use value of that work. Admittedly, it is still quite difficult to think of use value and work as being part of the project of contemporary art, let alone its central tenet or a means by which to identify and evaluate its potential or worth. After all, isn't the most obvious way to defeat the commodification of art to make a supremely useless work? However, what I propose here is precisely a rethinking of utility that abandons entrenched oppositions between utility and non-utility as if they were simply antinomies, relegating use value to applied art whereas art's 'artness' is made to depend upon the condition of its non-utility.

One project that is relevant here is Grizedale Art's ongoing attempt to re-imagine and reclaim the nineteenth-century English radical John Ruskin. Over the last decade, Grizedale Arts have sustained and developed a highly unique and cutting-edge commissioning programme by simply asking artists what kinds of things they would do if they decided to make themselves useful. Here, the emphasis is no longer on the production of tangible art objects but rather on the production of ideas, solutions and new knowledge.11 While Ruskin is

9. http://www.taniabruguera.com/cms/486-0-Immigrant+Movement+International.htm.

10. Ibid.

11. www.grizedalearts.org.

usually seen as a conservative figure, and commonly held to be emblematic of all things Victorian and backward-looking, Grizedale is keen to resuscitate his role as an activist in early workers' education movements or 'Mechanics Institutes' as they were called (where art played an integral and integrated role in a rounded and multidisciplinary approach to learning and improvement). In this way, through an active and imaginative recycling of a previously fixed history, Grizedale Arts is attempting to release the use value that resides in the anachronistic social radicalism of John Ruskin's work – as opposed to the contemporary exchange value of his work which results, more often than not, from the continual revalidation of his more conservative opinions.

To ask the question 'what kind of work is the work of art?' is an attempt to identify how artists, critics, curators, writers, radicals, etcetera are attempting to open up spaces of critical autonomy, however short lived these may be, within the current confines of a globalized neoliberal economy. It is an attempt, therefore, to reopen a territory within which the complex relationships between arts' ethical and aesthetic functions can be understood as complex forms of interaction and, as such, analysed more clearly within the age of the global image. It is, perhaps, the only way we can now imagine any future for a meaningful art.

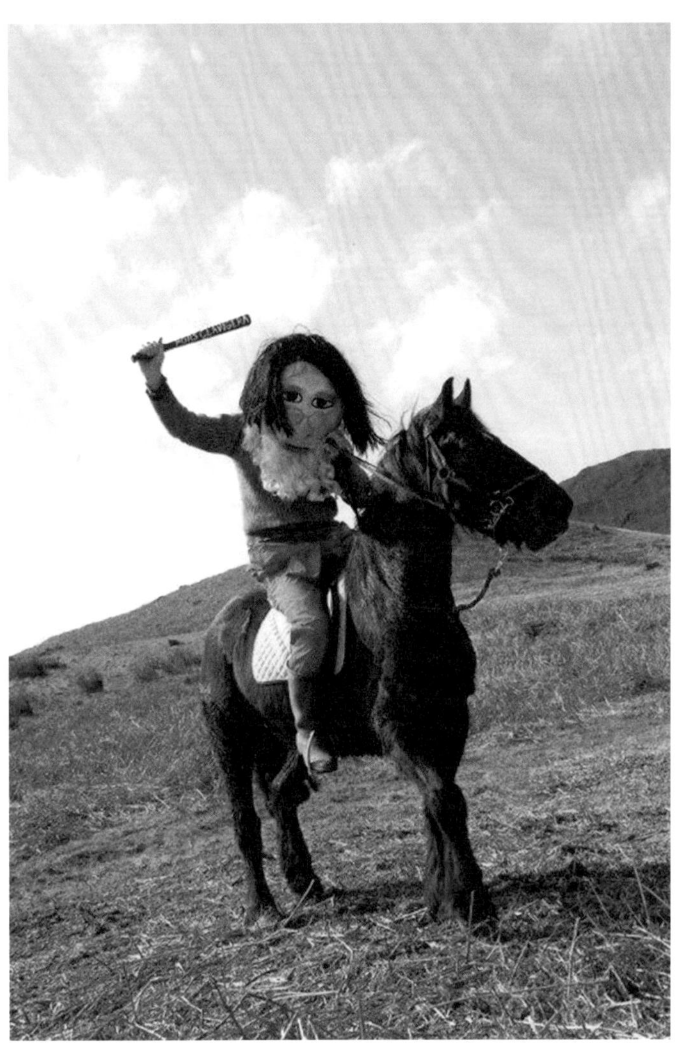

Johan Hartle

Rightist Hobbies and the End of Art

According to philosopher and cultural theorist Johan Hartle, the rightwing populist criticism of art is anything but democratically inspired. The democratic legitimacy of art is in fact destroyed by the present 'culturalist paradigm', which is dominated by a romantic, nostalgic longing for the restoration of cultural unity. Instead of a 'leftist hobby', this attempt at restoration is actually the ultimate 'rightist hobby', which is blind to the diversity and contradictions so characteristic of the modern age.

1. Leftist Hobby. Wilders as Art Philosopher

Wilders expressed it clearly: The institutionalized and subsidized Dutch culture is, in his by now winged words, a 'leftist hobby', a cultural curiosity of a social elite. As a tolerated partner in the present Dutch government coalition, the rightwing populist politician Wilders is a mirror and an allegory of the Rutte cabinet. His utterances often make the implicit claims that underlie government policy explicit, which is true here as well.

By suggesting that public institutions have been appropriated by private ('leftist') interests, Wilders poses a seemingly democratic question about the legitimacy of public institutions. In doing so, he also alludes to the universalistic tradition of the modern Western concept of art, and even the tradition of avant-garde and institutionally critical art – rather surprising for a rightwing populist politician!

In order to understand the universalistic claim of the Western concept of art, it can be helpful to look at the development of Kant's philosophical aesthetics. As late as the year 1787 (thus three years before the publication of his seminal work on aesthetics, the *Critique of Judgment* (Kritik der Urteilskraft), Kant maintained that it was impossible to establish a philosophical justification for the judging of taste.[1] Since aesthetic preferences always depend on physical and cultural conditions, and thus are conditional and not universal, empirical and not transcendental, Kant had not planned to investigate aesthetics. In the *Critique of Judgment*, the construction of potential universal aesthetic judgments remained dependent on the construction of an ideal community: the *sensus communis*. Through the *sensus communis*, Kant could allude to a universal sense of aesthetics that differs from all merely empirical cultural contexts.

This construction was necessary as a regulatory and normative framework, but it has always remained shaky. Nonetheless, thinkers from Hegel to Bourdieu have fallen back on this universalistic norm in order to criticize the reduction of art to specific cultural contexts. Philosophical reflection on the present economizing should consider this tradition and make it clear that in the seemingly democratic sheep's clothing of the criticism of the elitist art system there is a 'culturalist' and anti-democratic wolf.

2. The End of Art. Hegel as a Critic of Conservative Cultural Policy

The title of this essay refers directly back to the often misunderstood theme in Hegel's series of lectures on the philosophy of art, *Über die Philosophie der Kunst*.[2] Few philosophers have

---

1. Immanuel Kant, *Kritik der reinen Vernunft* (Hamburg: Meiner, 1990), A22/B25 ff.

2. Georg Wilhelm Friedrich Hegel, *Philosophie der Kunst. Vorlesung von 1826* (Frankfurt/M: Suhrkamp, 2004), 54 ff.

emphasized (and problematized) art's universalistic claims so extensively as did Hegel. According to him, the greatest potential of art (the ideal) was realized in the society of the ancient Greeks. At that time it was possible to worship the beauty of art directly. This claim had a social-theoretical background: the 'highest potential' of art, as realized in antiquity, had explicitly practical dimensions.

In a more or less homogenous society such as the Greek *pólis*, in which religious and cultural practices are not differentiated, art represents a general, connected way of life. The Greek city state and its culture (religion, art) were a happy compromise between the 'Oriental despotism' of previous societies on the one hand, in which the subject was completely subordinate to the state, and 'modern' subjectivism on the other. Whereas the 'internalized' modern subject often comes in conflict with the hostile outside world, the individual in the *pólis*, according to Hegel, was able to integrate his or her subjective freedom within objective social and political structures. Classical art is the manifestation of this. Thus the ancient temple was not only an architectural form; it organized a way of life and expressed that directly in a material manifestation. This is the ideal of art that Hegel recognizes in ancient (Greek) art.[3]

3. See Georg Wilhelm Friedrich Hegel, *Vorlesungen über die Ästhetik II*, (Frankfurt/M: Suhrkamp, 1986), 25 ff, and Hegel, *Philosophie der Kunst*, op. cit. (note 2), 146, 150. My

Hegel's famous claim that art's highest potential could only be realized in the past, and that therefore art *in that sense* was past history, has to do with this interpretation of ancient cultural life. In modern society, because a diversity of ways of life exist side by side, the absolute idea of art cannot be manifested by specific material works of art. Only at the level of the concept's contradictory movements (through intellectual debates and abstraction) can the universal still be represented; art strives to become philosophy, without ever being able to reach that goal.[4] Beauty loses to reflection. Its highest potential comes to an end.[5]

interpretation is strongly inspired by Annemarie Gethmann-Siefert. See for example: Annemarie Gethmann-Siefert: *Einführung in Hegels Ästhetik*, (Munich: W. Fink, 2005), 30, 47, 50 and 97.

4. The idea that modern art had actually become philosophy (of art) was the pseudo-Hegelian narrative that brought Arthur C. Danto media acclaim in the 1980s and 1990s.

5. Also see Gethmann-Siefert, *Einführung in Hegels Ästhetik*, op. cit. (note 3), 107 ff, 131 ff. For Hegel's criticism of Schelling, see 152.

According to Hegel, this development is unavoidable. And from this perspective, a nostalgic return to a mythical unity of the people, such as remained important in the conservative tradition of German mythology from Schelling to Heidegger, is just as dangerous as it is naive; for post-ancient, Christian, 'romantic' art can never offer a stable accommodation for a *Geist* that has outgrown art. Yet, precisely such a romantic-nostalgic project – in other words, the attempt to revive cultural unity or to artificially re-establish it – is the central element of conservative cultural policy. Conservative political projects, from Thatcher to Rutte, are structurally tied to this.[6] They cannot tolerate social diversity. They are the cultural-political manifestations of what I call the 'culturalist paradigm' in art.

6. For Thatcher's cultural policy, see: Stuart Hall, 'The Emergence of Cultural Studies and the Crisis of the Humanities', *October*, vol. 53 (summer, 1990), 11-23.

3. *Habitus*, Art and Social Elite

Pierre Bourdieu's empirical investigation into the social definition of cultural preferences also touches upon the question of what relation exists between art's claims to universalism and its specific cultural contexts. Bourdieu ascertained that even avant-garde art is favoured by more or less homogenous social groups, and in fact particularly so. Art that seemingly is no longer socially representative also remains indirectly connected with certain social milieus, according to him. He describes the capacity to enjoy the pure form of contemporary art as the privilege of a highly educated (sometimes apparently leftist) citizenry – a capacity that is related to financial and symbolic privileges. Thus, Wilder's 'leftist hobbies' is not so far off at all.

According to Bourdieu, art can be described as an expression of a specific *habitus*. 'Habitus' simultaneously refers to what one possesses (*habitus* as the participle of the Latin *habere*) and what one has internalized (habits and physical practices). The habitus is the result of a differentiated socialization process; during this process, the conditions are created for the 'proper' way of perceiving art, such as progressive art demands. The creation of an institutional framework and the relative autonomy of this art are, says Bourdieu, the result of a historical struggle. Autonomy becomes possible through intra-aesthetic debates in which dependence on external power structures is temporarily driven back. The relative autonomy of art is thus possible because there is a tension between its own claims and its reduction to ideology and the influence of social elites. Autonomy then only exists when the logic of producing art can be defended against the inclination to be dependent on economic forces and on the cultural narcissism of social elites. Bourdieu understands artistic freedom as a merely gradual distance from the field of power. At the same time, this autonomy is merely *relative* because art production always necessarily remains dependent on economic structures: without money, institutions and artists cannot work.

The seemingly innocent world of art is thus always susceptible to private social appropriation. It is always in danger of falling back into the 'culturalist paradigm' – not only with rightwing populists, but also and particularly among circles of 'enlightened' art lovers. Bourdieu has sought for theoretically-based answers in order to defend art's claims of universalism, and within that framework has also collaborated with progressive artists such as Hans Haacke and Andrea Fraser. Both have analysed in their work how patriarchal power structures and elitist appropriation influence the aesthetic field.[7] It is through such criticism of forms of private appropriation that the universal potential of art can temporarily and partially be realized.

7. Pierre Bourdieu, 'Foreword: Revolution and Revelation', in: *Museum Highlights: The Writings of Andrea Fraser* (Cambridge, MA: MIT Press, 2007), xiv-xv; Pierre Bourdieu and Hans Haacke, *Free Exchange* (Cambridge: Polity Press, 2005).

4. Art as 'Rightist Hobby' and the Defence of Aesthetic Universalism

As is apparent from the above, the 'culturalist paradigm' exists in at least two forms: art can be understood as an expression of a specific national culture or as the de facto property of a specific social milieu. Both of these forms of 'culturalizing' art are not 'leftist, but 'rightist'. They are based on exclusive constructions of cultural identity and the symbolic reinforcement of social inequality. Both aspects of *art as a rightist hobby* have clearly crystallized in the present Dutch art debate, and the cutbacks will only establish them all the more strongly.

Self-criticism has – luckily – had a long tradition in the history of art. To this end, the critical sociology of art and artistic practice have forged various alliances. In the history of progressive art, there have been a number of reasons to critically consider the institutional conditions under which art operates. The defence of art's public and universal content was undoubtedly one of the central motivations in this regard. It is only against this background that, for example, Hans Haacke's statistical surveys on the social makeup of visitors to museums or the Guerrilla Girls' posters on the lack of female artists in public collections can be understood. On the basis of its own autonomy and its own claims to universalism, art became potentially critical – particularly when it came to the exclusive and culturalist appropriation of art itself.

It goes without saying that this art is not so easy to consume as the populist criticism of elitist art would like it to be. As Bourdieu puts it: 'The modal readability of a work of art (for a given society in a given period) varies according to the divergence between the code which the work under consideration objectively requires and the code as an historically constituted institution.'[8] In other words, art itself also requires a particular institutional level. There is a

8. Pierre Bourdieu, 'Outlines of a Sociological Theory of Art Perception', in: Randal Johnson (ed.), *The Field of Cultural Production: Essays on Art and Literature* (London: Polity Press, 1993), 224.

connection between institutional codes and the intellectual standard of art. Owing to the objective standard of reflective art, which is established through historical discourse and preserved there, social criticism is also manifested in progressive art institutes.

It is ironic, but not surprising, that those art institutions which recognize that art can be a hobby of social elites, and which problematize this in their projects, are precisely those that are seen as awkward for the rightwing populist agenda. With the cutbacks, organizations that participate in debates criticizing the roles of institutions and society as a whole in today's art discourse accordingly have been taking some hard knocks. Where theoretical reflection on art (and the institutional requirements for its adequate reception) is willingly damaged, art's metamorphosis into a 'rightist hobby' will be the result.

Universalism is not a corporatist compromise, and certainly not the general opinion of the majority. The democratic legitimacy of art is not restored by the 'culturalist paradigm', but destroyed. With the government's economizing, institutional conditions are being eliminated, without which the criticism of art's elitism can hardly still take place. That is why opposition to the cutbacks cannot simply defend the remains of the status quo. Rather, it must go on the offensive and raise the question of the exclusive structure of the art world, without falling below the formal and discursive level of contemporary art practice.

Willem van Weelden

Erotic Uprising, or the Schooling of the Body

An Interview with Franco Berardi

Someone not to be overlooked in a publication on autonomy is
Franco 'Bifo' Berardi, the *éminence grise* of the Italian Autonomia
movement, which reached its peak in the late 1970s; in the last few
years, however, the ideas behind it have been making a comeback.
Inspired by Gilles Deleuze and Felix Guattari's *Anti-Oedipus*,
Berardi, alongside figures like Antonio Negri, Mario Tronti and
Franco Piperno, was a leader of the revitalization of the left
and known as an activist for his free pirate station, Radio Alice.
Fleeing the law in his own country – where Negri and others were
imprisoned for suspected involvement in the Red Brigades and the
death of Aldo Moro – he stayed for years with Guattari in Paris,
where he became acquainted with Guattari's work on schizoanalysis
in the La Borde clinic. In the 1990s, he above all focused on the
impact of the new media, by developing a media theory based on a
fusion of an unorthodox form of neo-Marxism, psychoanalysis and
communication theory.

As a teacher, Berardi has a post at the Accademia di
Belle Arti di Brera in Milan, where he teaches the social history of
communication. After the dot-com crash at the beginning of the
millennium, the increasing surveillance after 9/11 and the uprisings
of the alter-globalists, he wrote the probing essay 'What is the
Meaning of Autonomy Today? Subjectivation, Social Composition,
Refusal of Work' in 2003,[1] in which he describes the increasing
precarity of what he calls the 'cognitariat', the new proletarian
class of workers in the creative industry,
who have become the new exploited
class as a result of the flexiblization and
fragmentization of work in a collapsing
financial system. His analyses primarily
address the psychopathological aspects of the new developments,
and his more recent writings are straightforwardly sombre diagnoses
of the network society. Yet Berardi has remained a militant figure,
who currently is concentrating on setting up knowledge institutes
and knowledge networks outside the regular educational system,
such as scépsi, European School for Social Imagination.[2] In Italy, he
can be considered a driving force behind
the student protests and is a source of
inspiration for the Occupy movement.

Reason enough to visit him in December 2011 in Barcelona,
where in collaboration with the Museu d'Art Contemporani de
Barcelona (macba) he organized the conference kafca: Knowledge
Against Financial Capitalism, and to ask him what he thinks about

1. 'What is the Meaning
of Autonomy Today?
Subjectivation, Social
Composition, Refusal of Work',
2003: republicart.net/disc/real-
publicspaces/berardi01_en.htm.

2. scepsi.eu

the possibilities for the Autonomia   3. kafca.eu
movement today.[3]

WILLEM VAN WEELDEN — *To repeat the title of your famous essay from 2003 as an urgent question for once: What is the Meaning of Autonomy Today?*

FRANCO BERARDI — To begin with, I would like to say that right now autonomy is more of a keyword than ever! The only problem that must be tackled is giving it the right context. The concept and practice of Autonomia was conceived and organized in the 1960s and 1970s in an economic and social context of growth, development and expansion. Autonomia in that period, at the height of modern civilization, was seen as excess. Fundamentally, Autonomia meant the possibility of creating a space for self-organization of the general intellect, for work that in broad terms is conceived outside the socially accepted sphere of labour. Nowadays, the situation is totally different, and not just because we are now, and for the coming decades as well, in a process of increasing barbarity and of what I would like to call 'decivilization'. So we cannot conceive of Autonomia as excess anymore. The era of affluence, well-being and prosperity is over. Now we must see Autonomia as a manner of inventing a new, humane way of living and of situating a humane living space outside that barbaric order. At the same time, there is the confrontation with a physical space that is more and more characterized by war, ethnic and other violence and increasing financial and cultural impoverishment. So again, Autonomia must be reinvented more than ever, but in doing so we must think about wealth and peace in an entirely different manner. How is it possible to be 'rich' in a world that is steadily growing poorer? How is it possible to be peaceful and happy in a world that is increasingly caught up in violence and war? This conflict is the new framework for today's Autonomia.

    Coming back for a moment to the announcement that *Open* in its present form under SKOR is ceasing to exist – closing, you might say – I would like to suggest a nice title for the last issue under SKOR: '*Open* is Closing Down.' Because that's indeed the reality we must face, that

the openness of civilization, which was produced through
conflict and an alliance between the working class and
the bourgeoisie, a kind of open democracy, has come to
an end. We have to think up a new kind of openness. For
Open, this could mean starting a new European magazine
that we produce collectively, in more languages, fanning
out from the Netherlands to Spain, the UK, Italy, Germany,
and so forth. We have to face up to this closure operation,
because we know that predatory financial capitalism snaps
up everything, all of the resources, all of the money, all of
the valuable time, and that, inevitably, this process will
destroy everything. But to think that this is the end of
modern, social civilization – no! It is the closing down and
cordoning off of the democratic illusion, and thus that is
simultaneously the beginning of the possibility to create a
new space for autonomy. Of course, this does bring with it
an urgent methodological question: How are we going to
do this, how can we define autonomy in a society where
more and more people are armed and violent? But before
you can think about techniques and methods, it is important to emphasize that the current mindset comprises a
dual momentum: the closing down of what was once open
and the simultaneous creation of a new autonomy that
escapes this process of (en)closure. So, autonomy more
than ever!

wvw — *In* After the Future: The Post-Futurism Manifesto, *which you included in your book* Precarious Rhapsody: Semiocapitalism and the Pathologies of the Post-Alpha Generation[4] *precisely 100 years after Marinetti's* Futurist Manifesto, *you write that the separation between poetry and mass communication must be abolished and that the power of the media must be given to the poets and the sages again. This statement is reminiscent of the old credo of the Autonomia movement, which argued for the abolition of the separation between art and daily life. Even though the context has completely changed, has the movement remained the same in terms of ideology?*

4. Franco Berardi, *Precarious Rhapsody: Semiocapitalism and the Pathologies of the Post-Alpha Generation* (London: Minor Compositions, 2009).

FB — As I said before, the late 1960s and early 1970s were

characterized by prosperity. There came a turnabout in 1972, when the club of Rome published *The Limits to Growth*. This report offered a perspective that is again topical now: exhaustion. Never before in the history of society had exhaustion been a possible prospective. The Club of Rome pointed out the possibility of the depletion of natural resources, but there was also an exhaustion of psychic energy and an exhaustion in the imagining of growth. At the same time, the then-president of the USA, Richard Nixon, unilaterally changed the economic rules by decoupling the dollar from the International Monetary Standard, which is based on the price of gold. That was the moment of the arbitrary, arrogant independence of the dollar, and with it the confirmation of the superiority of the American economy.

The result was the dissolution of the principle of commensurability, which had been the most important harmonizing and balancing instrument of international world trade. The abandonment of the principle of commensurability means that nothing can be traded on the basis of a shared standard anymore. The standard is gone, and as a result we have entered the era of incommensurability. At the level of the economy, this means violence: prices are no longer determined by a common standard, but by whoever is the strongest. From this perspective and from a cultural point of view, you can say that what occurred in the 1970s, the promise of endless growth that turned into a perspective of irreversible exhaustion, can most certainly be compared with the present situation.

At that time, the question was how to redefine what wealth is; we must recognize that this is also the question today. When the Autonomia movement spoke about the refusal of work in the 1970s,[5] it meant that the general intellect was becoming more important and that the daily drudgery of physical work and poverty could be overcome by a free application of that general intellect. Today, just like 40 years ago, we can say that this misery is primarily caused by the cultural expectations we circulate in our information economy. Changing those expectations could now mean that we no longer associate wealth with having lots of material possessions or money.

5. Mario Tronti, 'Struggle Against Labor', in: *Operai e capitale* (Turin: Edizione Einaudi, 1966).

Wealth is living with the power to create solidarity and a communal spirit.

The political role of the Autonomia movement is basically to communicate this idea, as a necessary form of cultural contagion. Autonomy as frugality does not mean renouncing and giving up, but the capacity to be happy despite time and body. And thus I think that the hippie movement was the most important cultural experience of the last 50 years. So we have to go back to that. It's about confirming that love is ultimately the only thing that's truly important – and then not understood in the Christian sense, but in a materialistic sense. It's about the availability of body and time.

> wvw — *Do you have an idea that the coming generation, 'the new cognitariat', recognizes this appeal and takes it to heart? Are young people inspired by the hippie era? Or is that just a marketing term for them? Do you see any hope on the horizon in this regard?*

FB — It would be better to call the new generation 'the connective generation', to indicate the effect of the media, but also to emphasize their lack of physical experiences. I once referred to this generation as the generation that learned more words from a machine than from their mothers. For the past few years I was pretty pessimistic, which is expressed in *Precarious Rhapsody,* a book about the psychopathology of this generation. But now I'm inclined to reconsider that pessimism. Not because my analysis was no good, but because I see things shifting. I was pessimistic about the new generation because over the past 20 years I have observed in them an incapacity, caused by virtualization and precarity, to have either an exuberant physical relationship with themselves or with others. Whereas the only way to create solidarity and empathy is through the body. Solidarity is enjoying the body of the other. Solidarity is not an ethical or political value; it is corporality. The whole area of youth culture is changing, because the call for change is now becoming an existential reality. My own future, my post as a teacher for instance, is at stake now that the neoliberal economy and its related ideology are coming apart at the seams.

Erotic Uprising, or the Schooling of the Body

So a reorganization of the mental self is a necessity for everyone.

Of course it is interesting that people are occupying places and that all sorts of things are happening, but I want to look further than the direct political effects of the admission that a future cannot be offered anymore. It's about the deep anthropological effect of rediscovering the city as an erotic place, a place where you can touch and be touched. A nice expression that I recently picked up in Paris was 'Let's occupy each other'.

It's not about a political protest against something, but much more about a psychotherapeutic process, of rediscovering a common body. The generation that learned more words from a machine than from their mothers is suddenly beginning to speak! Which makes this physical psychological process a rediscovery of language!

> wvw — *What do you think is the most important idea for a reconfiguration of the 'cognitariat', now that this class recently received the cold message that it no longer has a future? How could the energy that has been released be bundled?*

FB — The first step is the reactivation of the social body as an erotic body, a body of solidarity. If this first step is not taken, nothing is possible. And that first step is now being taken in different ways. But you are actually asking for a possible kind of politics, and that goes beyond psychotherapy. In Bologna, we have started an experiment; there, and in other cities, the key word is now *Insolvenza*, 'insolvency' or 'inability to pay'.[6] The refusal of work has now become the refusal to pay! Vouchers are being handed out with the inscription *Santa Insolvenza* – you know that there already is a *San Precario*. These vouchers give you free admittance to public transport. But there are also food vouchers with your name, date of birth and address on them and the amount of provisions you need, along with the words, 'Dear cashier of this supermarket, please let me have these groceries for as long as I am still not getting a basic income from the European Bank', and on the other side it says, 'Debt has become the universal

6. th-rough.eu/writers/ bifo-eng/right-insolvency- and-disentanglement-general- intellects-potency .

form of human relations'. We will go into the supermarkets
with this type of voucher around Christmas time.

But as a concept, *Insolvenza* has many more
layers of meaning, for it is not just about the refusal to
pay; it is particularly about the refusal to pay the symbolic
or semiotic debt, if you will. It's about breaking the sense
of guilt, the idea that you would be 'guilty'. Thus the idea
is not to take on the bankers of this world for once, but
to deprive them of their power. To rid our lives of their
power! That's the true meaning of insolvency. The next
step would be to effectively use the force released by this.
That means that the general intellect, the techies, the doctors, the poets, can work freely in spaces that we will have
to create for that purpose. When the health care and the
sanitation systems collapse, when as a manner of speaking
you don't even have the money to die anymore, it will be
a matter of survival; then the Europeans will become just
like the Americans. What will we do then? We'll set up
hospitals where doctors, social workers and technicians
get the opportunity to voluntarily work in a space where
you can get free assistance. Creating such a space is by no
means a question of money.

WVW — Precarious Rhapsody *was in many ways a furious
tome, but when I saw a video recording of one of your
public speeches at the Brera
Academy, your anger aroused
a feeling of hope.*[7] *Do you think
that a change in education at
the institutional level is one of
the possibilities?*

7. 'Teaching Insurrection: Franco
Berardi Bifo @ Brera Academy,
Milan': th-rough.eu/writers/
bifo-eng/teaching-insurrection-
franco-berardi-bifo-brera-
academy-milan, 14 March 2011.

FB — I spoke in Brera on 14 March 2011; it was the beginning of a process of uprising in Italy, where education
has been completely destroyed over the past three years.
Eight billion euros' worth of cutbacks have been put
through and 130,000 teachers have been fired, at all levels
of the Italian educational system. At the Brera Academy,
the majority of the teaching staff are now 'precarious
workers', working without a contract or rights, for a lower
salary. The situation is extremely uncertain. I have made
it clear that I do not want to teach under such conditions.

The first act of Saint Insolvency: the creation of the human megaphone, produced by a time-out. Photo Mario Carlini/Iguana Press

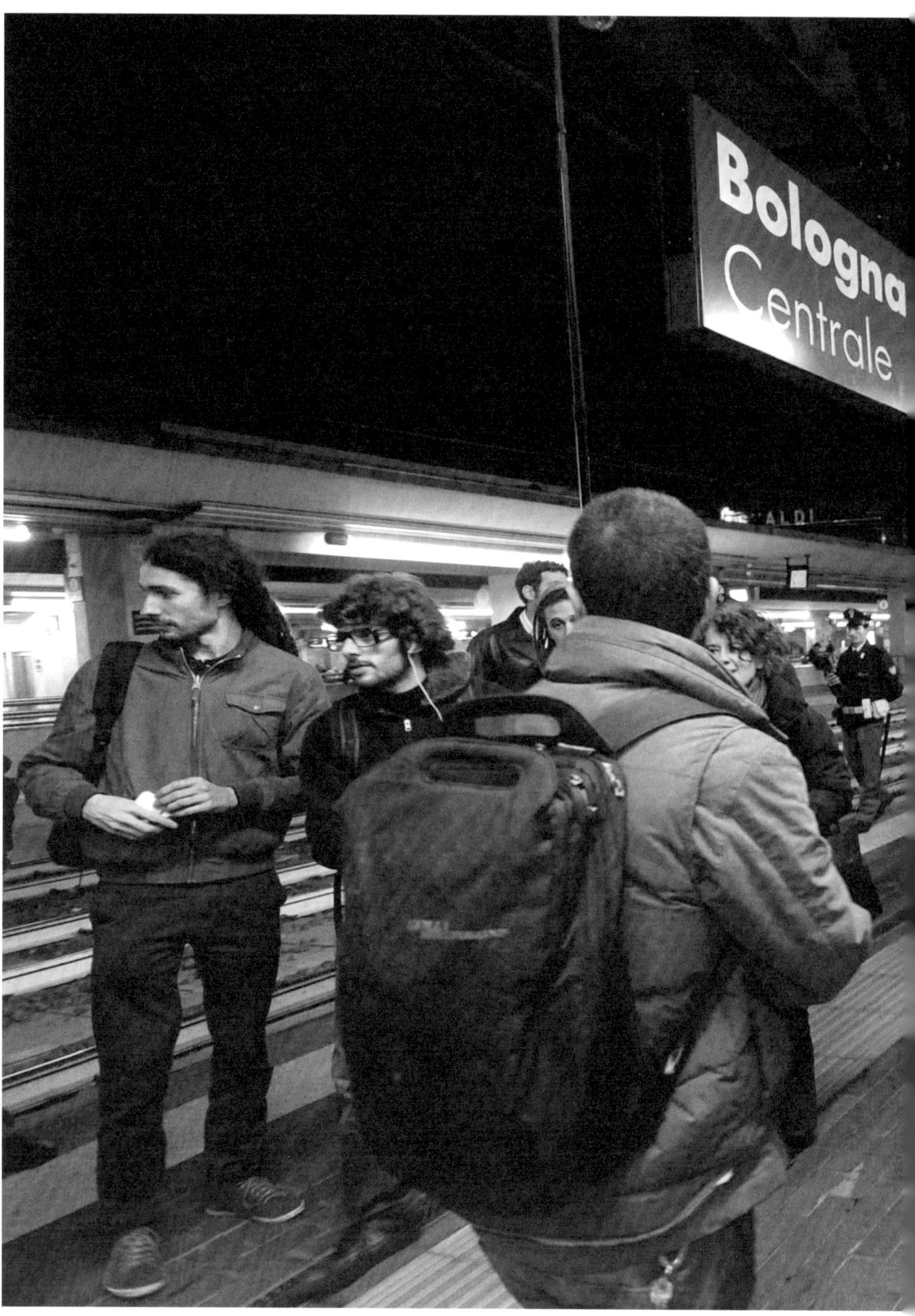

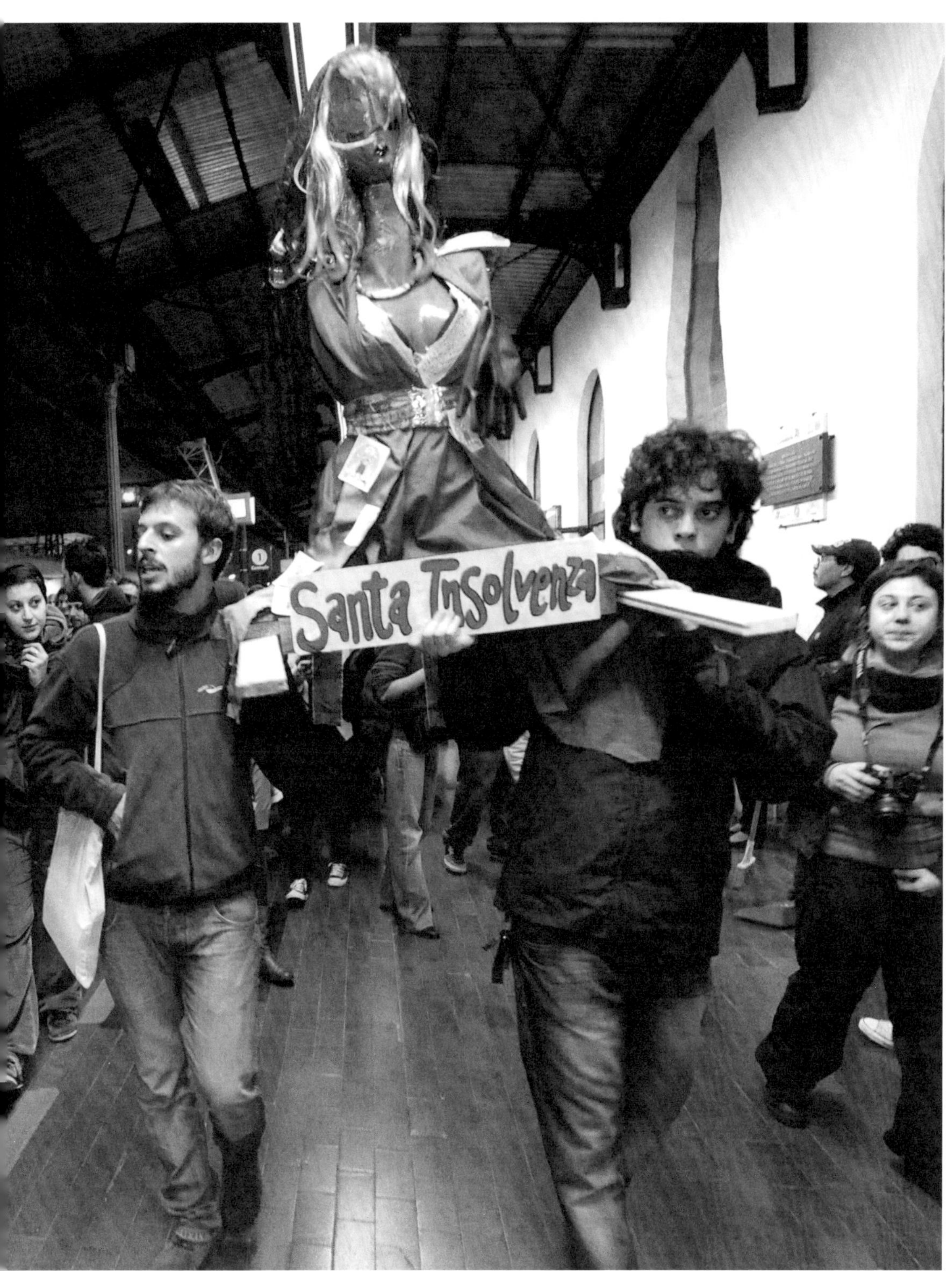

Erotic Uprising, or the Schooling of the Body   41

I only want to teach about uprising, outside the academy.
Originally the idea was to do this in a bank opposite
the academy, but the police managed to prevent that.
So then we occupied the Bourse. Universities and art
institutions are tremendously important. The question,
however, is whether we indeed should fight for the defence
and restoration of the old humanistic universities and
knowledge centres, whether this should be the focus of our
resistance. I don't think so. Not because of the cutbacks,
but because the university is an old institution, created in
the time of a rising bourgeoisie when industrial production
and humanistic values could still be synthesized from the
spirit of the Renaissance. We are now seeing a profound
change in all of society, especially in the area of the
production and imparting of knowledge. The Internet is
naturally very important in changing people's relation to
knowledge. Universities are becoming superfluous in terms
of transmitting knowledge, but necessary for the creation
and transference of power. Public schools and public universities in Italy have mainly become places for conferring
power; the transmittance of knowledge lies with industry,
where large corporations pay directly for applied research.
After the Treaty of Bologna in 1999, the corporations went
into the universities, and the universities are now modelled
on the Research & Development structures of the business
world.
   Why should we have to defend such a system?
We are now seeing a financial aggression that is out to
transform all universities into corporate structures, and in
the process banish the humanistic and critical traditions.
We must form new institutions for the production of
knowledge that can adapt to network conditions and to the
fragmentalization and transformation of knowledge. At the
same time, these institutions must be capable of coming
face-to-face with the interdisciplinarity of knowledge that
is bound up with the hyperspecialization of technology.
We must set up institutions that couple the exchange of
knowledge with sensibility. For you can't be a technologist
if you're not also a poet. I am not against specialization,
but hyperdisciplinarity must begin with the ascertainment
that you first and foremost are a thinking and feeling body,
and only after that, an engineer or a designer. That's the

new starting point for the university of the next 500 years!

> wvw — *In San Marino, you founded* scépsi, *the European School of Social Imagination, and here in Barcelona you have organized the three-day conference* kafca: *Knowledge Against Financial Capitalism, as part of the* scépsi *programme. Can you say something about how that initiative came about and how it is financed?*

fb — In order to start up scépsi we needed support, which we found in an association of civilians from the Republic of San Marino. These civilians are relatively well-off and for years and years have benefited from their country's independence and role as fiscal shelter for the Italian Mafia. San Marino is a tax haven of course, and scépsi is fiscally registered there. In May of 2000, these civilians made a seminar possible and promised to pay for an annual meeting. So it's not a case of the Republic of San Marino paying us. Here in Barcelona, the macba helped us with the financing of the kafca conference, and next summer we are organizing a conference in Kassel, Germany with the help of the *documenta*. In this way, we try to organize conferences and seminars within art institutes or institutes related to art. But in principle, every university or knowledge institute can act as a host for a scépsi initiative.

In the future – for this is only the first year of our existence – the idea is to become independent and to be able to support ourselves financially. For a conference or gathering, we need an average of about 20,000 euros in order to fly people in, provide accommodations and arrange food for them. That's still doable. In the next two, three or four years we will have to find financing for each case separately. But in the distant future, we must assume that the economic idea of exchanging money in the field of knowledge will have disappeared. And as a result, knowledge will again be what it is supposed to be: free! Teachers, researchers and lecturers must also accept such a free relation, but they will have to be fed in exchange. That's what happened in the twelfth century when Irnerio, the founder of the University of Bologna, came from Germany to Bologna as a celebrated scholar: the city gave him excellent accommodations and good food in order to teach medicine, theology and philosophy there. We want to reintroduce this old principle in the field of knowledge. It's a process of reciprocal help and the nourishing of reciprocal love. That's what we need, not money. But as long as we are still in the transitional situation, flights, hotels and meals have to be paid. The key question of course remains how to imagine the university in an era of deep transition.

> WVW — *In some of your writings you talk about the psychological vulnerability that is produced by the subjectivating power of the network society. On the one hand you emphasize the importance of the Internet for the distribution of knowledge, but on the other hand you also see the Internet as the echo chamber of that psychopathology. What possibilities do you see for escaping from these repressive and unhealthy forces and using the network for constructive change?*

FB — This is about the paradoxical relation with technology in the general sense, not only about electronic digital technology. Technology is an important force, but at the same time it's a pitfall that produces alienation, which in the case of virtual technologies has a specific character. Virtual technologies have expanded our cognitive power and simultaneously introduced a process of acceleration of what you could call the disembodiment of communication. You see this for instance with the media activism of the last 20 years. This has primarily been aimed at the potential of the networks – video activism was a new application of the capacity to produce images that are an accusation – but at the same time, of course, it participated in the game of disembodiment and alienation. That is the reason why media activism, despite all of its critical potential and the effect that it has had, has proved incapable of overthrowing the power of the media.

Not that we suddenly must forget media activism and media technology, but I think that a change has occurred over the last six months and that we are now concentrating on another space: the street. The problem with this new phase is that a battle is going on in media activism while work is simultaneously being done on reactivating the social body. Just look at Facebook: it embodies an extreme paradox. From a critical point of view, a homogenization and thus a complete reduction of human sensibility is taking place, along with a standardization of relationships and the perception of them. The infinite complexity of human relationships is reduced in Facebook to a few standardized functionalities. And its success has contributed to the fact that the immeasurable wealth of the Internet has been reduced to the blue of its house style and the rather simplistic icon with the raised thumb: I like! But we mustn't forget that that enormous wealth is still there! Young people who make their debut on the Internet with a Facebook account think that the Internet coincides with Facebook. Therefore we must instruct them that Facebook can have a certain convenience, for example when undertaking spatial actions, but above all that the Internet is outside of that! Besides the blue of Facebook, there still are a whole lot of other colours to discover there. So I think that the rediscovery of the city and the street and the rediscovery of the body of the other will also have repercussions in the media sphere. When you are open to freely moving in other spaces, that will affect standardized spaces such as Facebook.

wvw — *Jean Baudrillard writes in one of his last books,* Why Hasn't Everything Already Disappeared?,[8] *that art in the modern period exists by the grace of its disappearance – not through the disappearance of reality, but through its own active disappearance. What's more, he even claims that it disappeared a long time ago, without even knowing that itself. He adds that art has survived its own disappearance. Is that also what Autonomia is nowadays?*

8. Jean Baudrillard, *Why Hasn't Everything Already Disappeared?* (London: Seagull Books, 2009).

FB — I always have deep respect for what Baudrillard comes up with, even though sometimes I don't immediately understand what he means. This of course refers to the fact that, ever since Hegel, talking about the disappearance of art has taken on so many forms. Which is why I'm actually pretty suspicious about the accuracy of that idea: art disappears and then comes back in order to disappear again. Of course, art disappears in the sense that it becomes something different. In the 1940s and 1950s, art was primarily about political engagement; in the 1970s, art was the environment, the surroundings, and its means were problematicized; in the 1990s it was NetArt, the experiment with communication. And now we can say that art is disappearing and becoming diagnosis and therapy. You could say that art is entering the economy of sensibility, in the sense of the politics of sensibility. But another problem is that I am completely unable to say what art is. Perhaps art is a method of approaching things without it being directly usable, while revealing the rich pragmatic potential that any situation offers. In that sense, art cannot disappear, because it has an experimental attitude. It is an experimental method in relation to the future and to the imagining of possibilities. So art is always disappearing because it is always becoming something else, but at the same time that's why it is always there. Thank God! And may it also be that way with Autonomia!

Hito Steyerl

Art as Occupation

Claims for an Autonomy of Life

Nowadays work, like art, has become an 'occupation', with autonomy having turned into a dominant ideology of flexibility and personal initiative. Now that art has 'occupied' life, according to the filmmaker and theoretician Hito Steyerl, she wonders how life can recapture its autonomy from art. Just as the white cube was once employed to criticize the narcissistic spectacle of artistic autonomy, she makes a case for using the black box as a zone in which to consider how the autonomy of life can be reinstated with respect to art as an occupation.

Let's start with a simple proposition: what used to be work has increasingly been turned into occupation.[1]

This change in terminology may seem trivial. But it reveals massive differences between two very different paradigms of activity. In fact, almost everything changes on the way from work to occupation: the economic framework, but also its implications for space and temporality. If we think of work in the sense of labour, it implies a beginning, a producer and eventually a result. Work is primarily seen as a means to an end: a product, a reward or a wage. It is an instrumental relation. It also produces a subject by means of alienation.

An occupation is the opposite to all of this. An occupation keeps people busy instead of giving them paid labour.[2] An occupation is not hinged on any result, it has no necessary conclusion. As such it knows no traditional alienation, nor any corresponding idea of subjectivity. An occupation doesn't necessarily assume remuneration either, since the process is thought to contain its own gratification. It has no temporal framework except the passing of time itself. It is not centred on a producer/worker, but includes consumers, reproducers, even destroyers, time-wasters and bystanders and in essence anybody seeking distraction or engagement.

The shift from work to occupation applies in the most different areas of contemporary daily activity. It marks a transition that goes way beyond the often described shift from a Fordist to a post-Fordist economy. Rather than in terms of earning it is seen as a way of spending time and resources. Thus it clearly accents the passage from an economy based on production to an economy fuelled by waste, from progressing time to time spent or even idled away, from a space defined by clear divisions to an entangled and complex territory.

Perhaps most importantly: occupation is not a means to something, as traditional labour is. Occupation is in many cases an end in itself.

Captive, concept, receipt: these are just three notions related to the term of occupation. Others include catch, purchase and accept. The term occupation is derived from the Latin *occupare* (to take possession of, seize, occupy, take up, employ). The various meanings of the word occupation relate to activity, service, distraction, therapy and engagement; that is to many of the meanings of the thing formerly called work. But also to conquest, invasion and seizure. In its military meaning, occupation refers to extreme power relations, spatial complication and 3D sovereignty. It is imposed by the occupier to the occupied, who may or may not resist it. The objective is often expansion but also neutralization, stranglehold, the quelling of autonomy. Occupation also makes one think of the countless occupational programmes, which are meant to cushion

1. I am ripping these ideas from a brilliant observation by the Carrotworkers' Collective, found here: http://carrotworkers.wordpress.com/on-free-labour/.

2. Carrotworkers' Collective, 'On Free Labour' http://carrotworkers.wordpress.com/on-free-labour/: 'The European Union language promoting "occupation" rather than "employment", marking a subtle but interesting semantic shift towards keeping the active population "busy" rather than trying to create jobs.'

the full impact of unemployment in rich countries. Programmes that are not designed to create waged labour, but rather involvement, pastimes or activity schemes.

Occupation often means endless mediation, eternal process, indeterminate negotiation and the blurring of spatial divisions. It has no inbuilt outcome or resolution. It also refers to appropriation, colonization and extraction. Occupation is permanent, processual, uneven. From the occupied to the occupier it means completely different things.

But occupation can also be turned around and used in protest, as we have witnessed in the hundreds of occupations of schools, factories, banks, streets and other spaces, which took place over the past years globally.[3]

Of course these occupations – in all the different senses of the word – are not the same. But the mimetic force of the term operates in all of the diverse meanings and draws them towards each other. If the term occupation refers to all of these situations, then they resonate with each other. There is a magic affinity in the name itself: if it sounds the same, the force of similarity works within it.[4]

3. For a detailed description of just one, very influential example: The Occupation Cookbook or the Model of the Occupation of the Faculty of Humanities and Social Sciences in Zagreb; accessible at: http://slobodnifilozofski.org/?p=1915. For a list of occupied universities in the UK as of November 2010 see: http://anticuts.com/2010/11/27/list-of-university-occupations/, I have to leave out many of the most innovative and inspiring examples worldwide.

4. Walter Benjamin, 'Doctrine of the Similar', in: *Selected Writings*, eds. Michael Jennings, Howard Eiland, Gary Smith. Vol. 2, part 2, 1931-1934 (Cambridge, MA: Harvard University Press, 1999), 694-711.

Occupation as Art

In the context of art, the transition from work to occupation has additional implications. Because what happens to the work of art, then? Does it too transform into an occupation? Partly, yes. What used to materialize exclusively as object or product – as (art) work – now tends to appear as activity or performance.[5] By now, the traditional work of art has been largely supplemented by art as a process – as an occupation.

5. One could even say: the work of art is tied to the idea of a product (tied up in a complex system of valorization). Art-as-occupation bypasses the result of production by immediately turning the making-of into a commodity.

Art is an occupation in the sense of keeping people busy, spectators and anyone else alike. In many rich countries, it is a quite popular occupational scheme. The idea that it contains its own gratification and needs no remuneration is quite accepted in the cultural workplace. The paradigm of Cultural Industries is an example of an economy that was supposed to function by producing even more occupations (and distractions) by people who were in many cases working for free. Additionally, there are occupational schemes in the guise of art education. More and more post- and post-postgraduate programmes shield prospective artists from the pressure of (public or private) art markets. Art education tends to take longer and longer, and creates zones of occupation, which yield fewer 'works' but more processes, 'knowledge', engagement or relationality. It also tends to produce more and more educators, mediators, guides or even guards, whose occupation is again processual (and ill- or unpaid).

In poorer areas, the immediate grip of art seems to be lessening. But art-as-occupation in these places can be part of ideological deflection, or even very concretely profit from labour stripped of rights.[6] In turn this or any other squalor can be exploited by artists who use misery as raw material. Art 'upgrades' poorer neighbourhoods by aesthetisizing their status as urban ruins and drives out the inhabitants after the area becomes fashionable.[7] In many cases it is interesting to note that the ruined character of these places itself derives from a status of occupation. Buildings need to be at least marginally occupied in order to retain some functionality. So janitors or security firms are brought in to 'occupy' the space – that is, to keep it empty in order to safeguard its function as private property. This allows in turn for the development of artistically viable ruin architecture – referred to as a 'photo opportunity'[8] on a Detroit street sign; material for countless coffee table books.

Generally, art is part of an uneven global system, that underdevelops some parts of the world, while over-developing others[9] – and the boundaries between both areas interlock and overlap. Some parts are forcefully immobilized, their autonomy is denied and quelled – in order to keep other parts mobile and autonomous.

But, you may ask, apart from occasional exposure, I have nothing to do with art whatsoever. How can my life be occupied by it?

Here is a checklist: Does art possess you in the form of endless self-performance?[10] Have you found yourself curating your Facebook friends? Or wondered how you got caught up in the endless production of productivity and the

6. See Nicolai Ouroussoff, 'Abu Dhabi Guggenheim Faces Protest', *The New York Times*, 16 March 2011. Available online at: http://www.nytimes.com/2011/03/17/arts/design/guggenheim-threatened-with-boycott-over-abu-dhabi-project.html.

7. Central here is Martha Rosler's three-part essay, 'Culture Class: Art, Creativity, Urbanism', *e-flux journal* 21 (December 2010); 23 (March 2011); and 25 (May 2011).

8. This blog entry shows the sign and emphasizes that it too is an artistic intervention: http://www.detroitfunk.com/?p=5132. Interestingly, the Detroit ruin scenery (often referred to as set for 'ruin porn' by locals) became the backdrop for a fiction film about the communist occupation of the USA by China. (*Red Dawn 2*; http://www.guernicamag.com/spotlight/2281/leary_1_15_11/).

9. At this point it is beneficial to reconsider and recontextualize Gayatri Spivaks well known but nevertheless pertinent reminder that there is indeed an 'other side of the international division of labor from socialized capital, inside *and* outside the circuit of the epistemic violence of imperialist law and education supplementing an earlier economic text.' Gayatri Spivak, *A Critique of Post-Colonial Reason: Toward a History of the Vanishing Present* (Cambridge, MA: Harvard University Press, 1999), 269. This list could be made to include contemporary art next to imperialist law, the redistribution of wealth from poor to rich, and an institutionalized system of maintaining hegemonial knowledge as well as defining aesthetic value; and it could be made more precise by emphasizing that the 'other side' is in many cases next door.

10. See: Invisible Comitee, *The Coming Insurrection* (Los Angeles: Semiotext(e), 2009), 16ff: 'Producing oneself is about to become the dominant occupation in a society where production has become aimless: like a carpenter who's been kicked out of his workshop and who out of desperation starts to plane himself down. That's where we get the spectacle of all these young people training themselves to smile for their employment interviews, who whiten their teeth to make a better impression, who go out to nightclubs to stimulate their team spirit, who learn English to boost their careers, who get divorced or married to bounce back again, who go take theater classes to become leaders or "personal development" classes to "manage conflicts" better – the most intimate "personal development," claims some guru or another, "will lead you to better emotional stability, a more well directed intellectual acuity, and so to better economic performance".'

subjection of subjectivity? Do you wake feeling like a multiple? Are you on constant auto-display?

Have you been beautified, improved, upgraded or attempted to do this to anyone/thing else? Has your rent doubled because a few kids with brushes were relocated into that dilapidated building next door? Have your feelings been designed, or do you feel designed by your iPhone?

Or is access to art (and its production) on the contrary being withdrawn, slashed, cut off, impoverished and hidden behind insurmountable barriers? Is labour in this field unpaid? Do you live in a city that redirects a huge chunk of its cultural budget to fund a one-off art show? Is conceptual art from your region privatized by predatory banks?

All of these are symptoms of artistic occupation. While on the one hand artistic occupation completely invades life, it also cuts off some of its parts from circulation. Occupation means both: forcefully seizing and keeping out, inclusion and exclusion, managing access and flow. It may not come as a surprise that this pattern often follows fault lines of class and political economy.

Life and Autonomy

But beyond all this, art doesn't stop at occupying people, space or time. It also occupies life as such.

Why should that be the case? Let's start with a small detour on artistic autonomy.[11]

Artistic autonomy was traditionally predicated not on occupation, but on separation. More precisely: on art's separation from life.[12] As artistic production became more specialized in an industrial world marked by an increasing division of labour, it was also more and more divorced from obvious functionality.[13] While it became seemingly independent from instrumentalization, it simultaneously also lost social relevance. As reaction, different avant-gardes set out to break the barriers of art and to recreate its relation to life.

According to their hopes, art was supposed to dissolve within life and to infuse it with a revolutionary jolt. What happened was rather the contrary. To push the point: life has been occupied by art. Because gradually, art's initial forays into life and daily practice turned into routine incursions and then into constant occupation. Nowadays, the invasion of life by art is not the exception, but the rule. The autonomy of art was the idea to separate art from the zone of daily practice, as well as from mundanity, intentionality, utility, production and instrumental reason: in order to distance itself from all social

'Acting on the Onmipresent Frontiers of Autonomy', in: *To The Arts, Citizens!* (Porto: Serralves, 2010), 146-167.

12. Peter Bürger, *Theorie der Avantgarde* (Frankfurt am Main: Suhrkamp, 1974), 49-73.

13. The emphasis here is on the word obvious, since art evidently retained a major function in developing a particular division of senses, class distinction and bourgeois subjectivity. It became more divorced from religious or representational function. Its autonomy presented itself as disinterested and dispassionate, while at the same time mimetically adapting the form and structure of capitalist commodity. This is somehow an unsystematic rip of Adorno's ideas in *Aesthetic Theory* and Bürger's conclusions.

11. These paragraphs are entirely due to the pervasive influence of Sven Lütticken's excellent text

coercion and the rule of efficiency.
But this incompletely segregated area
then ended up incorporating everything it seceded from in the first
place; but this time within its own
aesthetic paradigms. The incorporation of art within life was a political project (both from the left and
the right). The incorporation of life
within art is an aesthetical project,
which coincides with an overall aestheticization of politics.

A similar process of over-inclusion
of life also characterizes the museum,
as art's default institution. By first
including more and more mundane
objects as well as non-objects and
then transgressing its own borders,
the museum has wound up expanding way beyond its initial boundaries. It has proliferated in places
where society has been abandoned
(or never existed), replacing former
public spheres and factories with
sites of occupation. Many of these
art spaces emphasize education and
engagement of audiences and tend
to downgrade the production of
content (which is often assumed to
be for free). Spectatorial attitudes
are closely managed to turn from
reflection to engagement, from con-
templation to immersion, from passing aesthetic judgement to being
entangled in social networking and
competing economies of attention.
An art institution becomes a way of
life, instead of a site separated from
everyday life. And it turns its focus
away from traditional works of art to
emphasize overall occupation.

It has often been described how
artistic activity
has become an
occupational role
model.[14] Networking, endless meet-

14. For example Brian
Holmes: 'The Flexible Personality': http://eipcp.net/
transversal/1106/holmes/en.

ings and greetings, all-out affective
and performative labour: all of these
have entered the repertoire of the
former work force.

On all of these levels art has not
only invaded life, but occupies it.
This doesn't mean that it's omnipres-
ent. It just means, that it has established a complex topology of both
overbearing presence and gaping
absence – both of which impact on
daily lives. The uneven occupation of
life by art is not exactly what avant-
gardes had in mind. Yet nobody
would doubt that it is quite effective.
A fractured map is created which
features varying degrees of occupational intensity. These zones are very
much shut off from one another, yet
interlocked and interdependent. It
is a check-pointed system, complete
with gate keepers, access levels and
close management of movement and
information. Its architecture is aston-
ishingly complex.

One example of this complicated topology is the figure of the
intern (in a museum, a gallery or
most likely a project). The intern
is a prime figure of contemporary
occupation. The term intern is linked
to internment, confinement and a
detention which may be involuntary
or voluntary. She is supposed to be
on the inside of the system, yet she
is excluded from payment. She is
inside labour but outside remuneration: stuck in a space that includes

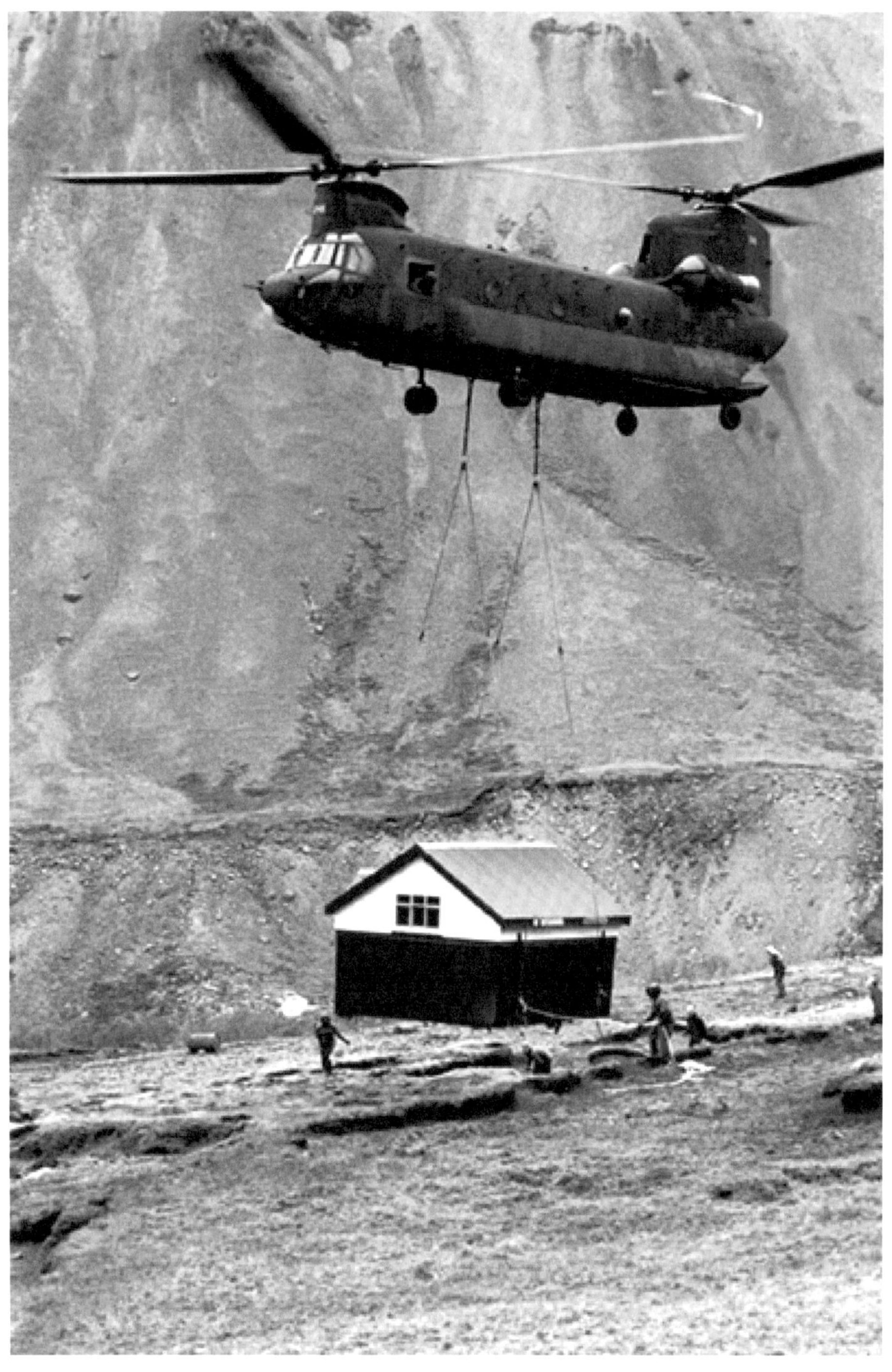

the outside and excludes the inside simultaneously.[15] As a result she works to sustain her own occupation.

15. 'The figure of the intern appears in this context paradigmatic as it negotiates the collapse of the boundaries between Education, Work and Life.' Carrotworkers' Collective: http://carrotworkers.wordpress.com/on-free-labour/.

Division of Labour

Of course, the avant-gardes – even if they had wanted – could never have brought about this change on their own. One of the reasons is rather a paradoxical development at the root of artistic autonomy. According to Peter Bürger, art acquired a special status within a bourgeois capitalist system because artists somehow refused to follow the specialization required for almost any other profession in the context of an ever more radical division of labour. Thus, the division of labour in the realm of arts remained not only incomplete but was again and again openly defied by artists. This contributed to art's claims for autonomy. But with the development of neoliberal modes of production the division of labour started to be reversed in many other occupational fields too. The artist-as-dilettante and biopolitical designer was overtaken by the clerk-as-innovator, the technician-as-entrepreneur, the labourer-as-engineer, the manager-as-genius and (worst of all) the administrator-as-revolutionary. Multitasking, as a template for many forms of contemporary occupation, marks the reversal of the division of labour – the fusion of professions, or rather their confusion. The assumed role of the artist as creative polymath serves as a role-model (or excuse) to legitimate the universalization of professional dilettantism and overextension in order to save money on specialized labour.

If the origin of artistic autonomy lies in the refusal of the division of labour (and the alienation and subjection going along with it), this refusal has now been integrated into neoliberal modes of production to set free dormant potentials. Thus autonomy has spread to the point where it tipped into a new dominant ideology[16] of flexibility and self-entrepreneurship. During this transition, autonomy started acquiring new political meanings, too. Workers,

16. It is interesting to make a link at this point to classical key texts of autonomist thought as collected in Sylvere Lotringer and Christian Marazzi (eds.), *Autonomia: Post-Political Politics* (New York: Semiotext(e), 2007).

feminist and youth movements of the 1970s started claiming autonomy from labour and the regime of the factory. Capital reacted to this flight by designing its own version of autonomy: the autonomy of capital from workers. This transition has been described in detail by many different theorists in the case of Italy[17] departing from the movements of the Autonomia Operaia. The rebellious, autonomous force of those struggles was turned into a catalyst for the capitalist reinvention of labour

17. Toni Negri has detailed the restructuring of the North Italian labour force after the 1970s, while Paolo Virno and Bifo Berardi both emphasize that the autonomous tendencies expressed by the refusal of labour and the rebellious feminist, youth and workers' movements in the 1970s was recaptured into new, flexibilized and entrepreneurial forms of coercion. More recently Berardi has emphasized the new

relations as such. The desire for self-determination was rearticulated as a self-entrepreneurial business model, the hope to overcome alienation was transformed into serial narcissism and over-identification with one's occupation. Only in this context does it become clear why contemporary occupations that promise an unalienated lifestyle are somehow believed to contain their own gratification. But the relief from alienation they suggest takes on the form of self-oppression, which arguably could be much worse than traditional alienation, which at least exposed subjects to something other than themselves.[18]

The struggles around autonomy and above all Capital's response to them are thus deeply ingrained into the transition from work to occupation. As we have seen, this transition is based on the role model of the artist as someone who refuses the division of labour and leads an unalienated lifestyle. This is one of the templates for new occupational forms of life that are all-encompassing, passionate, self-oppressive and narcissistic to the bone.

conditions of subjective identification with labour and its self-perpetuating narcissistic components. See inter alia Toni Negri, 'Reti produttive e territori: il caso del Nord-Est italiano', in: Giovanni Caccia (ed.), *L'inverno è finito. Scritti sulla trasformazione negata (1989-1995)* (Rome: Castelvecchi, 1996), 66–80; Paolo Virno, 'Do you remember counterrevolution?', in: Michael Hardt and Paolo Virno (eds.), *Radical Thought in Italy: A Potential Politics* (Minneapolis: University of Minnesota Press, 1996); Franco 'Bifo' Berardi, *The Soul at Work: From Alienation to Autonomy* (New York: Semiotext(e), 2010.

18. I have repeatedly argued that one should not seek to escape alienation but on the contrary embrace it as well as the status of objectivity that goes along with it.

Black Box (Unplugged)

'To strike is to attack the function of a space and to suspend the rhythm of its time in a determination location.'[19]

How then can we salvage life from art as occupation? How can life regain its autonomy from art?

19. Inoperative Committee, *Preoccupied: The Logic of Occupation* (Somewhere: Somebody, 2009), 7.

The problem is obvious: if art is occupation, then there is hardly any place to hide from it. There is no way to escape being incessantly linked to the production, consumption or discussion of art, to reproduce or mirror it as life or style, of being forced into the relentless performance of art, self, value, education, life or to prevent the collapse of all these categories into each other. No escape from being drafted into an incessant, stultifying and inflationary circle of reproducing life as art and vice versa. As Robert Smithson once soberly stated: life in a gallery is like fucking in a cemetery. We could add that spreading the gallery into life is even worse: like not fucking anywhere else.

This might be the time to start exploring the third meaning of occupation: the meaning it has taken on in countless squats and takeovers historically. As the occupiers of the New School in 2008 emphasize, this type of occupation tries to intervene in the form of occupational time and space itself, instead of simply blocking and immobilizing a specific area.

'Occupation mandates the inversion of the standard dimensions of space. Space in an occupation is not

Black Box.

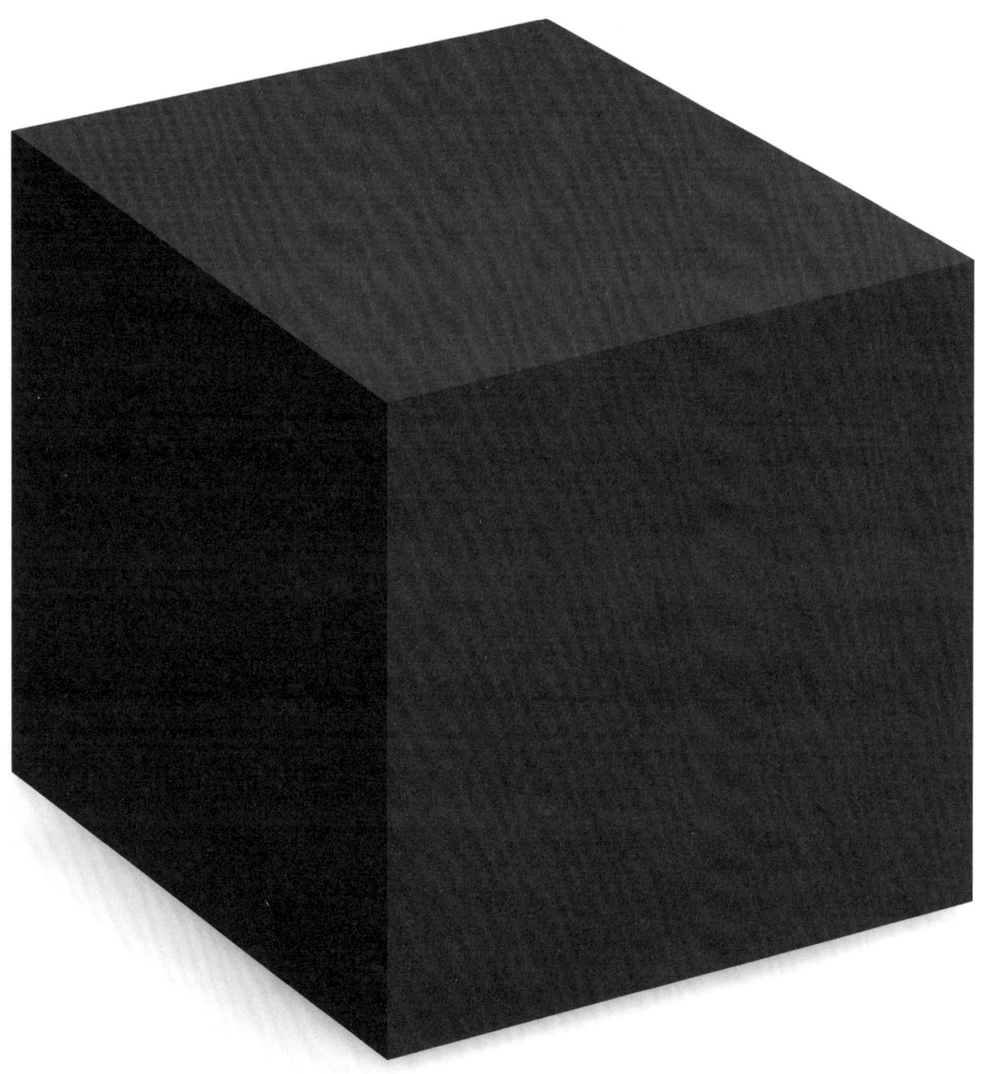

merely the container of our bodies, it is a plane of potentiality that has been frozen by the logic of the commodity. In an occupation, one must engage with space topologically, as a strategist, asking: What are its holes, entrances, exits? How can one disalienate it, dis-identify it, make it inoperative, com-munize it?'[20]

20. Ibid., 11.

To unfreeze the forces that lie dormant in the petrified spaces of occupation means to rearticulate its uses, to make it non-efficient, non-instrumental, non-intentional, to disable its utility, capacity of being efficient, utilitarian and a tool for social coercion. In short: it means to reclaim its autonomy along the lines of what used to be thought of as artistic autonomy. Now: to free an art space from art as occupation seems a paradoxical task, especially as art spaces have spread way beyond the traditional gallery. But on the other hand it is not too difficult either to imagine how any of these spaces might operate in a non-efficient, non-instrumental and non-produc-tive way either.

One example: an unexplored potential for autonomy unexpectedly lies in the cinematic Black Box in or outside an art space. As artists emp-tied out the White Cube to reveal its framing and its power, exposing the horror and narcissist spectacle of artistic autonomy running empty – so can we partially oppose its results by using the Black Box. If the White Cube was about highlighting and producing art as sacralised commod-ity – perhaps the Black Box can help achieve the autonomy of life from art-as-occupation. Because, if we unplug the Black Box and stop any projection, constant visibility and performance cease. The Black Cube becomes a zone of respite. Turn off the lights. No WIFI, no context, no show, education, iPhone, discourse, network, distraction. Go there to disengage, uninvolve, deproduce or simply breathe. Nobody can see you: there's no point in producing yourself as subject/spectacle. A place to sleep, to whisper, sleep again. Play hide and seek. Have sex or prefer not to. Swap files or kisses. Close your eyes. Unperform. Enjoy the autonomy of life from art and its countless derivatives. Of course, this is not going to solve the problem. But at least it provides some quiet to think it through. The result may be quite simple: if art is occupation of life – why don't we turn around the tables and go occupy its spaces, too?[21]

21. Ibid. 'The problem with this practice of spatial inversion is that it requires a particular mode of temporality which makes such actions more of less conducive. What blocks the physical reinterpretation of spatial function is the time of "emergency," when everyone is in a perpetual crisis due to the encroach-ing police or some force of repression. When this state of exception structures the time of the event, everyone becomes smothered with fear, and meetings dominate the use of the territory. To escape this downfall, buffer zones are necessary, multiple rooms, hallways, and passages to defuse the incoming threats. Recon-figurations of space are use-ful for not only mediating the barrage of internal and external policing opera-tions, but also for providing a release from the pathetic injunction to "mobilize".'

Christoph Brunner,
Roberto Nigro,
Gerald Raunig

Re-Territorialize!

New Dimensions of Present Forms of Activism

Against the background of Foucault's analyses of the philosophical significance of the cynic, philosophers Christoph Brunner, Roberto Nigro and Gerald Raunig at the Zurich University of the Arts are investigating present-day forms of activism such as the Occupy movement. By means of three themes – creating new forms of living, inventing new modes of organization and re-appropriating time – they show the pioneering potential of such activism.

It is 17 September 2011. A demonstration march through lower Manhattan chooses as the destination of its *dérive* a small park near the enormous construction site of the World Trade Center. Zuccotti Park is a formerly public, now privatized square belonging to the real estate corporation Brookfield Properties, named after its chairman John Zuccotti. On older maps of the financial district, however, this square has a different name: Liberty Plaza. The demonstrators have not chosen to occupy this territory because of a universalist invocation of freedom, but rather because they want to set a further component of the abstract machine in motion that has drawn lines of flight throughout the entire year, especially through the Mediterranean region. And the most intensive line of this abstract machine was probably the Egyptian part of the Arab Spring with its centre in Tahrir Square, the 'Place of Freedom'. By purposely occupying another place of freedom at the edge of Wall Street, the precarious occupiers seek not only to interrupt subservient de-territorialization, the flows through the global financial centre, but they also take up the practices, with which current activisms de- and re-territorialize their times, their socialities, their lives in new ways.

At the end of the 1970s the work of some authors like Foucault, Deleuze and Guattari – to name only a few of a larger movement – engaged in a trajectory focusing more and more on the analysis of the transformations that trouble a society and require a new type of political organization. In a word, they were addressing questions concerning the transformation of the political. At issue was the search for new forms of existence, new lifestyles, dif-ferent types of social and political organization as a result of the deep changes that shook the ground of our contemporary societies. All in all these issues involved a major question concerning the production of subjectivity, which also include struggles against subjection, against forms of subjectivity and submission.

The ground on which these reflections took shape was the crisis of the two extreme models of political organization, which dominated the history of the twentieth century: Leninism and anarchism. By the time these authors were writing, they were phantasms of defeat, voluntarism and disenchantment. Their collapse left open the question of the machines of struggles that the movement must make use of in order to be capable of winning.[1] It went hand in hand with the crisis of global projects of society, based on closed ideologies. It was no longer a matter of founding political projects in abstract syntheses, but in open processes of analysis, critique, verification and singular realization. The focus on concepts and practices such as molecular revolution, transversal struggles, minoritarian becomings and microphysics of power, among others, is to be situated in the wake of these social, political and intellectual displacements. Foucault's elaboration of the notions of government and governmentality, which emerged in 1978, should be interpreted in connection with such issues.[2] In fact, on the one hand, his reference to the question of governmentality called for a different approach to the problem of the constitution of the state

1. See Félix Guattari and Toni Negri, *Communists Like Us* (New York: Semiotext(e), 1990), 103.

2. Michel Foucault, *Security, Territory, Population: Lectures at the Collège de France 1977-78* (New York: Palgrave Macmillan, 2007).

and to the analysis of mechanisms of power; on the other, it called into question the effectiveness of a kind of revolutionary utopianism and the efficacy of some political experiences.

Foucault showed that the state does not have a unity, individuality and rigorous functionality; that it was probably nothing more than 'a way of governing, a type of governmentality, a series of relations of power that gradually take shape on the basis of multiple and very diverse processes'.[3] However, by the same token, his critique aimed at the heart of the social and political transformations of struggles, since his analyses suggested that from a molecular point of view, each attempt at ideological unification of struggles was an absurd and indeed reactionary operation. To be sure: such a critique in no way prevented Foucault from looking for what the different forms of struggle may have in common.[4]

Foucault recognized the immediacy and transversal character of the new forms of struggles emerging in the last decades of the twentieth century. He draws our attention to the fact that these struggles are more and more centred on the status of the individual and are struggles against the 'government of individualization'. His attentiveness to the peculiarities of the new forms of struggles emphasizes the political and philosophical meaning of his last analyses, in which 'the critical ontology of ourselves . . . must be conceived as an attitude, an ethos, a philosophical life in which the critique of what we are is at one and the same time the historical analysis of the limits imposed on us and an experiment with the possibility of going beyond them'.[5]

Therefore, the reference to a sort of ontology of actuality is not the attempt to give back a *static* picture of what is going on in a society; it is rather the attempt to make a diagnosis of the forces crossing a society; the attempt to map out the lines of actualization emerging in a society. Foucault's analyses of new forms of struggles are all the more important since they sketch out lines of forces at the forefront of the contemporary political scene in the movement of movements crossing the worldwide spread of conflicts.

Today the struggle against the forms of subjection, against the submission of subjectivity is becoming more and more important, even though – as Foucault stresses: 'The struggles against forms of domination and exploitation have not disappeared. Quite the contrary.'[6] This focus on subjectivity and its forms of struggles raises questions on the status of individual and processes of individuation. By the same token, these issues need to be situated in the context of their genesis, that is in the development of liberal and neoliberal societies, because of the importance such societies attribute to the notion of the individual. Foucault devotes consistent analyses to the development of liberalism and neoliberalism as the general framework of biopolitics, and of the politics of the self.[7] His last effort to go through an analysis of the Christian hermeneutics of the subject

3. Ibid., 248.

4. Michel Foucault, 'The Subject and the Power', in: J. Faubion (ed.), *Power* (New York: The New Press, 1997), 326-348.

5. Michel Foucault, 'What is Enlightenment?', in: P. Rabinow (ed.), *Ethics* (New York: The New Press, 1997), 319.

6. Foucault, 'The Subject and the Power', op. cit. (note 4), 331-332.

7. Michel Foucault, *The Birth of Biopolitics: Lectures at the Collège de France 1978-79* (New York: Palgrave Macmillan, 2008), 22.

and the Hellenistic culture of the self represents the attempt to figure out new political practices for the creation of a new subject and a new politics.[8]

In no way it can be suggested that Foucault's reading of liberalism was liberal. Such an interpretation would entail a profound misunderstanding of Foucault's argument, which, on the contrary, orbits the attempt of figuring out ways of going beyond actual forms of existence and of producing new spaces of freedom. The question that resonated in Foucault's last problematizations of an aesthetics of existence as production of new forms of subjectivity echoes with the contemporary Occupy movements around the globe.

In his last course, with the title 'The Courage of Truth',[9] Michel Foucault explored the scandalous life of the Cynics, to which he applied the colourful term of 'philosophical activism'.[10] It was not his intention to attribute a privileged position to the activity of the philosophers, even less to reduce activism to a cognitive capacity. Rather, the Cynic philosopher served as a backdrop for a more general form of activism, of changing the world, of newly inventing worlds. For Foucault in later years, philosophical activism was an 'activism in the world and against the world'.

The Cynic philosopher is, first of all, the exemplary, anecdotal, almost mythical figure of Diogenes, with no permanent residence, at most a tub, living his life completely in public, scandalously all the way to masturbating in public, practicing *parrhesia*, the manner of 'saying everything', even if it is associated with great risk, which in Cynicism conjoins the art of existence with the discourse of truth.[11]

Foucault's endeavour of a 'history of life as possible beauty' situates this old Greek Cynicism as the pivotal point of a whole genealogy of scandalous, disobedient, self-forming forms of living.[12] Foucault sees historical actualizations of Cynic activism in the minoritarian heretical movements of the Middle Ages, in the political revolutions of modernity and – somewhat surprisingly – in the theme of the artist's life in the nineteenth century. And here we would add to the Foucaultian genealogy the new activisms of the twenty-first century: the anti-globalization movement, social forums, anti-racist no border camps, queer-feminist activisms, transnational migrant strikes and Mayday movements of the precarious. And since last year there has been a tremendous intensification of these new activisms in the wider Mediterranean region: from the waves of university occupations to the revolutions of the Arab Spring, all the way to the movements of occupying central squares in Greece, Spain and Israel. Day-long sit-ins at the Kasbah Square in Tunis, revolutionary occupations of Tahrir Square in Cairo, Acampadas in the Puerta del Sol in Madrid, tents in the Rothschild Boule-

8. In this regard, see Maurizio Lazzarato's critical remarks on subjectivation and micropolitics in I. Lorey, R. Nigro and G. Raunig (eds.), *Inventionen* (Zurich/Berlin: Diaphanes, 2011), 161-173.

9. Michel Foucault, *The Courage of Truth*, trans. Graham Burchell (London: Palgrave Macmillan, 2011).

10. The original French term 'militantisme' is translated in the English version of the course as 'militancy'. For another recent development of 'activist philosophy' see Brian Massumi, *Semblance and Event: Activist Philosophy and the Occurrent Arts* (Cambridge, MA: MIT Press, 2011).

11. 'You recall that, etymologically, *parrhêsia* is the activity that consists in saying everything: *par rhêmia*. *Parrhêsiazesthai* is "telling all".' Foucault, *The Courage of Truth*, op. cit. (note 9), 9.

12. Ibid., 162.

vard in Tel Aviv. Much could be said about what these new activisms have in common. They are all about appropriating real places, about a struggle against precarization, against extreme competition and against the drivenness of contemporary production, largely dispensing with representation and weaving a transnational concatenation of social movements. There are, however, three specific vectors on which these activisms enter new territory: in their search for new forms of living, in their organizational forms of radical inclusion and in their insistence on re-appropriating time.

1. Inventing New Forms of Living

When Foucault brings art into play, following the revolutions in his genealogy of the Cynics, it is not classical aesthetics or an existentialist theory of art that concerns him, but rather art that is 'capable of giving a form to existence which breaks with every other form', a form that forms itself, newly invents itself, an 'aesthetics of existence'.[13] Aesthetics as ethics, as the invention of new 13. Ibid., 187. modes of subjectivation and of new forms of living (together), existence as aesthetic object, life as a beautiful work. This ethico-aesthetic aspect of forming life is by no means to be understood as an individualistic stylization of life: even though dandyism and existentialism certainly also belong to the genealogy of the aesthetics of existence, the term does not refer to an aesthetization of the artist's existence. Instead, Foucault's examples go in the direction of relationship, of exchange, and not in the direction of the pure and autonomous implementation of a self-relation.

Forming life as living together takes place at the microphysical and the macrophysical level, in the forming of the individual body, in the forming of social relations. In his lecture, Foucault explicitly says about this: 'By basing the analysis of Cynicism on this theme of individualism, however, we are in danger of missing what from my point of view is one [of its] fundamental dimensions, that is to say, the problem, which is at the core of Cynicism, of establishing a relationship between forms of existence and manifestation of the truth.'[14] Philosophical activism is not about a model of 14. Ibid., 180. philosophical or artistic life beyond relations, at the edge of the world. Cynics live in the midst of the world, against the world, with the horizon of an other world; in Foucault's words, they have 'laid down this otherness of an *other* life, not simply as the choice of a different, happy, and sovereign life, but as the practice of an activism on the horizon of which is an *other* world'.[15] 15. Ibid., 287.

This understanding of an other life enabling an other world applies all the more to the collective Cynicism, or rather: the molecular Cynicism of the new activisms today. In this kind of molecular Cynicism, it is not the individual philosopher, not the dandyesque artist, not the existentialist activist that is at the centre, but rather the exchange relations of singularities testing disobedient, non-subservient, industrious forms of living. Such an activism based on relation does not succumb to a logic of connecting or accumulating individual points to make a whole. On the contrary, molecular Cynicism is based on its primary relational mode of existence. Relation defines

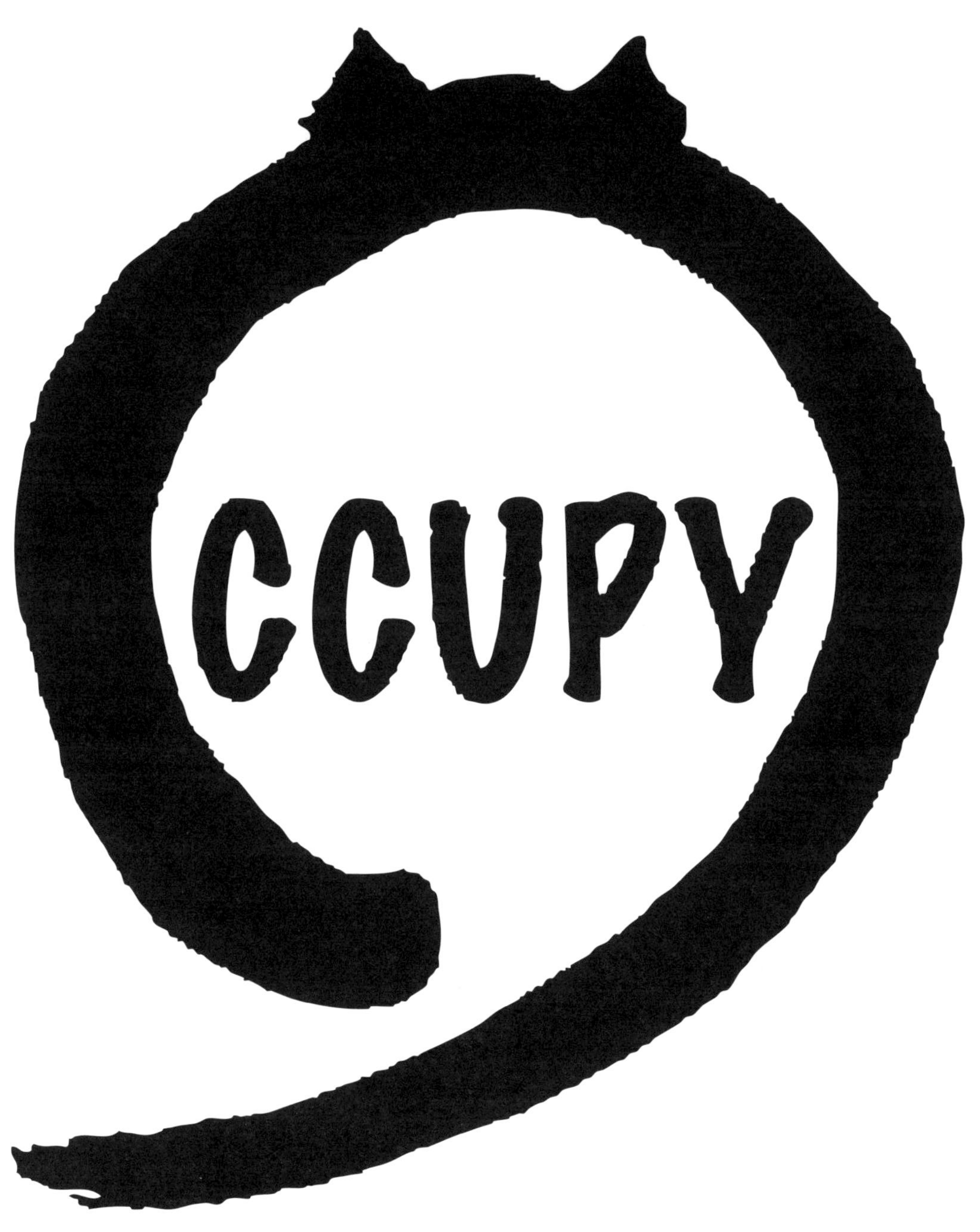
CCUPY

a qualitative *other world* where experimentations of what life might become or what a body can do are more relevant than a pre-figured capturing of situations through moral categories of good/bad, beautiful/not beautiful – hence the remarkable refusal of 'demands' in current Occupy movements around the globe.

If today's revolutions are not only taken as molar, as – in a narrow sense – political projects, but rather also as molecular revolutions, then the aesthetics of existence takes its place alongside the political project as a 'continual and constantly renewed work of giving form [to life]', to living together.[16]

16. Ibid., 162.

A contemporary concept of molecular revolution requires the ethico-aesthetic level of transforming forms of living into a beautiful and good life, as well as the becoming of forms of living together across continents: micro-machines, which in their singular situativity form disobedient modes of existence and subjectivation, develop arts of existence and life techniques, as well as translocally dispersed, global abstract machines. What accounts as beautiful in these practices is not a universal quality put into form, but a successful process of self-affirmative subjectivity that interlaces different modes of existence according to their very situated ecology. An aesthetic of existence as self-affirming defines the constitution of another world within and among existing worlds, not a subtraction or subsumption but a multiplication. Self-affirmative subjectivity moves beyond the individual through collective modes of expression – expression not as a unique form(ation) but a relational multiplicity 'self-enjoying' its existence.[17]

Such a process puts its operation into direct resonance with the capacity of heterogeneous elements to become collectively in and with their immediate social, mental and environmental ecology. An aesthetic of existence manifests nodes of truth and reality through the collective process of expression.

17. The notion of self-enjoyment is taken from Alfred North Whitehead. Whitehead describes self-enjoyment as the very process that enables an experience to come into itself, affirming its existence as what it is – relationally emergent and singular. On an activist philosophical scheme this activity of self-enjoyment is similar to Foucault's remarks on parrhêsia as the practice of manifesting truth or a world within and among other truths and worlds. On the concept of self-enjoyment, see Alfred N. Whitehead, *Modes of Thought* (New York: Free Press, 1968), 151. For an activist philosophical development of self-enjoyment see Massumi, *Semblance and Event*, op. cit. (note 10), 2-3.

The molecular revolution also comprises the 'ethical revolution' that is called for at the end of the manifesto of the Spanish occupiers of M-15. The multitude that occupied the many main squares of Spain beginning on 15 May for several weeks is not particularly interested in gaining symbolic space and media attention. The occupiers take over the occupied squares, they appropriate them and make them their own, even though they know they are only there for a certain time. This time, however, is decisive, an extraordinarily important time of their lives, the time of assemblies and the social time of living together, of residing and sleeping in the occupied squares. It is a time of finding and experimenting with heterogeneous und polyvocal truths/realities and new modes of collective expression. Their new ethico-aesthetic paradigm seeks revolution in the forming of their own lives and of living together. The call for an ethical revolution is thus not at all a kind of first demand for different, better politicians, nor simply the obvious demand that corrupt politics should resign as a whole. Instead, it is a demand to themselves, a call for fundamental transformations, for the fabrication of non-subservient machinic modes of living, for disobedient industries, for non-conforming forms of living together. Their ethico-aesthetic mode of existence becomes a 'laboratory of thought and experimenting for future forms of subjectivation'.[18] The ethics of such new forms of life and their experimental exploration yield an ethics of the event rather than a human ethics. As Félix Guattari points out, an aesthetics of existence 'has ethico-political implications because to speak of creation is to speak of the responsibility of the creative instance with regard to the thing created'.[19] Ethics is not a human affair but concerns the event of the creative instance with regard to the thing created. Machinic modes of living address mental, social and environmental ecologies as co-emerging. Experimental explorations for non-conforming forms of living therefore transform political and social ecologies through ethico-aesthetic practices across modes of existence without predetermining their actualization.

18. Félix Guattari, 'Entering the Post-Media Era', in: Sylvère Lotringer (ed.), *Soft Subversions* (Los Angeles: Semiotext(e), 2009), 301.

19. Félix Guattari, *Chaosmosis: An Ethico-Aesthetic Paradigm* (Bloomington/Indianapolis: Indiana University Press, 1995), 107.

2. Inventing New Modes of Organization

When today's activisms turn against a one-sidedly molar procedure, this does not mean that they neglect aspects of organization and re-territorialization. Yet the streaking of time and space finds its own molecular procedures. Molecular modes of organization are not organic, but rather orgic-industrious, not centred on representation, but non-representationist, not hierarchically differentiating, but radically inclusive. Molecularity does not focus on taking over state power, but it takes effect in the pores of everyday life, in the molecules of forms of living, across different materials of enunciation and technical modalities. Molar organization arises as striating re-territorialization, it focuses struggles on a main issue, a main contradiction, a master. In a molecular world of dispersion and multiplicity, a different form of re-territorialization is needed, inclusive and transversal, beyond individual or collective privileges. Transversality means that the movements of re-territorialization and de-territorialization do not pursue particular goals, they do not establish and secure privileges. Instead they smooth and streak territories by crossing through them. The special rights of every single singularity are diametrically opposed to all individual or collective privileges. Yet these special rights only exist where every singularity can fully live its own specialness, try out its own form of concatenation, streak its own time. There is no privileged position for the intellectuals, for art or activism. Molecular struggles are struggles that emerge incidentally and spread further through what is incidental to the incidentals. No master heads the molecular organization.

The Cynic philosopher is an anti-king. Philosophical activism is not practiced in the form of sects, communities, in the form of small numbers. Instead, there is no community at all in Cynicism; the Cynic form of philosophical activism is, according to Foucault, 'in the open, as it were, that is to say, an activism addressed to absolutely everyone'.[20] This kind of openness evolves in the practice of the new molecular activisms. In the language of the activists it places radical inclusion at the centre of assemblies, discussions and actions. An 'activism addressed to absolutely everyone', and yet nevertheless not operating universalistically, but transversally, like the tent camp in the Rothschild Boulevard in Tel Aviv, for example, following which the largest demonstration for social justice in the history of Israel took place in early September 2011. Radical inclusion means here, most of all, establishing an open milieu, in which the right to a place to live is not only demanded for everyone, but also acted out straight away in protest. The tent assemblages, the assemblies, the discussions are already living examples of the radical inclusion and transversality of the movement.

20. Foucault, *The Courage of Truth*, op. cit. (note 9), 284.

In the case of #occupy wallstreet, the tendency to radical inclusion is evident primarily in the invention and development of general assemblies. These are not so much 'general assemblies' in the conventional sense, but rather transversal assemblages of singularities, which renew the grassroots-democratic experiences of the anti-globalization and social forums movement, further developing them into a form of polyvocality – for instance in the invention, almost by chance and out of necessity, of a new procedure of 'amplification': because the police forbid them to use microphones, megaphones or other technical means, they began to repeat every single sentence from the speakers in chorus. The functionality of this repetition consists, first of all, in making the speech intelligible for hundreds of people in an open air setting. Yet the chorus as amplification here is neither a purely neutral medium of conveyance nor a euphoric affirmation of the speakers. It can happen that the chorus, whose voice is speaking the same thing, proves to be radically polyvocal and differentiated: one voice supports the speaker with hand signs, the next declares dissent with other hand signs, and the third has turned away from the speaker to better ensure the amplifying function for the others listening.

Another striking example of the self-affirmative and re-singularizing collective and inclusive practices of contemporary protest are the transversal modes of expression across different forms and media. Both form and media are detached from their representational function and turn into open platforms for expression. While techniques of the self through bodily amplification generate a-signifying means of enunciation a similar process occurs in the use of digital technologies. The singular-collective form of protest across the globe has given birth to new ways of living collectively through live video-streaming, writing and conceptualizing in de-territorialized online-zones and the actual occupation of physical space with its own modalities of living and producing together. The mass of digital technologies opposing the wall of policemen during marches in downtown Manhattan or the live capture of police violence against a sit-in at UC Davis are just one node of collectively constituting a differentiation of truths. Not one truth dominating the others, but a heterogeneous and singular multitude of enunciations. The technologies or technical assemblages insert themselves into the social and environmental ecologies as part of the new movements. The 'incorporeal materialism' of the digital inserts a layer of immediacy and at the same time the multiplication of timelines and spaces to the singular and local struggles and concerns at stake.[21] The processual multiplicities of these machines for enunciation operate aesthetically as much as ethically. In their aesthetics they self-enjoy their polyvocality in the videos produced on the ground of #occupy wallstreet and elsewhere, not representing particular groups but putting the immediacy of collective engagement into resonance with the expressive capacities of video itself. In other occasions through live streams the webcam and the activist's moving body, the architectural outline and the image processing develop into what Guattari calls 'existential operators'.[22] Such existential operators are forms of live, minority becomings, beyond the signifier and the sign moving towards a machinic productivity of self-affirming practices. This fundamental shift in the appropriation of time and space and their simultaneous collective sharing across different singularities calls forth a 'post-media' practice as part of the new and experimental aesthetics of existence.

21. Félix Guattari, *The Guattari Reader*, ed. by Gary Genosko (Cambridge, MA: Blackwell Publishers, 1996), 176.

22. Félix Guattari, 'Postmodern Deadlock and Post-Media Transition', in: *Soft Subversions*, op. cit. (note 18), 300.

3. Industrious Re-Appropriation of Time

Just as the Cynic philosopher seeks scandal in the offensive transparency of his life, the new activisms speak clearly by taking the empty promise of 'public space' at its word. This is the exercise, as widely visible as possible, of deviant modes of subjectivation, not or not only in the nakedness, placelessness and promiscuity of the Cynics, but most of all in playing with the paradox of the public: public space does not exist, and most of all not in the smooth spaces of urban centres, whether they are the touristic non-places of the Puerta del Sol or the Rothschild Boulevard, whether it is the privatized sphere of Zuccotti Park or the heavy traffic of Tahrir Square. And yet, or specifically because of this, the new activisms occupy the central squares, turn them into common-places, as a paradoxical provocation of normativity and normalization. And beyond this spatial re-territorialization, it is primarily the re-appropriation of time that marks the protestors' modes of action. In the midst of the nervous poly-rhythms of precarious life, in the midst of this mixture of drivenness and melancholy, they invent a surplus, in the midst of subservience they create a desire to not be taken into service in that way. In the midst of hurried timelessness, the precarious strikers insist on different time-relations, they streak the time in the patience of assemblies, in spreading out living, residing, sleeping in the squares, feeling their way to the first rudimentary possibilities of a new form of resistance, the molecular strike.

The occupiers take the space and time seriously that they set up, striate, streak,

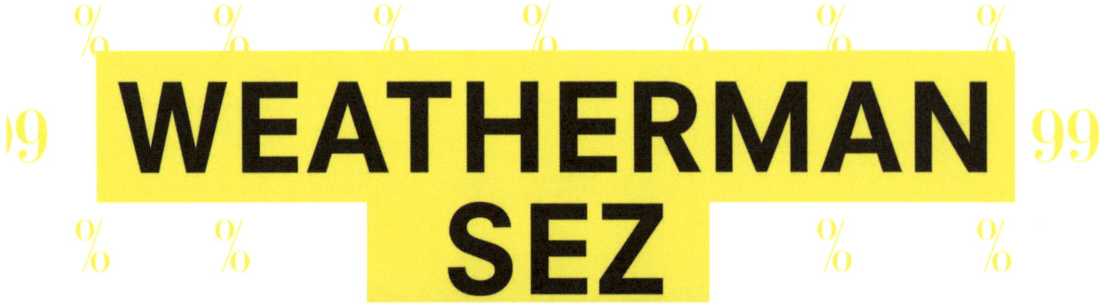
WEATHERMAN
SEZ

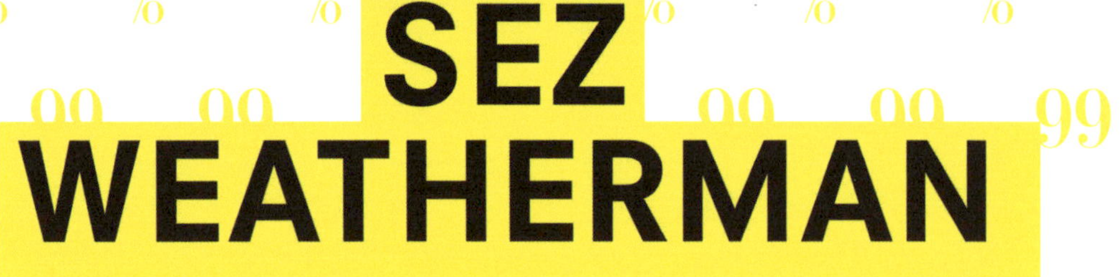
LIVE
Extended Forecast
SUN MON TUE WED
OCCUPY
OCCUPY
OCCUPY
OCCUPY
OCCUPY
OCCUPY
OCCUPY
OCCUPY
OCCUPY
OCCUPY
OCCUPY
OCCUPY
TONIGHT'S FORECAST
99%
6:23
THE WEATHER CHANNEL
weather.com
SEZ
WEATHERMAN

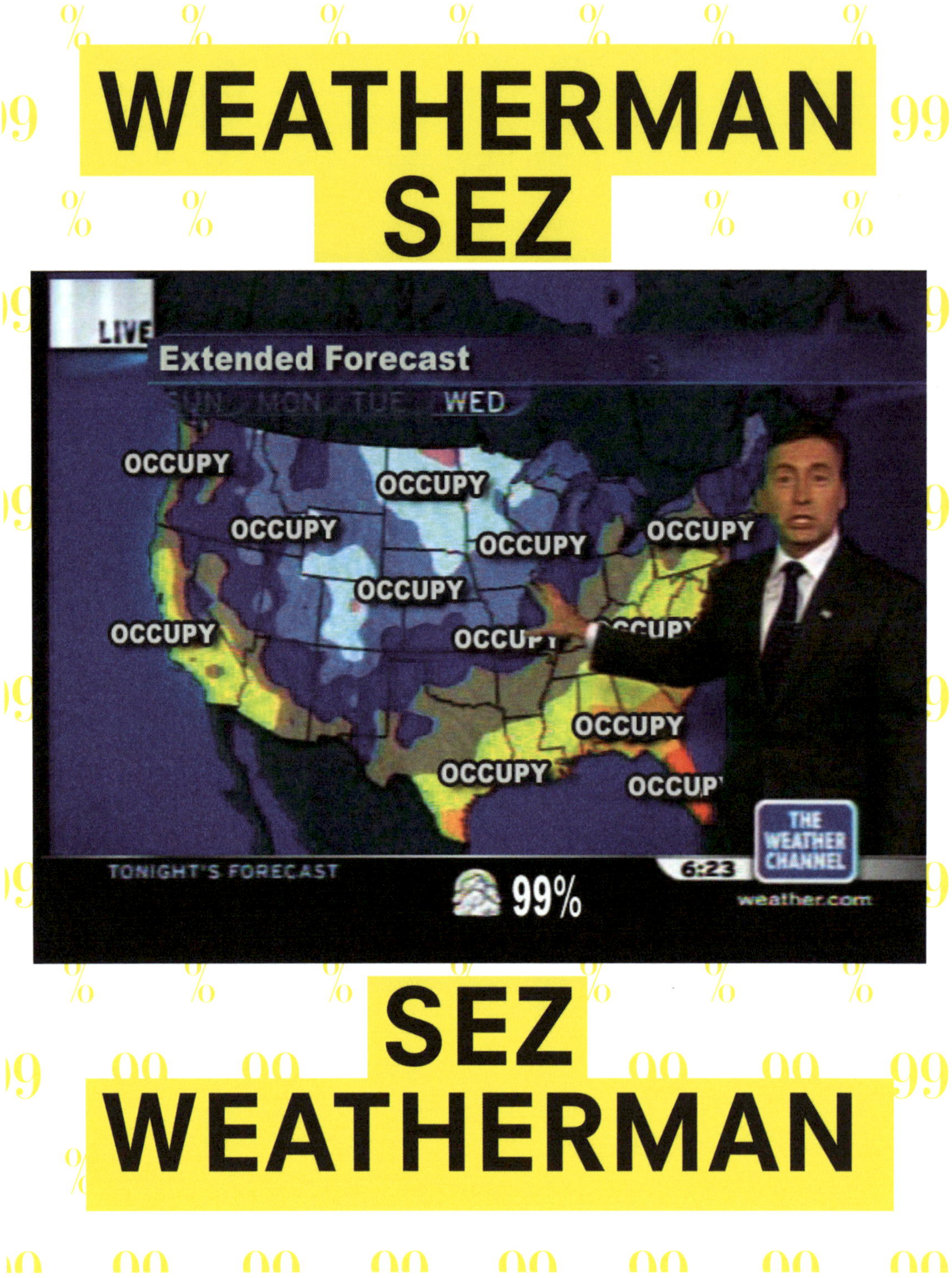

taking time for long, patient discussions and taking time to stay in this place, developing a new everyday life, even if only for a short time. In an otherwise boundless everyday life, the molecular strike spreads out these small new durations of everyday life. Its institution, however, first requires an evental break with subservient de-territorialization in machinic capitalism. The molecular strike is both: duration and break. It is not leaving, not dropping out of this world, no time-out. The molecular strike is the breach in the time regime of subservient de-territorialization that we drive in, in order to try out new ways of living, new forms of organization, new time relations. No longer a struggle merely to reduce working time, but rather for an entirely new streaking of time as a whole. In machinic capitalism, it is a matter of the whole, the totality of time, its entire appropriation. The molecular strike struggles for its re-appropriation, its streaking, piece by piece. The new Wobblies will not be Industrial Workers of the World, but rather Industrious Workers of the world, a gigantic industry carrying everything along with it, not submitting to subservient de-territorialization, at the same time a re-territorialization, an industrious refrain, a dangerous class that will no longer let its time be stolen.

Joost de Bloois

Without Exception: Art, Consensus and the Public Sphere

Artists and theorists have frequently deliberated the meaning of the idea of 'autonomy in art', and certainly since the protests against the cutbacks in art. Cultural studies specialist Joost de Bloois considers the present debate on this issue problematic because it is based too much on assumptions. Fundamental contradictions within the art sector as well as its complex relation to politics and the public domain are often ignored.

'Art demands exception, but it will not be excepted'[1]

'Autonomy' is not just the concern of the art world that is now, in the Netherlands, holding the 'short end of the stick', but, as self-legislation, immunity and territory, 'autonomy' is equally the concern of whomever is at the other end of that stick: in the Dutch case, that peculiar consortium of populists and neoliberals that rose to power after the 2010 elections. The irreducible ambivalence of current Dutch politics is the coupling of a global and de-territorialized neoliberal economic model and a populist ideology that is re-territorializing to the extreme. We are witnessing a rather odd work of mourning: the rapid dismantlement of the commons (of which the institutions of the welfare state are emblematic), which appears to be the prime goal of current austerity policies, is at the same time lamented and conjured by reserving the remains of the welfare state for those who are truly deserving, and who are now defined in strictly national terms. Equally, the protests we have seen so far against the unprecedented cuts in the very infrastructure of the Dutch art world seem to be characterized by a similar melancholia: claims of the universal significance of art were made to justify calls for the continuation of the state's mecenat; claims that echoed, seemingly without being aware of the dissonance, both the rhetoric of the twentieth-century vanguard and the jargon of social-democratic cultural policymaking. Although there is no doubt that where we come from is a lot better than what we are heading for, the fundamental ambivalences of the art world today, as well as the complexity and vicissitudes of its relation to politics and its assumed public role, remain largely unaddressed. This long overdue problematization might, in fact, be obstructed by the tacit assumptions of 'autonomy' that underpin current debates; assumptions that in particular fail to address art's relation to a public sphere that may increasingly be characterized as post-bourgeois, post-democratic and even post-cultural. What has become clear in the debates that accompanied the protests against the assault on the arts in the Netherlands is that the paradox that has sustained most of twentieth-century avant-garde practices, and has effectively served as the ground for art's politicization throughout that century, has become inoperative: in the current liberal-populist constellation, the creed that 'art is *exceptional* and therefore may claim the *universal*' is reduced to nothing more than an oxymoron that, as such, is negligible. Yet, it is precisely this oxymoron that continues to determine debates today, and that obscures the complexity of art's (real or potential) autonomy as well as its closely related public significance. Therefore, we might ask whether 'autonomy' truly remains 'the elephant' in the room', that is to say, 'the only matrix at our disposal'

1. Gerald Raunig paraphrasing Kafka at the Autonomy conference, Van Abbe Museum Eindhoven, 7-9 October 2011.

to think about art's public and political significance and to give shape to the responses and strategies in relation to the neoliberal restructuring of the art world and the cultural sphere.[2] I would precisely like to argue that any meaningful conception of 'autonomy' today has to thoroughly account for the intimate correlation between art and contemporary capitalism and, perhaps particularly in the Netherlands, the advent of a liberal-populist consensus and the transformations of the public sphere that have resulted from this.

2. Statements made by John Byrne and Charles Esche at the Autonomy conference in Eindhoven.

'Relative Heteronomy'

As Jorinde Seijdel writes in her book on the prevalence of 'amateurism' in today's art world: throughout the twentieth century, the history of art's autonomy has foremost been the history of art's increasing *professionalization*.[3] Practically speaking, 'autonomy' resulted from a fundamental operation of exchange: art shrugged off its direct, precarious, ideological dependency on higher powers by confining itself to the ever proliferating framework of the institutions of the bourgeois state (art schools, museums, art education, etcetera). In our contemporary neoliberal context, however, 'professionalization' has been given a meaning that seems fundamentally at odds with still current notions of autonomy. Firstly,

3. Jorinde Seijdel, *De waarde van de amateur* (Amsterdam: Fonds BKVB, 2010).

the increasing demand for direct valorization of art's institutions (disguised as the urge to 'professionalize'). Secondly, the ever growing symbiosis between art and the market, or rather: art and the very basic tenets of the economy. Over the past decades these two forms of professionalization have grown ever closer. On the one hand, we see a veritable boom of professional training programmes such as MFA's, curatorial programmes and, most of all, the double helix of 'art and research'. This so-called 'educational turn' in the art world cannot be seen apart from the increasing economization of knowledge work.[4] It drags the art world into academic institutions that now operate under the premises of the Bologna treaty, which precisely reorganizes higher education along the lines of neoliberal political economy.[5] On the other hand, we witness how art has become inextricably bound up with dominant modes of capital accumulation; in recent decades of art theory, this has been extensively documented, most notably in post-operaist and post-autonomist theory. The shift from Fordism to post-Fordism, from material to immaterial labour, has

4. See Marion von Osten and Eva Egermann, 'Twist and Shout: On Free Universities, Educational Reforms and Twists and Turns Inside and Outside the Art World', in: Paul O'Neill and Mick Wilson, *Curating and the Educational Turn* (London/ Amsterdam: Open Editions/De Appel, 2010), 277.

5. Also, in many cases, this academic institutionalization of art becomes the only available means of making a living as an artist outside of the speculative art market (as Douglas Fogle recently put it in *Frieze* magazine: 'If you can't wait tables, you can always teach'). See http:// www.frieze.com/issue/ article/art-rules/.

turned art from a relative anomaly into *the* model for contemporary capital accumulation. The artist now functions as the new Stakhanov, the new flexible, precarious superworker: the artist, often simultaneously fulfils her role as creative worker, as the eternal intern 'who has nothing to offer but her free labour',[6] and as the *homo debtor*, the indebted subject who perpetually invests in her own 'human capital'. Equally, the valorization of art seems to perfectly fit the now dominant mode of capital accumulation, since it *operates through speculation* (at least in the most prominent part of the artistic economy). Furthermore, the modus operandi for the valorization of art is largely that of today's capitalism: it operates through derived capital accumulation such as city branding or the never-ending circus of biennials and festivals.[7]

Crucially, art has become largely indistinguishable from the 'creative industries' (design, fashion, media, etcetera), now championed by Dutch government policies, and therefore of other designer and luxury goods. As Isabelle Graw argues, in this context, even Bourdieu's concept of art's 'relative autonomy' is too optimistic. Rather, we should speak of the 'relative heteronomy' of art today: 'Autonomy is no longer the dominant structural characteristic of the field of art. Considering the dominance of the economic system within society, it is necessary to shift the emphasis toward a definition of the artistic field as "relatively heteronomous". In concrete terms, this means that the external constraints are placed in the foreground.'[8]

The creative economy (and its synonyms such as 'cognitive capitalism' or 'immaterial labour') has not so much shifted art towards the centre of capital accumulation, but rather appropriated its modus operandi: art is effectively superseded by the creative economy and is now exiled at its outer margins. *Art qua art* is at best a niche among others. 'Art' is but one of the many composite private/public circuits that constitute neoliberal society (and that have come to replace 'the social fabric'). Consequently, it is doubtful whether art, as such, is powerful enough to change its own exorbitant position under neoliberalism in any significant way. Let alone that it may claim its, politically vanguardist, 'exceptional universalism'. This is not to say that art cannot, and even less: should not act politically; however, in our current context, we will have to be very specific about art's political radius (and where to put the emphasis in the notion of 'political art'). As we will see, the voluntarist deadlock into which a large part of the debate driven by contemporary conceptions of 'autonomy' (at least in the Netherlands) has manoeuvred itself, does not allow this radius to be addressed.

6. See Hito Steyerl, 'Art as Occupation: Claims for an Autonomy of Life', http://www.e-flux.com/journal/art-as-occupation-claims-for-an-autonomy-of-life-12/.

7. Equally, the valorization of art depends on what we might call the 'derivatives' of the art world: art criticism, curatorial discourse, media exposure, etcetera.

8. Isabelle Graw, *High Price: Art between the Market and Celebrity Culture* (Berlin: Sternberg Press, 2010), 141.

In this context, both sides of the debate concerning the cuts in the art world in the Netherlands seem rather anachronistic. State Secretary for Culture Halbe Zijlstra intriguingly disregards the reality of the art market and its intertwining with contemporary capital accumulation by inciting artists to become 'cultural entrepreneurs' who need to give up their 'addiction' to government subsidies as their supposed *only lifeline*.[9] The rationale behind Zijlstra's policy is that art, in recent decades, sided with the wrong kind of economism: still too Keynesian (too much state-sponsored valorization, rather than *immediate* valorization), and too much emphasis on Third Way social-democracy for his taste. This explains why the current policies attack the educational and institutional infrastructure, which now needs to be subjected to the regime of immediate value-extraction. At the same time, we see how the Dutch art world reacts with a similar disregard for the real significance of art's autonomy today. We hear the mantra of art's fundamental 'valuelessness', of art's autonomy opposing principles of exchange, valorization and commodification, when in reality this relation is at best ambiguous. Although the energies that went into the protests against the indeed unprecedented cuts in the arts in the Netherlands should by no means be underestimated, these perhaps also display a peculiar misreading of the developments within the art world over the past 30 years and seem to fall back on an absolute (all too romantic and pre-Adornian) notion of autonomy that is, even more worryingly, effectively translated as dependency on the state, without taking into account the extent to which that state has redesigned itself along neoliberal lines.

'Autonomy' is assumed to be a self-evident attribute that correlatively turns both the art work and the artist into fiercely independent *subjects* – who inevitably get in the way of any meaningful rethinking of 'autonomy' within today's political economy. Because art seems bereft of any effective positioning concerning its autonomy (or lack thereof) in relation to neoliberal modes of capital accumulation, artists and other defenders of art's cause have lapsed into an anachronistic voluntarism. To give but what is probably the most outspoken example of this tendency: Dutch artist Jonas Staal's neo-Beuyssian call for 'creative man' as the antipode of the neoliberal homo oeconomicus.[10] Remarkably, in Staal's appeal, the *generic* aspect of Beuys's *Jeder Mensch ein Künstler* – its address to unleash undefined potentiality – is immediately

9. This appeal, again, seems to be a slightly anachronistic notion (one imagines Victorian entrepreneurs with top hats and cigars): What could be the meaning of 'entrepreneurship' in a financial economy? This perhaps most of all reveals the *disciplining* function of the notion of 'entrepreneurship': perhaps art has sailed too close to the heart of financialization for its own good and it now needs to be dragged back into the world of the atomized producer-consumers?

10. See Jonas Staal, 'De hardwerkende Nederlander en de scheppende mens. Een aanval op een van ons, is een aanval op ons allen', in: *Open Noodnummer: Over de nieuwe politiek van cultuur*, http://www.skor.nl/nl/site/item/open-noodnummer-over-de-nieuwe-politiek-van-cultuur.

muted by the fact that the emphasis is very much on 'every man an *artist*': it presupposes a subject whose autonomy, as the guarantor of creativity, is always already considered a given (and whose historically limited agency, for example under neoliberal rule, thus remains unquestioned; its historical situatedness becomes a burden that can simply be shrugged off). Staal's *détournement* of Beuys's call to arms implies that *before producing anything else, man must produce himself*. Here, autonomy paradoxically becomes the timeless attribute of an equally timeless subject that acts as the guardian of its own potentiality, thus forbidding time to impede its autonomy. Consequently, Beuys's generic appeal is transformed in a productivist and thus subjective project, which is, practically, expressed in quasi-Leninist terms of an artistic-political avant-garde that needs to *bring about* 'creative man'.[11] The microcosm of the artistic event is projected onto the macrocosm of society, implying that the microcosm of art some-how *directly influences* the public sphere – an idea that conveniently remains unproblematized because of its voluntarist assumptions. Staal's proposals start from the voluntarist assumption of an autonomous subject that is then seamlessly equated with a political and artistic vanguard that, paradoxically, is presented as both *self-organizing* and as a *model* for a truly democratic society. This stance is at the root of what Boris Buden calls 'the new robinsonades' that haunt many contemporary theories of political and artistic autonomy.[12] Buden denounces the tendency for *'self-proclaimed autonomy* that believes it is able to arm itself with positive contents *from its own sources* and thus challenge neoliberal capitalism. . . . It needs a pre-historic and pre-political – and thus also a universalistic – identity to be able to become a political subject at all.'[13] At best, this leads to moralistic denunciations of the 'collaborating' neoliberal art institution (leaning heavily on Schmittian notions of enmity), to the moralistic denunciation of the art world's 'elites', and to inevitable appeals for an avant-garde of the righteous.

Such conceptions of autonomy take as a given that the alternative to neoliberal capitalism is somehow to be *designed*, and more importantly, that art and politics are somehow *on a par* since both are in the busi-

11. This is precisely expressed in the project 'Allegories of Good and Bad Governement' that was hosted by the W139 arts center in Amsterdam, May 2011; it brought together artists, key figures from the cultural sector and (local) politicians in a carefully designed setting (part camping site, part open office space). For Jonas Staal the project offers a model for 'a training camp for ideological recalibration and experiments in shared living on a micro-level'; part managerial leadership programme, part 're-education facility', the project could involve a series of discussions between '*experienced* artists and designers', politicians, aldermen and other prominent figures. See http://koerskunst.nl/landelijk-tentenkamp-voor-politici-en-kunstenaars/. For a detailed critique of the work of Jonas Staal, see Joost de Bloois, Ernst van den Hemel and Femke Kaulingfreks, 'Futloze wereld: Over medeplichtig kunstenaarschap volgens Jonas Staal', *nY* 2011:11, 342-358; see also Staal's reply in the same issue.

12. See Boris Buden 'Commentary on Branka Ćurčić: Autonomous Spaces of Deregulation and Critique: Is a Cooperation with Neoliberal Art Institutions Possible?', http://eipcp.net/transversal/0407/buden2/en.

13. Ibid., my italics JdB.

ness of designing things. As Jacques Rancière, whose work often serves as a reference for justifying such correspondences, reminds us: there is a *relation of resemblance* between art and politics that is not a *relation of equivalence*.[14] In examples such as Staal's, this relation collapses into equivalence, which leaves curiously unchallenged notions of artisthood and art's relation to capital accumulation. We witness a similar confusion of resemblance and equivalence in current strategies of *hyperidentifying art as labour*, in particular as *precarious labour*.[15] The rationale behind this identification is that, if labour is increasingly flexible, if cognitive capitalism has recourse to the immaterial labour of communication, creativity and affect, then the artist is no longer the exception to the rule of labour, but becomes, as we have seen, if not the new model worker, at least a metonymic working subject. Indeed, the notion of 'precarity' has effectively been used as a rallying cry attempting to politically align artists and other members of the creative class with the 'precariat',[16] and to provide the former with a renewed, if not guiding political role. However, these alliances

14. See for example Jacques Rancière, *Les Écarts du cinéma* (Paris: Éditions la Fabrique, 2011) and *Tant pis pour les gens fatigués: Entretiens* (Paris: Éditions Amsterdam, 2009).

15. See for example, Pascal Gielen and Paul de Bruyne (eds.), *Being an Artist in Post-Fordist Times* (Rotterdam: NAI Publishers, 2009); Pascal Gielen, *The Murmuring of the Artistic Multitude: Global Art, Memory and Post-Fordism* (Amsterdam: Valiz, 2009); and *Open* 17 (2009): *A Precarious Existence: Vulnerability in the Public Domain.*

16. See Guy Standing, *The Precariat: The New Dangerous Class?* (London: Bloombury, 2011).

and identifications are problematic: if, under cognitive capitalism, the worker's greatest asset becomes her symbolic, communicative and affective capital, than obviously the creative class is in a much better position than, say, cleaners and postmen; it is questionable whether the assertion of fairly allegorical relations between types of immaterial labour, based on affective proximities, can serve as an impetus for social and political mobilization.[17] As Franco Berardi shows: the generalization of precarity among the workforce is foremost an attempt to *dis-identify working subjects from their labour* (among other things 'precarity' means being perpetually *in and out of work*).[18] Today, it is therefore at best questionable whether labour still serves as a privileged site for emancipatory political mobilization. Structurally, the shift from Fordism to post-Fordism, from *productive* capital accumulation to *unproductive* capital accumulation, has resulted in a generalized disidentification with labour. We might even say that, ironically, the only places where one still is allowed to identify as a worker are the supposed ivory towers of the art world and the world of academic critical theory. Unproductive capital accumulation turns workers into debtors: being in debt is an isolated, passive position; a

17. For an attempt at theorizing such affective proximities, see for example Maiko Tanaka, 'Notes for Further Action Research' in Binna Choi and Maiko Tanaka, *The Grand Domestic Revolution GOES ON* (London/ Utrecht: Bedford Press/ Casco, 2010).

18. See Franco Berardi, *Precarious Rhapsody: Semiocapitalism and the Pathologies of the Post-Alpha Generation* (London/New York: Autonomedia, 2009).

position of dependency that predates bourgeois or proletarian subjectivity. It is unlikely that we will see labour's replacements, debt and rent, act as an impetus for sociopolitical mobilization.[19] Against this background, artists perform roles that make any identification as a traditional working subject virtually impossible. For Isabell Lorey, artists act 'simultaneously as service providers, producers and entrepreneurs of themselves'[20] – they constitute a fragmented working subject; this fragmentation is accentuated by the ever increasing degree of abstraction of artistic activity: the artist, from producer, is increasingly becoming a mediator for assembling and transmitting knowledge and information; artist, researcher and curator are becoming more and more indistinguishable. This makes for a feeble mobilizing force indeed, which makes any recourse to an unproblematized notion of 'autonomy', or the idea of a mobilizing vanguard, obsolete. More often than not, the identification of art and (precarious) labour results in the aesthetization of precarity and informality, reinforcing the notion that precarity is a *state of being* rather than a socioeconomic condition to be overcome by means of collective engagement.

19. See Maurizio Lazzarato, *La fabrique de l'homme endetté: Essai sur la condition néolibérale* (Paris: Éditions Amsterdam, 2011).

20. Isabell Lorey, 'Virtuosos of Freedom: On the Implosion of Political Virtuosity and Productive Labour', in: Gerald Raunig et al., *Critique of Creativity: Precarity, Subjectivity and Resistance in the 'Creative Industries'* (London: MayFly Books, 2010).

Liberal-Populism, Consensus and the Public Sphere

Any reconsideration of 'autonomy' today, especially in the Dutch context, needs to take into account the issue of *consensus*. In fact 'consensus' might be the dirty little secret of the protests against the neoliberal restructuring of the art world. Jacques Rancière defines 'consensus' as the conflation between a socioeconomic model (in this case, neoliberalism) and a supposed national ethos.[21] This is exactly what is at stake in the notion of the 'Hardworking Dutchman', *de Hardwerkende Nederlander*. The concept, or should we say: the conceptual persona of the Hardworking Dutchman can be found throughout the political spectrum: from the populist far right – who gave it names: Henk and Ingrid – to the socialist far left, to the now ruling liberal and Christian democratic parties. The Hardworking Dutchman expresses what we could call the *liberal-populist consensus*. This liberal-populist consensus imposes, by means of national identity, a neoliberal socioeconomic model. The Hardworking Dutchman emphatically *does not* see himself (collectively) as a 'worker', but as a *hardworking individual* who knows how to take care of himself (ironically, not unlike the very same artists that act as the Hardworking Dutchman's lazy and unproductive counterpart). Populist, even racist assumptions are thus seamlessly inte-

21. Jacques Rancière, *Moments politiques. Interventions 1977-2009* (Paris: Éditions La Fabrique, 2009).

grated into a larger neoliberal project. As Étienne Balibar argues: this liberal-populist consensus *equates the national and the social*, and is therefore all the more compelling (we see this for example in the populist defence of what remains of the welfare state: health care and pensions are now the private interests of the Hardworking Dutchman rather than being considered as commons).[22] The liberal-populist consensus leaves little room for political citizenship as any opposition to the economic policy of neoliberal privatization is immediately denounced as treason against Dutch morals. The liberal-populist consensus conflates arguments of *economic profitability* with *popular will* and *democratic decision making*; this is why the much invoked Dutch notion of *draagvlak* ('public support', which art is supposedly lacking) is such a poisonous term: it brings together, to the point of indiscernibility, the three mutually exclusive principles mentioned above. The notion of 'public support' thus becomes a perversion of the bourgeois idea of art as a common good: if it fails to generate *private* profits than it cannot be *publicly* supported, such is the will of the people . . . The liberal-populist consensus is a *disjunctive synthesis* if ever there was one, but not necessarily in the way Deleuze and Guattari envisioned.[23] It is the logic of the 'AND' that, far from offering lines of flight, effec-

22. See Étienne Balibar, *Droit de cité* (Paris: Presses universitaires de France, 1998).

23. See Gilles Deleuze and Félix Guattari, *L'Anti-Oedipe* (Paris: Éditions de Minuit, 1972).

tively boards up the public sphere and public debate. We should add to this the populist *rhetoric of the hyperbole* which effectively evacuates the political arena of any serious exchange of ideas: those who oppose the populist rant are invariably dismissed as insane, sick, cowardly, etcetera (they are pathologized and never to be taken seriously); the populist re-enactment of the 1980s culture wars clears the public arena from its dissident voices by endless, self-exhausting non-debates: populism thus pays lip service to neoliberal policies, which it consistently albeit never outspokenly supports, by taking out vocal opponents to these policies (the populist political economy is probably best translated as the oxymoronic 'neoliberalism in one country').

In this context, *autonomy as self-proclamation in the public sphere* is a highly problematic conception. It effectively bypasses any analysis of the actual conditions of that public sphere, which, to start with, is always already partly privatized under neoliberalism. The reaction against liberal populism is oddly regressive: although it, to a large extent, relies on the strategies and results of, for example, institutional critique and many other twentieth-century criticisms of the alleged public accessibility and political significance of art and its institutions, it seems reluctant when it comes to acknowledging its own significance within the liberal-populist sociopolitical consensus. In particular under the aegis of theories of cognitive capitalism and immaterial labour, art is perhaps more politicized than ever, yet this politicization, paradoxically, often seems to amount to merely denouncing and discarding the political economy these theories bring to light. Simply dreaming up a counter-hegemony of the commons and the affective against the politics of privatization and nationalist sentiment might not be the most favourable strategy. Fundamentally, the liberal-populist consensus discards the (remnants) of bourgeois and social-democratic culture, of which the public accessibility of art and knowledge was an essential component. Even the most virulent anti-bourgeois art of the twentieth century still proceeded from the public status conferred to art by bourgeois ideology, and its supposed role in such things as democratic and participatory citizenship. Post-Fordist societies are also post-democratic societies, and this has vital consequences for any political role that art might envision. The liberal-populist consensus precisely says that *there is no such thing as the common*, unless the common is defined in purely negative terms: we have to protect the remnants of the welfare state as long as they serve our private interests (we want health care, albeit as an insurance of sorts for healthy people, and most of all, we desire the police). It thus comes as no surprise that 70 per cent of the Dutch electorate are in favour of the cuts;[24] it

is unlikely that they will get even a glimpse of the amount of militant mobilization within the Dutch art world today . . .

If conceptions of 'autonomy' today mostly hinge on art's self-legislated agency in the public sphere, it is all the more surprising to see that the architecture of that 'public sphere' remains merely an object of denunciation. The liberal-populist consensus endorses the politics of privatization, not just in economic but in sociocultural terms as well. The fragmentation or nichefication of the commons, the replacement of the labouring subject by the hardworking individual, national and local politics becoming more and more a depository for populist resentment (that is: precisely these levels of policymaking art has to deal with): all of these developments cannot be merely rejected as obstacles on the path to radical self-organization, but need to effectively be taken into account in any critical assessment of 'autonomy' today. Even more worryingly, it seems that the relative ease with which a certain philosophical lexicon of radical democracy has been picked up by the art world obscures its sociopolitical situatedness and, consequently, political radius rather than enlightens it. It appears as if the rhetoric of *demos* and *event* is projected onto the segment of the art world that is not entirely market driven, and that therefore is closely associated with government policies, and that is now championed as the locus of radical democracy. Event-based

24. See http://www.nrc.nl/nieuws/2011/07/03/meerderheid-nederlanders-staat-achter-bezuinigingen-op-cultuur/.

and relational art that previously acted as the restorer of the social tissue or as spearhead of the creative economy is now wishfully turned into a model for radical emancipatory politics. In reality, however, it is precisely this type of artistic practice that is now under liberal-populist fire and threatens to lose its central place in government policies; a precarious situation that invalidates the radical claims made at the very moment these are uttered.

Therefore, any rethinking of 'autonomy' today has to take into account its profound ambivalences, in particular autonomy's relation to a neoliberal capitalism that, as Paolo Virno argues, produces nothing but ambivalent subjects.[25] What characterizes today's capitalist societies, as well as their critiques, is *the absence of a reassuring third term*:[26] little to nothing stands between individual lives and the processes of capital accumulation. There are no ontological, libidinal or anthropological safe havens. We can no longer be assured of the inherently emancipatory nature of creativity or desire, and therefore these can no longer act as the prerequisites for autonomy. In this context, the voluntarist conception of autonomy makes little sense; in this context, autonomy, as it was in Adorno's case, is in a sense always *composite*.

Maybe, today, 'autonomy' as the *conditio sine qua non* for whatever radical politics or whatever counter-hegemony to neoliberalism simply makes too little sense to still act as a political and practical catalyst. What if 'autonomy' keeps us inevitably stuck in a rather tedious narrative of good news/bad news in which, as the critic Jan Verwoert writes, the good news is invariably that 'the inherent theatricality of politics puts us [artists, intellectuals and cultural producers] in a position of power' and the bad news is invariably that, in truth, 'the potential of art to make a sense that would politicize the crowds is minute and negligible'.[27] If invoking 'autonomy' becomes repetitive moralistic denunciation, if tackling the inevitable relation between art and capital becomes obsessing about appropriation, and criticism consists of allegories of enslavement, maybe it is time to change the record.

25. See Paolo Virno. *A Grammar of the Multitude* (New York: Semiotext(e), 2004) and Paolo Virno 'The Ambivalence of Disenchantment', in: Paolo Virno and Michael Hardt (eds.). *Radical Thought in Italy: A Potential Politics* (Minneapolis: University of Minnesota Press, 1996).

26. See Paolo Virno, *Multitude: Between Innovation and Negation* (New York: Semiotex(e), 2008).

27. Jan Verwoert, *Tell Me What You Want, What You Really, Really Want* (Berlin: Sternberg Press, 2010), 98-99.

column

JORINDE SEIJDEL

ANYONE, ANYWHERE, ANYTIME

ON AUTONOMY AND ANONYMITY

Reflecting upon Anonymous, the activist Internet movement that can be anyone and that has no leader or external management, the following question comes to mind: could autonomy and anonymity perhaps have something to do with each other, in thinking about new forms of critical art and culture? The term 'anonymous', from the Greek *anoonumos*, means 'nameless', 'unnamed' and also 'incognito' or 'unmarked'. The advent of the so-called autonomous subject in the modern age was specifically coupled with the naming of that subject and with a rational process of individualization. This 'calling by name' also literally resulted in a personality culture and a theory of authorship, not least within the arts, in which the identifying, the determining of a person's individuality is of great importance, and which has produced strict value structures. The social order and political administration that is attendant on this is based on people's uniqueness, on what makes them recognizable and identifiable. Distinctive identities cannot be ascertained from anonymous subjects, or at least not without difficulty: the anonymous subject, which is in fact a contradiction in terms, undermines the logic and culture of the autonomous subject, in that it does not let itself be controlled just like that. It's not for nothing that messages without a sender are almost always distrusted in our culture: the anonymous subject becomes the object of suspicion.

From the perspective of these modern ideological conceptions, anonymity and autonomy would thus appear to be mutually exclusive. One can immediately qualify this, however. For instance, you can assert that a condition and situation of anonymity in fact also implies a degree of autonomy in the sense of freedom and the room to move with respect to the dominant system. This autonomous anonymity or anonymous autonomy was found by a number of artists and activists in the 1990s, for instance, in the form of the 'multiple use name' Luther Blisset ('author' of the novel Q) and later Wu Ming, both of them explorations of new forms

of authorship and identity, and spinoffs of the
Italian counterculture's Autonomia movement.

Not being able to be identified because
of a voluntary, self-chosen anonymity, an act of
resistance, has its advantages and offers new oper-
ational perspectives. But in our society, anonymity
can also stem from a directly or indirectly imposed
status of not being heard or seen, as a result of
not being identifiable according to the system, an
exclusion and exceptionalness that actually attacks
personal autonomy. Under laws made by others,
the individual then cannot follow those laws — a
bizarre condition of illegality.

At the same time, you can wonder what the
unique identity of the subject still comprises,
if anything, in an era when identities are more
makeable, fluid and reproducible than ever, and
can no longer be pinned down in time and space.
The autonomy of the subject has long been beset
by immaterial shadow presentations in the form
of avatars, data bodies and online personas, new
'life forms' and subjectivities that never totally
coincide with their original. On the Internet,
anonymous cultures and anonymous information
exchanges flourish, and autonomy arises from a game
of (non-)identities and collective desires instead
of from the manifestation of a singular absolute
identity and its free will.

And then we are back to Anonymous,
whereby unidentified persons agitate to protect
the free exchange of information on the Internet,
and who have become famous and infamous for
their DDoS attacks and Operation Avenge Assange.
Anonymous sees itself as a spontaneous collective of people who serve a common goal, and in
that sense is comparable with Occupy, which does
not work with obvious leaders or representatives
either, and likewise campaigns on behalf of and
for everyone without unequivocally sanctioned
principles. The interesting thing about these
movements is that from this interplay of anonymity and autonomy a form of politics seems to be

arising, a community that is taking shape, which
comes close to what Jacques Rancière describes
as a new distribution or reorganization of the
sensory, that is to say, of the structuring of
perception that determines what can be seen or
not seen and said or not said in a society. This
is not about the private interest of a specific
group or the injustice done to it or to another,
nor is it about finding a consensus. It's about
the demand to be heard and accepted as a partner
in the conversation. And so it is about a different group in society which speaks for the entire
society because their actions concern everyone.

Rancière seems to be saying that those who
are not perceived, and thus in fact are anonymous,
can only achieve a form of autonomy out of precisely that condition. A stimulating proposition
in every way. In the context of Anonymous, you can
counter this by the fact that 25 'suspected members
of Anonymous' were recently arrested by Interpol
and that they thus actually are identifiable, and
therefore traceable for the police. However, the
movement does not have any membership structure;
everyone can carry out activities in the name of
Anonymous. The arrests are real, but the idea of
the anonymity of a group that is not perceived, to
use Rancière's term, is guaranteed.

Sven Lütticken

Autonomy after the Fact

Art historian Sven Lütticken subjects the concept of autonomy and its relation to aesthetics and politics to a thorough analysis and places it within the context of post-war modernism, whereby autonomy is not interpreted as a fact but as an act. As Rancière has shown, the aesthetic and political characteristics of an act can never coincide, although some acts can function in different registers simultaneously.

The Italian Autonomia movement of the 1970s was one important effect of and response to the political and cultural event that was May '68. Recently, Autonomia has met with significant interest among those looking for alternative forms of contestation, beyond old-school organizational structures. In his collection of writings by authors associated with Autonomia, Sylvère Lotringer explained the relevance of the notion of autonomy in this context: 'Political autonomy is the desire to allow differences to deepen at the base without trying to synthesize them from above, to stress similar attitudes without imposing a "general line", to allow parts to co-exist side by side, in their singularity.'[1] How do such attempts at redefining autonomy socially and politically relate to the contested concept that is the autonomy of art? The modernist understanding of art was based on the process of self-criticism to which art subjected itself after its old social functions had atrophied; this historical process was seen as a progressive increase in autonomy. Ever since the politicization of artists and theorists in the wake of May '68, this ideology of artistic autonomy has been subjected to a prolonged and withering critique. In art, 'autonomy' has become a bad word. Could this tainted notion be made productive in art once again?

Autonomy is not empty freedom from outer constraints. It means being *self-ruling*; for Greenberg as for Habermas and, with important qualifications, for Adorno, modernism meant that art develops by making and challenging its own rules, reflexively, according to its own inner logic and 'learning processes'.[2] The socioeconomical underpinnings of such definitions of autonomous art are usually based on Max Weber's analysis of modern society as being marked by the functional self-differentiation of its spheres, including art. This autonomy of *art* underpinned the autonomy of the *art work* as a seemingly self-sufficient entity obeying its immanent logic, which is at the same time that of an art history. It is thus not surprising that autonomy has come to be associated with apolitical isolationism, with a retrograde ideology of High Art. However, this is not the whole story. As Terry Eagleton has noted, the notion of autonomy as referring to 'a mode of being which is entirely self-regulating and self-determining' may on the one hand provide 'a central constituent of bourgeois ideology', but on the other its emphasis on 'the self-determining nature of human powers and capacities' holds an emancipatory political potential.[3] Is any radical political project thinkable without *such* a concept of autonomy, however implicit?

In fact, while the term may have been suspect, avant-garde art movements that were critical of artistic autonomy strove for *an autonomy*

1. Sylvère Lotringer, 'In the Shadow of the Red Brigades', in *Autonomia: Post-political Politics* (Los Angeles: Semiotext(e), 2007), V.

2. Adorno was of course acutely aware of modern art's *Doppelcharakter* as being both autonomous and a (commodified) 'fait social', but this *Doppelcharakter* still distinguished modern art sharply from the culture industry, which was *only* a fait social.

3. Terry Eagleton, *The Ideology of the Aesthetic* (London: Basil Blackwell, 1990), 9.

that dared not speak its name. In the 1960s, neo-avant-garde groups from Fluxus to the Situationist International sought to *negate* the autonomy of art in favour of acts that would attain a greater degree of autonomy by not being containable within the framework of modern art. With the Situationists, this increasingly took the form of actions that seemed to represent an abandonment of the aesthetic in favour of the political, of one autonomy for another. The term *aesthetic* is, however, treacherous; it refers to art, but it is not a synonym for *artistic*. Developed in the late eighteenth century mainly by German philosophers such as Baumgarten and Kant as the philosophy of beauty and/or taste, aesthetics increasingly became a philosophy of art in the early nineteenth century, with Schiller, Schelling and Hegel.[4] The aesthetic is thus *a specific approach to art*, and with Jacques Rancière we can characterize the aesthetic project in terms of the dialectic of logos and pathos, of reason/freedom and the sensible – of autonomy and heteronomy.[5] The aesthetic thus understood is never 'purely' autonomous, for it needs heteronomy as its double.[6] The aesthetic is the constant questioning of art and thus of claims for art's autonomy, counteracting it from persistent problem to ideological given. This is why the comfortable assumption that art is structurally autonomous ultimately leads to aesthetic attrition: see much of the late-modernist painting of the 1960s and 1980s.

We thus encounter the constitutive paradox of all art since Romanticism: if it were ever possible for art to become completely autonomous, this would in fact mean that it would be insufficiently aesthetic, for the aesthetic is a constant renegotiation of autonomy and heteronomy. Aesthetic practice and theory thus problematize conceptions of autonomy in relation to the (un)reality of autonomy in specific forms of artistic production. The aesthetic thus understood always returns to haunt limited conceptions or forms of 'autonomous art'. Autonomy is not a fact; we cannot possess it. If anything, autonomy is an exceptional occurrence in the realm of social facts – including art and its institutions.

4. My reading differentiation here between the autonomy of art and aesthetic autonomy is indebted to Peter Osborne, 'Theorem 4 – Autonomy: Can It Be True of *Both* Art and Politics at the Same Time?,' see elsewhere in this issue of *Open*.

5. Rancière denies that his 'aesthetic regime' is a *historical regime of art*; rather, it is a régime of the *identification* of art. Rancière points out that this regime started with the reinterpretation of old art, not with the production of new art. However, such aesthetic reflection almost instantly became new aesthetic production – for instance in line drawings that were used to illustrate the earliest art historical publications, and in poetry.

6. My analysis is, again, indebted to Osborne.

However, I would argue that his reading of the aesthetic tends to privilege certain philosophical positions without sufficient regard for their counterpoints. A critical return to Kant or to early Schiller can be helpful in analysing the emergence of the foundational antinomies of the aesthetic, but one should be careful not to create a new cult of origins. I see no reason to privilege Kant over Schiller, and the early Schiller of the Kallias letters is not any less problematical than the 'late' Schiller of the *Letters on Aesthetic Education,* just as Adorno's melancholic modernism is not less problematical than the avant-gardism of Benjamin's 'Kunstwerk' essay. These positions are all part of the moving constellation – the set of interacting antinomies – that is the aesthetic regime.

Autonomy in and against Art: Institutional Critique

The artistic practices that have come to be known as Institutional Critique – from Hans Haacke and Michael Asher, starting around 1970, to younger practitioners – differed from both the historical avant-garde and the neo-avant-gardes of the late 1950s and early 1960s in their approach to the problem of 'the autonomy of art'. Whereas both the 'ludic' happenings and Fluxus artists and the much more politicized Situationist avant-garde sought to operate outside the institutions of art and the art market, Institutional Critique started from the realization that there is no 'elsewhere', no realm outside art, beyond recuperation. If one reads writings from the 1970s by practitioners of what was then not yet labelled as Institutional Critique, such as Haacke or Asher, the term autonomy hardly plays a role at all; it is certainly not used with any degree of consistency. This is all the more remarkable if one looks at a book such as Peter Bürger's 1974 *Theory of the Avant-Garde,* in which it abounds. Bürger analyses the historical avant-garde as an attack on modernist autonomy and the neo-avant-garde as an institutionalization of the avant-garde that negates its original intentions.[7] Does a similar diagnosis not underpin Institutional Critique?

7. Peter Bürger, Theorie der Avantgarde (Frankfurt am Main: Suhrkamp: 1974).

In Andrea Fraser's writings from the 1990s, which were shaped both by those of the 'first generation' prac-

titioners of Institutional Critique and by the work of critics/historians such as Peter Bürger and Benjamin Buchloh, the concept of autonomy was addressed explicitly and incisively.[8] Rather than presenting institutional critique simply as an attack on autonomy as a purely ideological notion, Fraser argued that 'the critique of the autonomy of the artwork' was 'rooted in a recognition of the partial and ideological character of the that autonomy and an attempt to resist the heteronomy to which artists and artworks are subject'. Therefore, '[the] critique of the art object's autonomy was less a rejection of artistic autonomy than a critique of the *uses* to which artworks are put: the economic and political interests they *serve'*.[9] In other words: what was criticized was *a lack of real autonomy*, the reduction of artistic autonomy to a sham. And this meant precisely that the autonomy that was the aim (an autonomy that still dared not speak its name) could not be traditional artistic autonomy, since such attempts had been shown to lead straight into heteronomy.

8. See Buchloh, *Neo-Avantgarde and Culture Industry* (Cambridge, MA/London: MIT Press, 2001), and 'Autonomy' in: *Texte zur Kunst*, no. 66 (June 2007), 'Short Guide', 32-34.

9. Andrea Fraser, 'What's Intangible, Transitory, Mediating, Participatory, and Rendered in the Public Sphere? Part II', in: Alexander Alberro (ed.), *Museum Highlights: The Writings of Andrea Fraser* (Cambridge MA/London: MIT Press, 2005), 57.

Far from being an abandonment of autonomy, Institutional Critique should thus be seen as an attempt to regain a degree of autonomy – an autonomy that cannot be that of

Andrea Fraser, *Official Welcome* (2001), performance at Kunstverein
Hamburg, 2003.

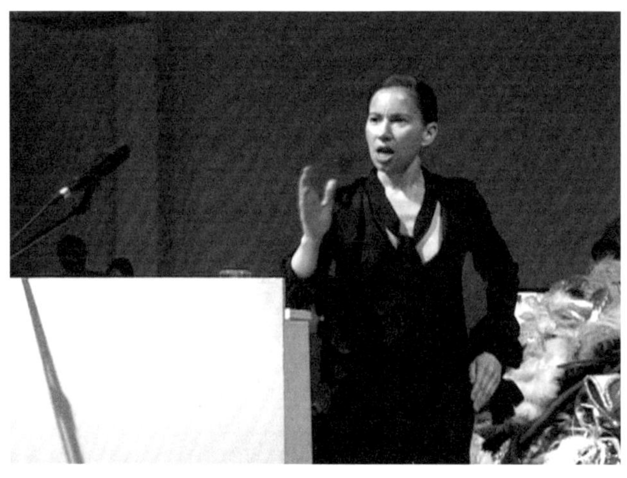

Hito Steyerl, *November*, videostill, 2004.
Creative Commons, courtesy: the artist

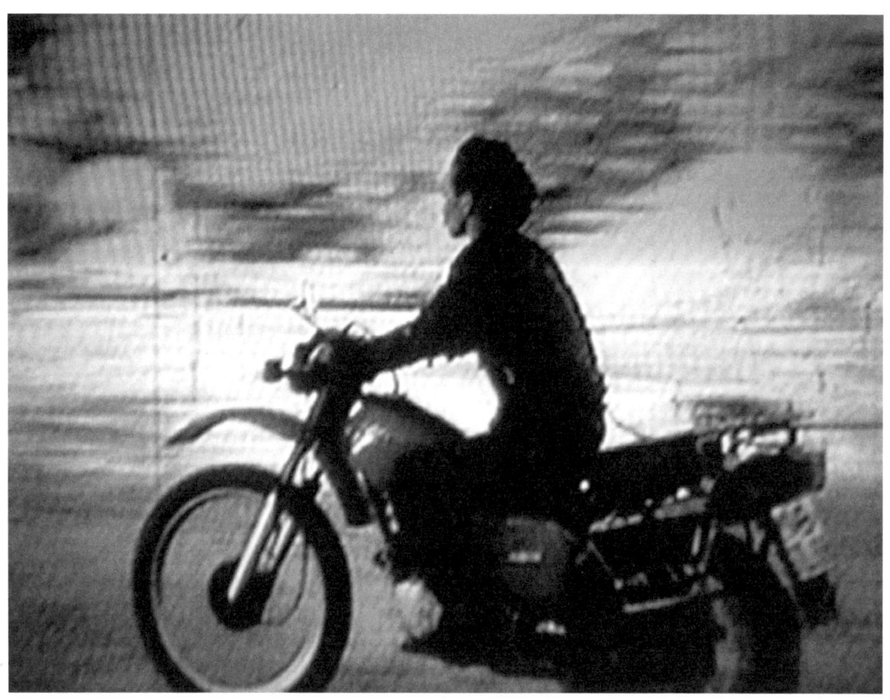

modernist paeans. A work by Hans Haacke such as *The Chase Advantage* (1976) uses the similarities between the 'modernist' Chase Manhattan Bank logotype and 1960s art such as Frank Stella's shaped canvases to investigate art sponsoring as a form of PR than can help gloss over unsavoury business practices. Supplementing the 'autonomous' logo with a montage of quotations and data, the panels that make up Haacke's work are object lessons in the heteronomy of art. If such a work seems to posit a viewer who has some degree of critical distance, a 1974 project by Michael Asher stressed the viewer's own implication in the heteronomous habitat of art. For his show at the Claire Copley Gallery in Los Angeles, Asher removed the partition wall separating the white cube from the back office, making visible *labour* as the repressed base of the shiny superstructural surface of art – an expanding and morphing form of cultural labour. In this respect, the work can be seen to announce a later shift in emphasis in Institutional Critique.

There are various genealogies of Institutional Critique, various periodizations of its development since the early 1970s. In Hito Steyerl's account, the third phase (after the artist's 'integration into the institution' and 'integration into representation') is marked by his/her integration *into precarity* – 'while institutions are being dismantled by neoliberal institutional criticism, this produces an ambivalent critical subject which develops multiple strategies for dealing with its dis-location.'[10] What changes with the rise of precarity, with the formation of a relatively large cultural lumpenproletariat, is that art's role as an economical factor becomes ever more part of people's lived reality.

The Marxian spin on the analysis of the artistic field as a differentiated autonomous sphere argues that – to quote Eagleton once more – the relative autonomy of such a field 'is itself a material fact with particular social determinations', since 'certain historically specific forms of consciousness become separated out from productive activity, and can best be explained in terms of their functional role in sustaining it. . . . Once an economic surplus permits a minority of "professional" thinkers to be released from the exigencies of labour, it becomes possible for consciousness to "flatter" itself that it is in fact independent of material reality.'[11] It is precisely this self-flattering that has become hard to sustain for ever more practitioners. Adorno, the self-critical modernist, noted that 'the autonomy of art is unthinkable without the obfuscation of labour'.[12] But who can really flatter themselves into thinking that they are released from the exigencies of labour? The dirty little secret that is

10. Hito Steyerl, 'The Institution of Critique' (2006), in: Alexander Alberro and Blake Stimpson (eds.), *Institutional Critique: An Anthology of Artists' Writings* (Cambridge MA/London: MIT Press, 2009), 492.

11. Terry Eagleton, *Ideology: An Introduction* (London/New York: Verso, 1991), 74-75.

12. 'Lässt überhaupt keine Autonomie der Kunst ohne Verdeckung der arbeit sich denken, so wird diese im Hochkapitalismus . . . problematisch und zum Programm.' Theodor W. Adorno, 'Versuch über Wagner' in: *Die Musikalischen Monographien. Gesammelte Schriften*, vol. 13 (Frankfurt am Main: Suhrkamp, 2003), 80.

labour infiltrates every conversation, every gesture.

In her work since the late 1980s, Andrea Fraser has placed new emphasis on the subject as the real battleground for institutional critique, which came to be redefined in terms of *performance*.[13] Fraser often foregrounds the pressures involved in self-performance in a series of performances mimicking lectures, guided tours and speeches whose monologues are replete with verbal slips and twitches. What we see here is a shift in institutional critique towards the subject, towards the site of subjectivation. Having started out by playing the museum volunteer Jane Castleton in *Museum Highlights: A Gallery Talk* (1989), Fraser soon let go of any suggestion that she plays specific characters. In pieces such as *Official Welcome* (2001), she instead turned herself into a jukebox of instable quasi-subjects beleaguered by performance anxiety. In this way, she anchored her performative art within a wider performative economy, using it to reflect on and intervene in it.

Here we see the emergence of a properly contemporary conception of autonomy: an enacted autonomy in the age of labour-as-performance.

13. The term Institutional Critique became established (belatedly) in part because of Andrea Fraser, who used it in her 1985 essay on Louise Lawler, 'In and Out of Place'. See Fraser's discussion of this in 'From the Critique of Institutions to an Institution of Critique' (2005), in: Alberro and Stimpson, *Institutional Critique*, op. cit. (note 10), 408-417. The term had already been employed in Mel Ramsden's 1975 essay 'On Practice': 'To dwell perennially on an institutional critique without addressing specific problems within the institutions is to generalize and to sloganize.' 'On Practice' in: Alberro and Stimpson, *Institutional Critique*, op. cit. (note 10), 176. However, thus usage was relatively imprecise and remained isolated.

This is autonomy not as the grand gesture of freedom, but autonomy as *work on and with constraints*. It situates the dialectic of autonomy and heteronomy *in the practitioner*. He/she is part of the problem, which is in fact the condition for his/her agency. Such autonomy does not invite an ideological use of the term as a cultural weapon or PR device. If anything, it is used to develop possible responses to the antinomies that shape and traverse one's practice. In this sense, its use is internal rather than external.

The Praxis of Autonomy

For Clement Greenberg, the history of art appeared as a series of rooms *en filade*, with works of art arranged in sequences that showed ever more rigorous solutions for formal 'problems'. However, for most of the 1950s this was not the dominant account of modern art; much more prominent was Harold Rosenberg's existentialist take on Abstract Expressionism, which he conceptualized as Action Painting. Rosenberg's reputation still suffers from a certain essayistic flightiness and from his 'inability to see', for which Greenberg chided him. Indeed, Rosenberg's seminal essay 'The American Action Painters' (1952) does not mention a single artist by name.[14] While this is certainly highly problematic, it has to be seen in conjunction with Rosenberg's valorization of the *act* over the work of art as tangible *fact* – as object with

14. Harold Rosenberg, 'The American Action Painters' in: *The Tradition of the New* (London: Paladin, 1970; first edition 1959), 35-47.

specific qualities. It was Rosenberg's contention that Greenberg's reduction of art to a series of observable facts was wrong; in so far as it becomes fact, the act is realized but its potential is curtailed.[15] The problem ultimately lies in the abstract and undialectical nature of Rosenberg's negation of the work of art as obdurate fact.

The Rosenberg of the 1950s and 1960s was no longer the Trotskyist Marxist he had been in the late 1930s, but the central role of the act in his philosophy betrays his continuing indebtedness to Marx and to post-Hegelian philosophies of *praxis* in general. One might say that these post-idealist philosophies exacerbated one type of Kantian autonomy, and abandoned another – for in Kant's critical system, autonomy has a twofold function. On the one hand, Kant posited philosophy as a discipline that needed to develop autonomously, in accordance with its own inner logic – albeit in dialogue with the sciences. This is the meaning of Kantian autonomy that Clement Greenberg would use: 'The essence of Modernism lies, as I see it, in the use of characteristic methods of a discipline to criticize the discipline itself, not in order to subvert it but in order to entrench it more firmly in its area of competence. Kant used logic to establish the limits of logic, and while he withdrew much from its old jurisdiction, logic was left all the more secure in what there remained to it.'[16] This understanding of autonomy is compatible with the Weberian notion of functional differentiation – law, science and morality all increasingly developing along lines of reflexivity, self-criticism.

The second sense of Kantian autonomy concerns not the *discipline* but the *subject* – a notion that is largely absent from Greenberg's historical narrative of modernism, even though his practice as a rather judgmental art critic depended on his stance as critical subject. In Kant's realm of practical reason, it is the moral and free subject that determines its own path and self-legislates. However, the Kantian subject is split between pure reason and practical reason, between the phenomenal and the noumenal world.

15. Rosenberg tantalizingly states that those artists whose work completely matches a theory are usually not the 'deepest'; while most people thought that the essay was mostly based on Pollock, this remark suggests that De Kooning, whom Rosenberg admired, was in fact a greater painter for being less of an Action painter (Ibid., 35). One may say that Rosenberg's writings constitute a missed encounter with works by both De Kooning or Pollock as sensuous fact; yet these works, in their factuality, are also a missed encounter with Rosenberg's writings. The developments of the late 1950s and 1960s forced Rosenberg to argue that, after all, it was crucial that the act *did* result in material traces. 'In emphasizing the creative act rather than the object created, Action painting, or – by the testimony of Allan Kaprow – the *idea* of Action painting, led logically to the Happening. Action painting is ambiguous; it asserts the primacy of the creative act, but it looks to the object, the painting, for a confirmation of the worth of that act ... Action painting is subjective, yet it is bound to a *thing*, even though a thing in process.' (Rosenberg, 'The Concept of Action in Painting', 224). Against happening and Fluxus artists, Rosenberg now stated that: 'To dissolve "the barriers that separate art from life" is an impossible ideal – the dream of a world in which all actions are intended to be forgotten at their moment of fulfilment.' (Harold Rosenberg, 'The Museum of the New' in: *Artworks and Packages* (New York: Dell, 1969), 156.) While Kaprow had drawn logical conclusions from the notion of Action painting, 'in art it is always a mistake to push a concept to its logical conclusion.' (Rosenberg, 'The Concept of Action in Painting', 226.)

16. Clement Greenberg, 'Modernist Painting' (1960), in: John O'Brian (ed.), *Clement Greenberg: The Collected Essays and Criticism, vol. 4: Modernism with a Vengeance, 1957-1969* (Chicago/London: University of Chicago Press, 1993), 85.

It is only as the transcendental subject of practical reason that the subject is free and self-governing, which is to say: autonomous. Adorno would be highly critical of this disembodied, abstract subject, which seemed to be a philosophical sublimation of socially imposed duty: you must.[17] Kant's autonomous will seems to be autonomous also from any lived reality. In attempting to restore a sense of lived ethics to the autonomous subject, Adorno was in a long line of thinkers who tried to overcome the limitations of the Kantian system by focusing not on ethical imperatives but on praxis, on the act – a lineage starting with Fichte, Schelling and Hegel. Rosenberg would anchor his theory of the act in a 'revolution against the given, in the self and in the world' that started with Hegel.[18]

It was, of course, the critique of Hegel in the 1830s and 1840s, by Marx and others, that would derive a materialist notion of praxis from the 'spiritualized' Hegelian subject. For Hegel, humans are subjects in so far as they participate in the dialectical progress of spirit; they are subjects in so far as they posit *objects* that are seen as cast-off refuse. For Marx, the subject could only consist of sensory human activity, of praxis, a praxis that can ultimately only be collective. In Brian Holmes's words: '[The] attempt to give oneself one's own law becomes a collective adventure.'[19] But this collective adventure clearly can be *willed* only very partially by individuals; this insight took hold only very gradually during the post-war decades, parallel to the decline of the traditional working class, which would ultimately make Bolshevist politics that attempted to forge a proletarian mass subject receiving its will from the Party look anachronistic. From the late 1960s, particularly from May '68 onwards, many attempted to forge new forms of action beyond party politics; Rosenberg, however, remained content with the depoliticized version of 'the act' as existential-aesthetic gesture within the Weberian domain of art that he had devised during the Cold War.

In a 1960 response to criticism from Mary McCarthy, Rosenberg drew a parallel between the radical artistic event taking place on the canvas and revolutionary political events: both demand spur-of-the-moment decisions from viewers, who must play a part in these events if they are not to pass them by. The editors of *ARTnews* helpfully visualized Rosenberg's parallel by juxtaposing black-and-white reproductions of Abstract Expressionist paintings with photos of 'students rioting in Japan'.[20] But Rosenberg insisted that artistic acts remain restricted to pictorial gestures on canvas while there was a

17. See Iain Macdonald, 'Cold, Cold, Warm: Autonomy, Intimacy and Maturity in Adorno,' in: *Philosophy & Social Criticism,* published online 26 April 2011, psc.sagepub.com/content/early/2011/04/12/0191453711402940.full.pdf.

18. Rosenberg, 'The American Action Painters', op. cit. (note 14), 42.

19. Brian Holmes, 'Artistic Autonomy and the Communication Society' (2003), http://www.nettime.org/Lists-Archives/nettime-l-0310/msg00192.html.

20. Harold Rosenberg, 'Critic Within the Act', *ARTnews* 59, no. 6 (October 1960), 26-28. This article would be republished, sans illustrations, in *Encounter* no. 93 (June 1961), 58-59.

parallel between painterly and other acts, but they should not be mixed. Rosenberg rejected the 'logical' conclusions that Allan Kaprow drew from the theory of action painting with his happenings. Against happenings and events, Rosenberg now stated that: '[To] dissolve "the barriers that separate art from life" is an impossible ideal – the dream of a world in which all actions are intended to be forgotten at their moment of fulfillment.'[21] Rosenberg's response to the total event of May '68 was as blasé as his reaction to the earlier artistic happenings; this surely, was retro-avant-gardism. In a piece about May '68 in Paris titled 'Surrealism in the Streets', Rosenberg remarked that the wall slogan 'Culture is the inversion of life' is itself culture, 'since it is inherited from the radical art movements of fifty years ago'.[22] However, Rosenberg showed no sign of being aware of the Situationist International, whose agenda shines through from this slogan. To some extent the Situationists remained indebted to old models, presenting themselves as successors to the First International; however, they re-politicized the act by pushing concepts to their logical conclusion and beyond.

Why bring Rosenberg into the discussion? The aim surely cannot be to create a new cult of the artist as free subject par excellence – the way that Action Painting was ideologized in the Cold War. If anything, Institutional Critique has taught us that the institution is inside us – and in an age of networked subjectivities, '[the] individual is defined . . . by the pass codes that delineate his or her area of access'.[23] But it is precisely this entanglement in structures and scripts that seems to create a need for returning to the notion of the act, or of action – as evidenced by the vogue for that other action theorist of the post-war era, Hannah Arendt, and her trias of *work-labour-action*. This ultimately takes the form of a crypto-idealist progression: the dumb *animal laborans*, labouring simply to consume and survive, needs to be complemented by the *homo faber*, who makes durable things, and ultimately by human action and speech.[24] As Richard Sennett has noted, this leaves one rather empty-handed when trying to deal with the material world.[25]

But was it not a crucial aspect of avant-garde practice to *transform labour*, to make labour itself the field of action? Rosenberg's aesthetic act seemingly abandoned this aim, but Rosenberg (via Kaprow and others) bequeathed a notion of action to the 1960s, to a period in which the culturalization of the economy started in earnest – in which culture became integral to labour. The more interesting and productive interventions in the 'new labour' of culturalized capi-

21. Rosenberg, 'The Museum of the New', op. cit. (note 15), 156.

22. Harold Rosenberg, 'Surrealism in the Streets', in: *The De-definition of Art* (Chicago/London: University of Chicago Press, 1972), 51.

23. Boris Groys, 'The Revolt of the Clerks, or Universality as Conspiracy', in: *Open* no. 22 (2011), 41.

24. Hannah Arendt, *The Human Condition* (Chicago/London, University of Chicago Press: 1988 [1958]), 173 etc.

25. Richard Sennett, *The Craftsman* (New Haven/London: Yale University Press, 2008), 6-7.

'Student Uprising in Japan' and on the page to the right, *Untitled Painting* by Robert Richenburg, illustrated in: Harald Rosenberg, 'Critic Within the Act', in *ARTnews* 59, no. 6, October 1952.

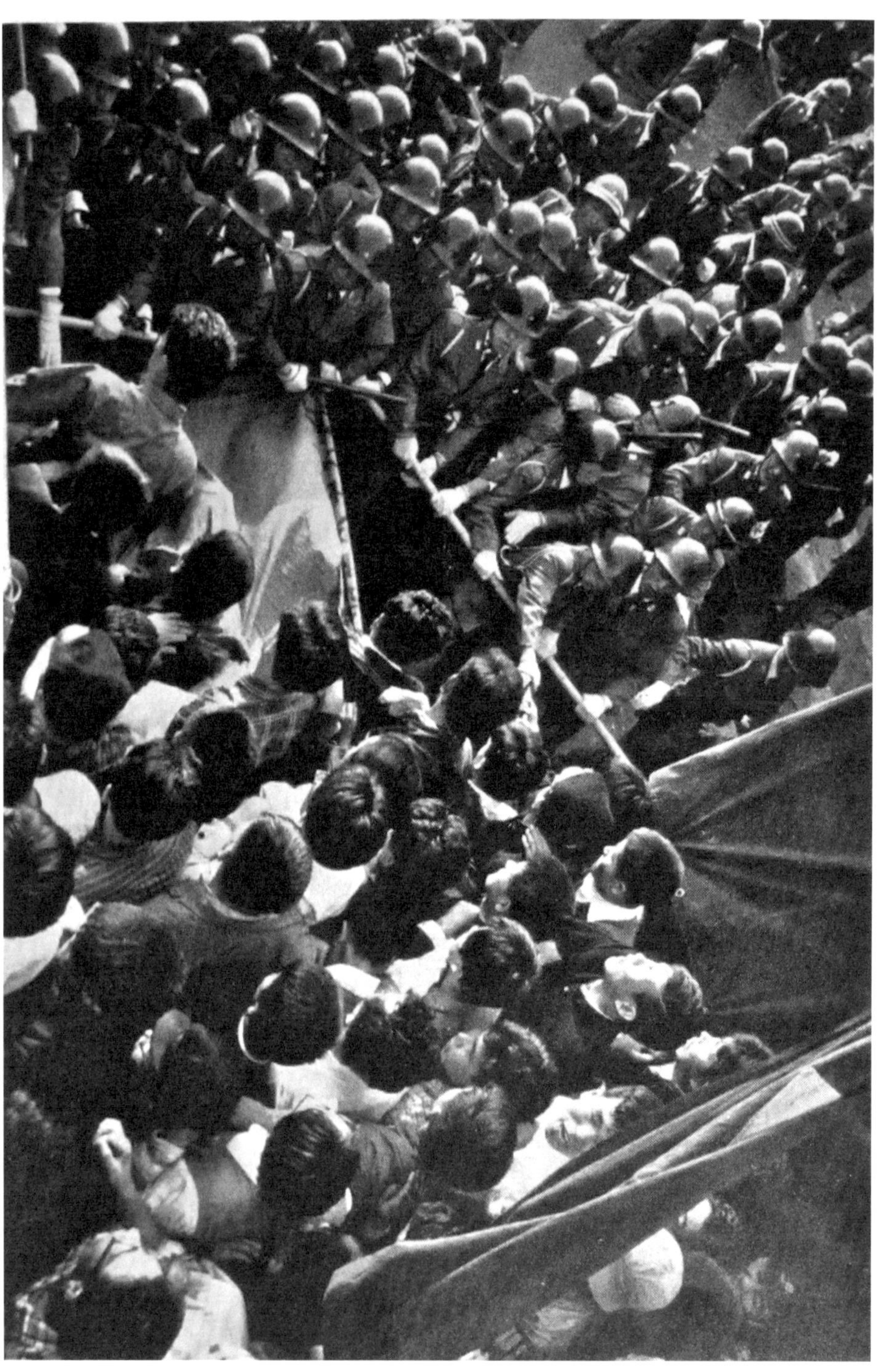

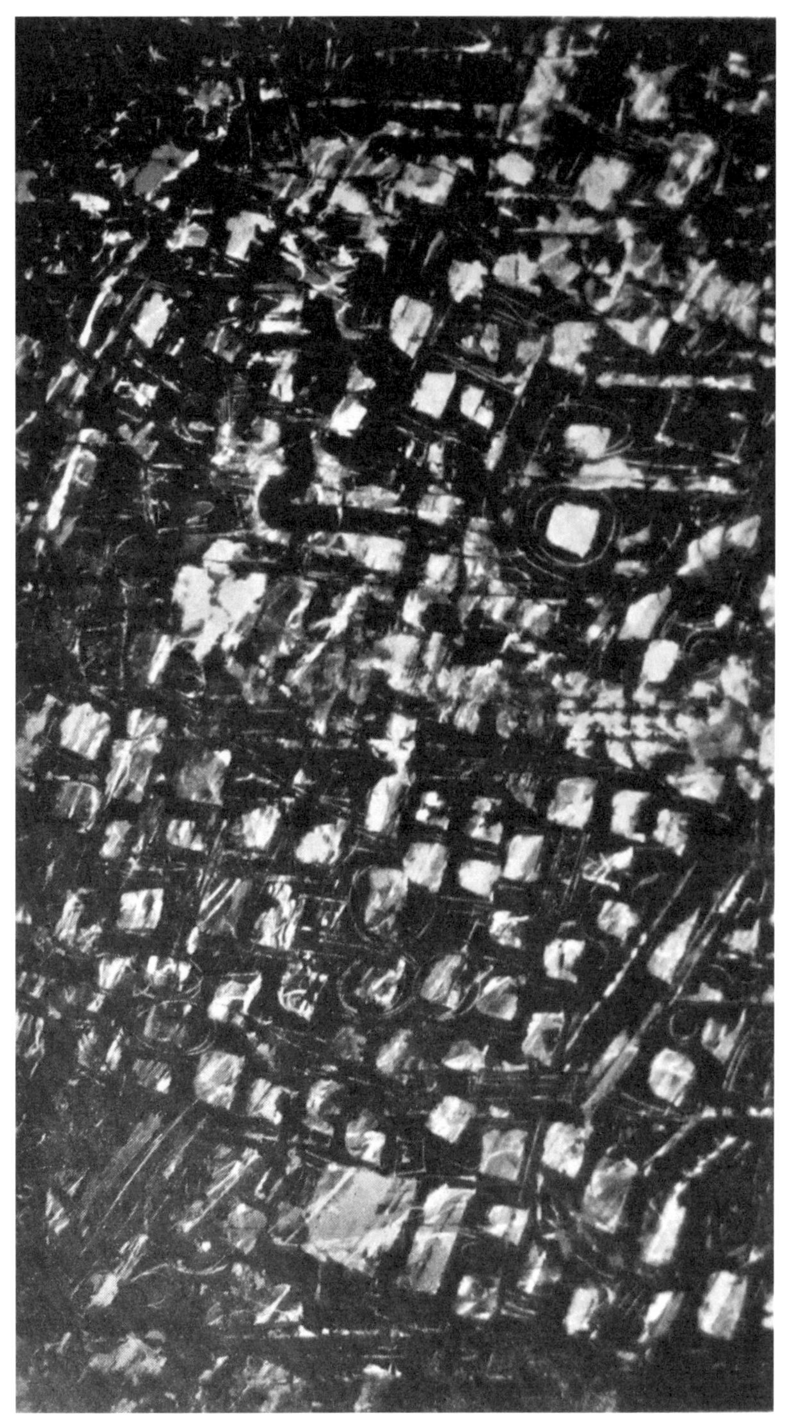

talism go beyond sub-existentialist voluntarism; they explore and explode the daily performance of the dialectic of heteronomy and autonomy.

Beyond New Labour: Activating Performance

We live in a culture of performance, and this 'performance' is as ambiguous as Rosenberg's notion of 'acting'. Rosenberg's writings were characterized by a constant slippage that he himself detected in the work of André Malraux: 'In Malraux's thinking, action constantly blends into acting: with historical script in hand, the only problem is which part to play and how to play it.'[26] Rosenberg was fascinated by Marx's passages on the 'Resurrected Romans' of the French Revolution; historical re-enactment could be all but indistinguishable from historical acts. And since socialism's basic proposition is 'an aesthetic one', the re-making of man and of society, why would such slippages not be possible and productive?[27] As for performance, today it stands both for one's quasi-dramatic *self-performance* and for one's economic achievement – and increasingly, the former is essential to the latter. This is what I call *general performance*. Using but not being limited to specific (artistic) disciplines, this economico-theatrical performance occupies different contexts and most of many people's time – it is *permanent* performance.[28] In the 'social factory' of post-Fordism there is no *sortie de l'usine*. Performance is ongoing, in different constellations and with different degrees of publicness. It is modulated: languid stretches alternate with intense moments.

General performance is at the heart of the new labour of post-Fordism. Or is it really a kind of substitute for labour, as Hito Steyerl has argued? Is it really a kind of *occupation*, a form of keeping busy?[29] The new labour can look like occupation, but ends up being a new type of work with even less security and less return than old industrial labour. The new labour is marked by the *inability to distinguish* between labour and leisure, between work and occupation, between working hours and free time, between performance and life – and ultimately between objective economical pressures and subjectivities that are constantly updated, upgraded, remodelled. As part of the erosion of the distinction between labour and non-labour, looking and reading have become productive of value – often for others. 'Every time you log into your Facebook account, you work for Mr Zuckerberg.'[30]

Michael Asher's 1974 gesture in LA, a somewhat theatrical revelation of labour, also created an interplay

26. Harold Rosenberg, 'Actor in History', in: *Act and the Actor: Making the Self* (Chicago/London: University of Chicago Press, 1970), 165

27. Harold Rosenberg, 'The Pathos of the Proletariat', in: Ibid., 36. See also: 'The Resurrected Romans', in: Rosenberg, *The Tradition of the New*, op. cit., 140-158.

28. See Sven Lütticken, 'General Performance', in: *e-flux journal* no. 31 (January 2012), http://www.e-flux.com/journal/general-performance/.

29. Hito Steyerl, 'Art as Occupation', see elsewhere in this issue.

30. Marten Spanberg, *Spanbergianism* (self-published, Stockholm, 2011), 37.

of gazes between office workers and visitors, who were both turned into (or revealed to be) self-performers; the latter became momentary co-workers of the former. A 1998 project by Hans van Houwelingen, which might be read as an update and critique of Asher's work: for *Guard on Art*, Van Houwelingen had asylum seekers that were not legally permitted to work patrol a space in a Dutch museum, functioning as museum guards and as a reminder of the policing of borders and of access to legal work in Western countries, and the sequestering of unwanted immigrants. The temporary museum guards in Van Houwelingen's project are the invisible reverse of neoliberal self-performers – and Van Houwelingen gave them a degree of (highly problematic) visibility by turning them into actors. Such projects suggest that, under certain conditions, neoliberal performance may malfunction and become, briefly, an act – and possibly the 'act of imagination' sketched by Negri.[31] Through such acts, such acting, that performance may morph into something that is more than was bargained for, more than was programmed.

31. Antonio Negri, *Art & Multitude. Nine Letters on Art, Followed by Metamorphoses: Art and Immaterial Labour*, transl. Ed Emery (Cambridge/Malden, MA: Polity, 2011), 31. See also xii: 'The beautiful is not the act of imagining, but an imagination that has become action.'

In Paul Chan's words, a work of art works by not working at all.[32] One specific form that this can take is that of a pointed intervention in today's labour regime, which

32. Paul Chan, 'A Lawless Proposition', *e-flux journal* no. 30 (December 2011), http://www.e-flux.com/journal/a-lawless-proposition/.

works only too well – except for the actual labourers. The 'culturalization' of labour in the form of general performance remains *sub-aesthetic* until its functioning is questioned, and until it is placed in conjunction with seemingly disparate form of work. The outlines of a genuinely aesthetic economy only become visible once work stops working. It is true that at times it appears as if the notion of work and labour have been reduced to an art-world preoccupation, having lost their galvanizing political potential in society at large.[33] However, it would be an intellectual capitulation to present this historical deadlock as an immovable fate; the Occupy movement but also actions by cleaners and domestic workers in the Netherlands indicate that there are possible points of departure for challenging it. For instance, Matthijs de Bruijne collaborated with the cleaners' union, realizing his Trash Museum in the context of collective actions.[34] This mobile museum contains objects founds by cleaners, together with written narratives by those cleaners. Here the object truly takes on the form of refuse.

33. See Joost de Bloois's cautions in this regard, elsewhere in this issue.

34. For instance, the group ASK! (Actie Schone Kunsten), founded in the context of Casco's project *The Grand Domestic Revolution*, sought to make visible the 'invisible labour' of domestic workers engaged in a struggle for rights. The political and/or aesthetic qualities of such undertakings must of course be evaluated.

In his critique of the idealist subject and is hubristic eradication of the non-identical, Adorno stressed the 'primacy of the object'.[35] The subject is at least

35. Theodor W. Adorno, *Ästhetische Theorie* (Frankfurt am Main: Suhrkamp, 1970), 477.

as much the refuse of the object as the other way round; object and subject are each other's *effect*. The object in question does not have to be thought of as a single physical entity. The very working conditions under which the subject labours have an 'objective' character, and in the cultural field these conditions are also *performing conditions*. To act in and against these conditions is not some form of voluntarist 'actionism' that knows no obstacles, but precisely an attempt to make these conditions visible as an obstacle, as a form of resistance shapes the subject, both enabling and disabling it. What Benjamin Buchloh decries in the post-Fordist culture of self-performance is the *lack of friction* between subject and its other – an obstacle, something that is not identical to the subject.[36] Of course, such friction is in fact produced all the time, but at the same time it is being neutralized and absorbed. In this sense, an act is a failed performance, a symptomatic interruption of *business as usual*. In other words: we are not talking about some grand existentialist-expressionist act, but about a glitch, about an interruption. Such an interruption can be caused voluntarily, but this is not a necessity; neither is the mere intention to create one sufficient. If Melville's character Bartleby and his refrain of 'I would prefer not to' are so popular these days in intellectual and artistic circles, is this not because Bartleby's act seems to spring from some kind of unreasoned, dumb resistance? Bartleby

36. Benjamin Buchloh. 'Que faire?', *Texte zur Kunst* no. 81 (March 2011), 147-151.

hardly seems to be a free subject. His autonomy comes from being object-like; his act of resistance is one of radical passivity. In today's performative economy, something as unplanned and unwilled as a burnout can become an act, a reclamation of self-legislation. The production of autonomy is not easily planned, but this does not mean that one should refrain from analysing one's situation. Ultimately, performance can only become act if and when it is perceived as such by someone. This someone need not be one of the actors; it can be an observer, now or later, who transforms the material through an interpretive act.

From May '68 to Occupy Wall Street, we have seen that certain films inspire forms of collective action; these actions in turn have an aesthetic component, or generate aesthetic reflections. Sometimes one act or action can be perceived politically as well as aesthetically. Who is to determine what the 'proper' register is for watching the chilling online video of UC Davis chancellor Katahi walking to her car through throngs of silent protesters after the notorious use of police brutality on campus?[37] Even if an act appears to fall squarely within art, or within the realm of politics, it may migrate in unforeseen ways. Hito Steyerl's film *November* (2004) recalls how, as teenage girls, Steyerl and her friend Andrea Wolf would be influenced by images of women from cheap exploitation flicks, and tried to make their own feminist karate flick. Andrea

37. http://www.youtube.com/watch?v=8775ZmNGFY8.

Hans van Houwelingen, *Guard on Art*, in the exhibition 'Power Up',
Museum voor Moderne Kunst Arnhem, 1998.
Photo by Hans van Houwelingen

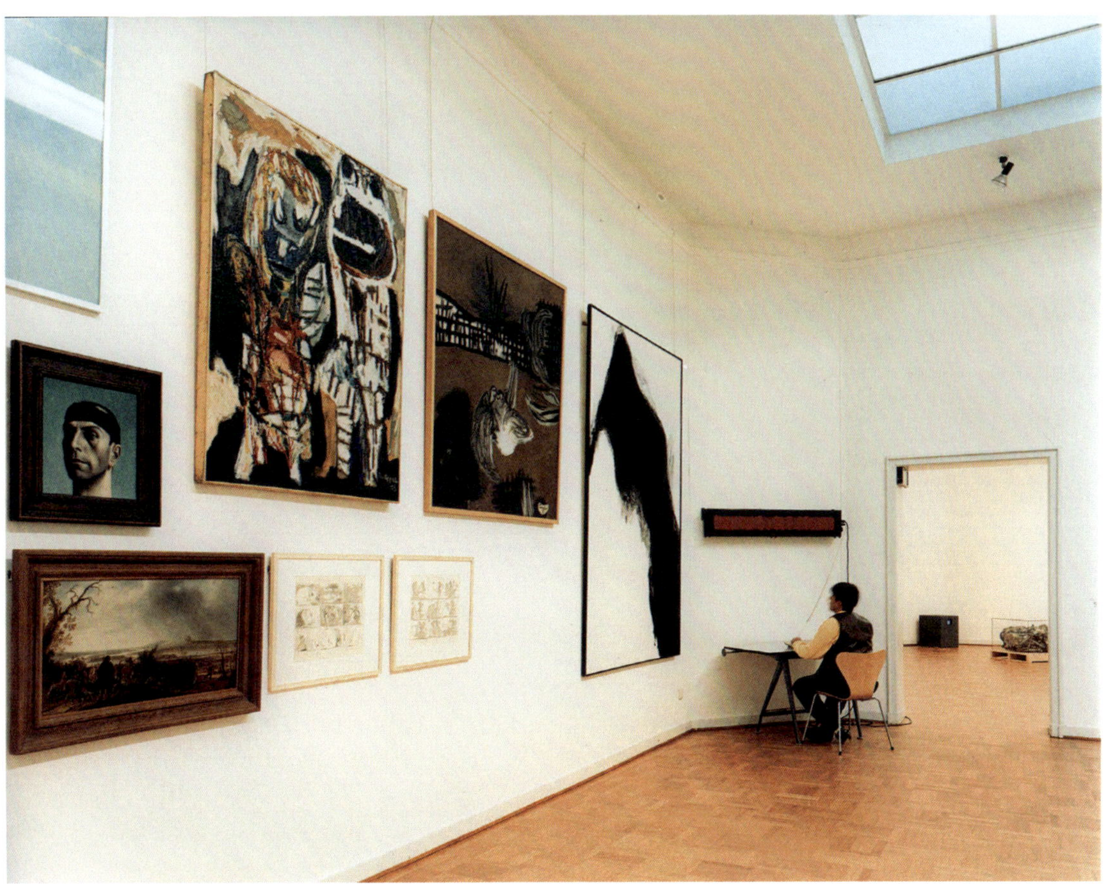

Wolf later joined the Kurdish PKK as a real fighter. After Andrea's death, Steyerl then made a montage in which fictional and 'real' martial poses and performances were placed in questioning constellation, possibly generating a next generation of unforeseeable effects.

If autonomy cannot be a structural fact but appears in an act within certain limiting conditions, such an act can be termed aesthetic to the extent that it foregrounds its entanglement in heteronomy. If the aesthetic problematizes the relationship of autonomy and heteronomy, then this means that an act can be termed aesthetic insofar as it lets autonomy *appear* sensibly as problem – in the heteronomous world of the senses and of social facts. Jacques Rancière is one of a number of philosophers who have issued stern caveats about the compatibility of the aesthetic and the political, in particular in so far as they involve different 'autonomies'. As Rancière's puts it: '[Aesthetic] art promises a political accomplishment that it cannot satisfy, and thrives on that ambiguity.'[38] But while an act's aesthetic and political qualities may never quite converge, some acts may function in different registers simultaneously, or successively. It may precisely be the *passage* from one aspect to the other that is of most interest – both politically and aesthetically.

38. Jacques Rancière, 'The Aesthetic Revolution and Its Outcomes: Emplotments of Autonomy and Heteronomy', *New Left Review* no. 14 (March/April 2002), 151.

Andrea Fraser

Autonomy and Its Contradictions

More than anybody else, artist Andrea Fraser has for decades painstakingly investigated the concept of autonomy, basing her work on the analyses of the cultural sociologist Pierre Bourdieu. She discovered that the different dimensions of autonomy are contradicting one another more and more sharply in their functioning. A more meaningful autonomy can be developed by approaching the concept from a psychoanalytic perspective, provided that certain conditions are accepted.

The conditions and contradictions of artistic autonomy have been a central concern of mine since the 1990s. I began my 1996 essay 'What's Intangible, Transitory, Mediating, Participatory, and Rendered in the Public Sphere, Part II', by enumerating four different aspects or 'dimensions' of artistic autonomy. First, I listed the 'aesthetic dimension', including 'the freedom of art works from rationalization with respect to specific use or function, whether moral, economic, political, social, material or emotional'. Second, the 'economic dimension', which emerged with 'the relatively anonymous bourgeois market and with it, the artistic commodity; the consequent separation of sites of production and consumption and with it, the separation of production from the demands it meets or satisfies in the places and processes of consumption'. Third, the 'social dimension': the autonomy of art as a field which, like the autonomy of other fields, in Pierre Bourdieu's analysis, is a condition of its capacity to impose 'its own norms on both the production and the consumption of its products' and to exclude norms and criteria dominant in other fields – especially the economic and political fields'. And, finally, the 'political dimension', which I frame in terms of 'the freedom of speech and conscience and the right to dissident opinion'.[1]

My characterization of the 'aesthetic' and 'political' dimensions of autonomy in that essay are perhaps particularly in need of elaboration, and I would now also add to this list what might be described, broadly, as a psychological dimension of autonomy. However, I still believe that any meaningful and productive discussion of autonomy in relation to art must include a clear articulation of which aspects of autonomy – these or others – are at issue, and how these aspects of autonomy are interrelating. The challenge that I became aware of in the mid-1990s, as I confronted some of the consequences of the services model that I was developing at the time, is not only that discussions of autonomy often blurred these different aspects, but that these different dimensions of autonomy often seem to function in contradiction to each other. I think that these contradictions have only become more acute since that time.

Bourdieu was a central influence in the development of my thinking about artistic autonomy and its contradictions. Bourdieu himself, to my knowledge, only used the term 'autonomy' to describe what I would call the social dimensions of artistic autonomy. He develops his theory of relatively autonomous social fields in the context of 'The Field of Cultural Production, or; the Economic World Reversed' and other essays from the 1970s and 1980s, which he later revised into the book *The Rules of Art*. Interestingly, he hardly uses the term in *Distinction: A Social Critique of the Judgment of Taste*, which is where he engages those aspects of art that are often central to discussions of autonomy in the context of art discourse,

1. Andrea Fraser, *Museum Highlights: The Writings of Andrea Fraser* (Cambridge, MA: MIT Press, 2005), 56.

and which I think of as the aesthetic dimension of artistic autonomy, such as traditions of disinterestedness, distancing, and freedom from rationalization with respect to specific functions, etcetera. He engages these as aspects of art in terms of the 'aesthetic disposition', but never in terms of 'autonomy'. However, clear links are to be found between these two sides of his analysis of culture, particularly in the homology between the social conditions of the relative autonomy of the artistic field, and the social conditions of the formation of the aesthetic disposition, both of which he links to the negation of the economic and, perhaps more broadly, of material interests, needs and forms of determination.

For Bourdieu, of course, all social fields are 'relatively autonomous' – otherwise they would not exist as or be recognizable as fields (he says somewhere that a completely heteronomous field would be, rather, an 'apparatus'). The relative autonomy of all fields, from this perspective is contingent upon their capacity to 'impose their own norms and sanctions' within their sphere and to exclude external or competing norms, values and so forth. In this sense, to say that fields are 'relatively autonomous' is not just to say that they are never completely autonomous, but also that they are autonomous only relative to other fields. What is particular to cultural fields as they developed in the west, in Bourdieu's analysis, is their tendency not only to exclude but also to negate and even invert economic

values specifically. With art in particular, this is then linked – although usually only implicitly in Bourdieu's work – to specifically aesthetic traditions of disinterestedness, the conditions of which, in his analysis of the aesthetic disposition, are also a negation of the economic. In this case of the 'aesthetic disposition', however, Bourdieu's emphasis shifts from the negation of economic values to the negation of economic and material determination more broadly, in the form of need, and of the uses and functions that would serve such need. The 'aesthetic disposition' is thus 'the paradoxical product of negative economic conditioning' in that it manifests the economic conditions that determine it precisely by negating economic conditioning and determination.[2]

2. Pierre Bourdieu, *Distinction: A Social Critique of the Judgment of Taste* (Cambridge, MA: Harvard University Press, 1984), 55.

This is where artistic autonomy becomes really problematic. It is at this juncture that one finds the homology between, on the one hand, the freedom from economic (and other forms of) rationality, which, in left traditions, has been won by artists through sacrifice and struggle, and, on the other, the freedom from economic rationality that is a by-product of economic privilege. It is here that one finds the structural logic of the objective collusion between avant-garde artists and economic elites that is performed in the art market and bourgeois art institutions, despite the apparent social and even political opposition between these positions.

Within the structure of this homology it also often seems that avant-garde negations of instrumentality are felt most acutely not by those in power and against whom they may be manifestly addressed, but by those who do experience themselves as subject to this instrumentality. I encountered this quite directly in my research in corporate collections, where the autonomy performed by the artists and curators seemed to be experienced by employees as no more than a particularly arbitrary and violent manifestation of managerial power, stripped of the logic economic rationality that governed their own working lives. I think it is extremely important to recognize that this is a matter of collusive homologies and not of the kind of cooptation that many avant-garde traditions have made it out to be. From there we might begin to be able to reflect more honestly and productively on what it is in our field, our practices, and even our politics, that serves to reproduce these structures.

Looking back over the past 30 or 40 years, it seems that efforts by artists to reject the privilege, elitism and idealism that has been associated with the aesthetic disposition have often led not to an emancipatory gain but to the development of even more rarefied cultural forms. For example, the rejection of specialized modes of artistic production and reception – commonly associated with the 'de-skilling' of Minimalism but in fact on-going through most twentieth-century art movements – most often ended up producing aesthetic forms that are even more obscure and demanding than the craft-based competencies it eschewed. A similarly bitter irony can be found in many cultural activist and culturally engaged political positions that often seem to slide into a aestheticization of politics or that replace an artistic vanguardism with a political – and often also intellectual – vanguardism that is no less demanding of cultural capital and competence, no less life-style determined and no more egalitarian, except perhaps in rhetoric.

On the other hand, it now also seems likely that many of the developments that have been identified with the artistic critique of autonomy, or at least some of the privileged forms of production and consumption associated with it, have been motivated more by a frustration with the limits that go along with artistic autonomy than by radical egalitarian impulses. The 'specific principle of legitimacy' of relatively autonomous fields in which producers produce for the recognition and evaluation of other producers – institutionalized in mechanisms such as peer-review – tends to generate increasingly specialized forms of production and consumption. While these mechanisms and the highly specialized discourses and practices they produce are more or less accepted in the sciences, in cultural fields they have been decried as elitist and obscure and cut off from the culture of everyday life. However, one can see in pop traditions, as well as in the more recent vogue of all forms of participatory art, a hunger of artists as well as art institutions for larger audiences and wider influence in which radical democratic rhetoric and corporate populism, if not marketing, often seem to merge all too seamlessly.

Another example of this may be found in activist and productivist positions that perform a protest against art's traditional lack of function, material effect and use value, but which seem most often to fall to the side of the instrumentalization or bureaucratization of art – most problematically not only by artists, but by public and other institutional funders. The expansion of these positions in and since the 1990s clearly have coincided with what is sometimes called the instrumental turn in cultural policy in the USA as well as Europe, as the end of the Cold War, European integration and globalization led to the collapse of traditional rationales for public subsidy in the West, such as national prestige and regional competition (although these seemed to have gained ground in the East), and as neoliberalism trampled on notions of social democratic public goods.

I ran up against these tendencies quite directly in the 1990s, when I was deeply involved in trying to work through a model of art making as service provision. By the mid-1990s, I ended up feeling that most forms of artistic autonomy were just too problematic and contradictory to defend, except perhaps for the political dimension of artistic autonomy, which I identified with free speech rights above all and which are not specifically artistic. However, as I learned in

the course of a study of censorship battles over art in 1999-2000, even this form of autonomy is often also reduced to a kind of artistic or professional privilege in the context of culture wars, as 'artistic freedom' specifically, and that in fact artists and art institutions rarely defend freedom of speech as political principle or a civil right. The reduction of free speech to a kind of artistic privilege is one of the most vicious forms of symbolic violence produced by such art controversies – and one in which, again, the art field often seems to collude with conservative forces, despite their apparently opposed positions.[3]

All that being said, practically speaking, I continue to be deeply

3. See my essay 'A Sensation Chronicle', *Social Text*, no. 67 (summer 2001). Reprinted in *Museum Highlights*, op. cit. (note 1).

committed to the autonomy of and cultural as well as educational institutions in the very basic sense of defending traditions of self-governance and self-regulation, peer review and freedom from market criteria as well as the immediate rationalization of art and other cultural and intellectual endeavours with respect to social use, economic value and political interest. Much more pressing, in my opinion, than the loss of autonomy in art is the loss of autonomy in the sciences, where research and practice is increasingly market directed and 'inconvenient' facts come under immediate political attack. In our political and economic context today, any critique of the professional or expert privilege historically associated with these forms of autonomy runs the risk of playing right into the hands of the rightwing populists who have so successfully identified class hierarchy with educational and cultural rather than economic capital and who are intent on destroying anything that gets in the way of their political agenda.

In this context, we must also be careful that some of the constructions and claims of artistic autonomy, as well as those emerging from the theoretical field with which the art world has become so closely allied, do not serve to weaken the autonomy of other fields, and perhaps even, ultimately, of the artistic field itself. I am thinking in particular of formulations that seem to reach for a kind of pure autonomy, a kind of pure freedom, in which avant-garde practices are sometimes identified with radical political practices, such as anarchist traditions and autonomia. I am also thinking of formulations that identify artistic autonomy as an essential property of the aesthetic, rather than as a historically specific social form. Such formulations have appeared, for example, in recent debates about the definitions of artistic research and requirements for PhDs in art practice, in arguments that artists should not be required to write book-length dissertations for PhDs or to formulate an explicit research methodology. Such requirements, the arguments often go, constitute an attack on artistic autonomy and the subjection of art to the criteria of academic fields. But it must be obvious at this point that such arguments themselves constitute an attack

on the autonomy of academic fields, which is itself based on their capacity to impose their own norms and sanctions within their sphere. Surely, if artists were as autonomous as they are made out to be in some of these arguments, they would not be pursuing academic doctorates in the first place. In this case it begins to look very much like some of the most apparently radical formulations of artistic autonomy are in fact often only the most expedient. Even more problematic is to see such artistic positions structurally aligned with the political and market forces that see academic standards only as impediments to the reduction of academic fields to instruments in their own economies.

Critical Art Practice

For artists invested in critical practice today, one of the most challenging aspects of the conditions and contradictions of artistic autonomy is their relationship to artistic critique. Historically and discursively, the notion of critical art practice is unthinkable without some notion of autonomy – even if one of the primary objects of artistic critique has been artistic autonomy itself. However, I think both of these terms need to be radically rethought if they are to be useful at all. In fact, I am beginning to wonder if the term 'critique' ever really can be made useful again – but I would much sooner toss 'critique' than I would 'autonomy'.

We use the term 'critique' incessantly in art discourse but it is even harder to pin down than 'autonomy'. Art's 'critical' capacity or potential can be linked to all of the dimensions of artistic autonomy I listed above. Art's capacity to negate or invert the values and principles of hierarchization dominant in other fields or in the social world is linked to the autonomy of art as a social field. The freedom of artists to question and challenge is linked not only to politically guaranteed free speech rights, but also to the practical and economic autonomy of artists as independent producers who control our own labour and the products of that labour to a relatively large degree. But then there is the link between critical art practice and the aesthetic dimension autonomy, which, once again, proves to be particularly problematic. That link can be found most clearly in the distancing that is one of the basic features both of the aesthetic disposition, in the form of disinterested pleasure, etcetera, and of critical art practices, through the operation of estrangement that may be found in almost all critical art strategies. (Here I would distinguish critical from political art practices and cultural activism, which may be much more direct and not rely on such forms of distancing.)

This distancing now seems to me to be the most problematic feature of both 'critical art practice' and of some conceptions, and perhaps also dimensions, of artistic autonomy. Developing on Bourdieu's scattered references to 'negation in a Freudian sense', I am beginning to believe that this distancing functions through an operation of

negation that often is more defensive than dialectical. Bourdieu himself seems to vacillate on this question a great deal. Sometimes he links artistic autonomy to 'a bad faith denial of the economic', with all its intimations of moral failing and fraud. At other times, he links negation to the social conditions of art as a relatively autonomous field, which he defends vigorously, particularly in the context of his anti-neoliberal activism; and, in language that parallels many representations of artistic critique, to art's capacity to achieve a 'partial anamnesis of deep and repressed structures'.[4]

In many ways, the complexity of negation in Bourdieu's work mirrors its complexity in Freud's. Freud beings his essay 'Negation' (1925) introducing negation as a mechanism of defence. However, while he describes negation as a form of denial, it is a denial that nevertheless also represents a partial lifting of repression. The key distinction he makes is between idea and affect: with negation, something may be admitted to consciousness as an idea, but is nevertheless distanced emotionally; it may be thought, but only negatively, as an idea that is rejected, dismissed, etcetera. More broadly, however, what is at issue is inside and outside: whether the idea or affect is owned and accepted or whether it is split off, expelled, projected or otherwise disowned, often, in a sense, by locating it outside of the boundaries of the self – which is also thus constituted, in some sense, by way

4. Pierre Bourdieu, *The Rules of Art: The Structure and Genesis of the Literary Field* (Palo Alto, CA: Stanford University Press, 1992), 3-4.

of these boundaries, as autonomous and perhaps we could even say as an autonomous field.

Freud then goes on to describe negation as a condition of the development of the intellectual function and even of thought, as well as of judgment, in some sense, precisely by virtue of the role it plays in distinguishing what is inside and what is outside, what is only subjectively or also objectively existing, and of whether something thought also exists in reality.

One question I have been preoccupied with lately is whether it is possible to distinguish, in practice, between defensive negation and critical negation. Can there be a 'critical' distancing that is not also a defensive disowning? This has led me is to consider substituting the term 'analysis' for 'critique', or at least to consider analysis as a necessary step following critique. If critique is indeed a moment of defensive negation that nevertheless allows a repressed idea to make its way to consciousness – but as split off and disowned – then we may still need a second step that allows for a recognition and reintegration of that idea as well as our affective investment in it. Such a second step might be called analysis, and my hope is that such analysis might finally lead us out of the now seemingly perpetual reproduction and expansion of contradictions in which we seem to be trapped in the art world today.

This is all very schematic, of course, and I don't believe that a psychological model can be transferred directly to a social field. However, this psychological model also has interesting implications for a discussion of autonomy. Autonomy is also a very much-debated term in the field of psychoanalysis. Part of the critique of autonomy that was important to my development in the early 1980s derived from Lacan's rejection of the notion of the autonomous ego, dominant in ego psychology, and of the Cartesian *cogito*; his identification of the autonomous self with the Imaginary; and the theory of ideology developed by Althusser in response to those formulations. This rejection of the autonomous ego was also central to many other Marxist as well as feminist critiques of the 'autonomous' subjects produced by and for capitalist and patriarchal institutions.

In my recent return to psychoanalytic frameworks—not Lacanian so much as object-relations, Kleinian, Bionian, and relational perspectives – I am finding that 'autonomy' figures most prominently as an unconscious fantasy of agency, often linked to infantile omnipotence. This fantasy of agency also serves a defensive function: it wards off anxiety associated with the frustrations, privations, discomforts and potential losses that go along with helplessness and dependency; or even against the trauma represented by the external world as such – overwhelming, impinging and determining – whether that external world is physically or only narcissistically injurious. In these perspectives, the tenacity and rigidity of that unconscious fantasy of autonomy and agency often appears as a key factor in the development of psychopathology.[5]

5. See, for example, D.W. Winnicott, 'The Use of an Object', *International Journal of Psycho-Analysis*, 50 (1969), 711-716.

Interestingly, it is also linked to art, particularly in object-relations theory, which posits infantile omnipotence as a developmentally necessary stage in which infants are protected from premature and traumatic subjection to reality and revelation of their own helplessness. Winnicott developed the theory of a transitional phase in which infants are gradually 'failed' by their environment and exposed to their own dependence. This phase is characterized by 'transitional objects' and 'transitional phenomenon' that are both found and made, inside and outside, subjective and objective: that belong to both reality and fantasy. Interestingly, Winnicott suggests this is a matter not only of infantile belief but also of adult collusion: sustained by an implicit, collective, unconscious if not conscious agreement and participation. And this transitional space, for Winnicott, is also the location of cultural experience.[6] In this, Winnicott agrees with Freud, who in his 'Two Principles of Mental Functioning' (1911) famously

6. See D.W. Winnicott, *Playing and Reality* (London: Tavistock Publications, 1971).

suggests that art brings about a reconciliation of fantasy and reality in a particular way: artists turn away from reality to fantasy, but then find a way to return from fantasy back to reality by moulding fantasy into a new kind of reality. Artists do this, according to Freud, without 'creating real altera-

tions in the outer world'. Instead, he suggests that fantasy is realized through the recognition and collusion of others who share the artist's dissatisfaction with reality, which itself is part of reality.

Clearly, Bourdieu read Freud: I'm convinced that he also read Winnicott. There is a passage in *Distinction* that recently jumped out at me in which Bourdieu links 'the suspension and removal of economic necessity' and the 'objective and subjective distance' from determination that characterizes the aesthetic disposition, to 'a child's relation to the world'. In what sounds very much like a reference to infantile omnipotence, he then mentions parenthetically that 'all children start life as baby bourgeois, in a relation of magical power over others and, through them, over the world'.[7]

From the psychoanalytic per-

7. Bourdieu, *Distinction*, op. cit. (note 2), 54.

spectives I'm interested in these days, the question raised by all of this is not whether artistic autonomy is fantasy or reality, but whether constructions of artistic autonomy, perhaps like some of those of critique, serve defensive functions, vis-à-vis negation, splitting, externalization, etcetera, that ward off affectively experienced and invested conflicts, social or psychological, by disowning the bad parts of them and expelling them from the boundaries of the ideally autonomous field, practice or self. Such defensive constructions of autonomy would thus serve to reproduce those conflicts on some level, perhaps especially as contradictions, by keeping them protected from potentially transformative engagement. Or, on the other hand, whether constructions of autonomy serve to enable a working-through of those conflicts, for example, by creating a space, like the analytic space or frame (which has certain homologies to the artistic frame), in which the a temporary suspension of immediate material consequences as well as familiar patterns of existence, relationships, thought, behaviour and, perhaps especially, judgment, provide for a possibility for new relationships and new experiences of relationships to emerge.

From these psychoanalytic perspectives, meaningful autonomy and agency can only develop out of an acceptance of dependency and determinisms; the taming of the anxiety provoked by dependency and a loosening of the defensive idealization, splitting, projection, and so forth, that we employ not only to manage that anxiety but also to put off the often unpleasant and only marginally achievable task of making real changes in ourselves or in the world. And I would like to imagine that this would be a form of autonomy that would also escape those problematic homologies with economic privilege and the not-so-magical power of the adult bourgeoisie.

Peter Osborne

Theorem 4: Autonomy

Can It Be True of Art and Politics at the Same Time?

It is a distinctive feature of much recent critical discourse that 'autonomy' has become increasingly derided in art, while being increasingly valued in politics. Indeed, autonomy is frequently claimed to be the very basis of politics, and hence of a politics of art – art activism – dedicated to the production of non-autonomous art. Yet it is not clear that the sense in which some art may be claimed, critically, to function auton-omously is well understood; or that the theoretical inti-macy of relations between claims for autonomy in art and in politics is fully appreciated. This short piece

(brutally brief)
approaches these
relations from a
historico-philo-
sophical angle and
a broadly Adornian
point of view. It
sets out from four
common miscon-
ceptions of the
autonomy of art,
and proceeds to
what Osborne takes
to be Adorno's less
inadequate concep-
tion, its political
limits, and the
dialectical entangle-
ment of its critique
with artistic
autonomy itself.

1. Aesthetic Autonomy

The autonomy of art is not – although it has often been thought to be – the same thing as the 'autonomy of the aesthetic'. Nor can the autonomy of the aesthetic provide a conceptual basis for the autonomy of art. It is a widespread historico-philosophical myth that it is the *logical* autonomy of aesthetic judgements of taste from other types of judgement (as theorized by Kant in his *Critique of the Aesthetic Power of Judgment* of 1790) that is the conceptual basis of the autonomy of art from other types of social practice. Over the last 200 years, this myth has been perpetuated to the level of a philosophical commonplace in part through the slippage created by the use of the term 'aesthetic' to mean 'of art'. The phrase 'aesthetic autonomy' has thereby come, in most places, to be used synonymously with 'autonomy of art'. However, with regard to autonomy, this identification of 'art' with 'aesthetic' is both philosophically incoherent and art-historically implausible. Philosophically, Kant's *Critique of the Aesthetic Power of Judgment* cannot, in principle, provide the conceptual ground for a philosophical account of the art work – which was actually the contribution of Jena Romanticism – since it has no account of (nor any interest in) the ontological distinctiveness of the work of art. Indeed, the whole of Kant's transcendental philosophy is systematically orientated towards the avoidance of all ontology. This is its methodological distinctiveness. Kant's thought on aesthetic requires objects that can 'occasion' the possibility of pure aesthetic judgement, for which his model is *nature*. The 'produced' and hence purpose-based character of the art work means that *no* judgement of 'artistic beauty' can be a pure aesthetic judgment of taste, in principle, for Kant (genius notwithstanding). Indeed, what Kant called 'aesthetic art' – an art appropriate to pure aesthetic judgments of taste – precisely *cannot* be viewed as autonomous qua 'art', or as an instance of any particular art, but only 'as if' a part of nature. *Aesthetic autonomy is indifferent to the art/non-art distinction.* This makes it interesting, in itself, of course, but not as an account of the autonomy of art. Correspondingly, historically, *autonomous art has largely been indifferent to the aesthetic/non-aesthetic distinction,* for 50 years at least; and in important cases much longer.

Is there, then, no 'aesthetic regime of art' – to use Jacques Rancière's now established phrase? Well, there is no strictly Kantian one; although there appears to be a Schillerian one. However, this Schillerian regime is *not strictly aesthetic*, in either of Kant's two main senses ('of sensibility' and pertaining to a 'critique of taste'), since Schiller's aesthetics involves the application to Kant's transcendental analysis of aesthetic judgement-power of a principle from Kant's philosophy of pure *practical* reason: namely, what in his 1788 *Critique of Practical Reason*, Kant called 'Theorem 4': autonomy of the will. Theorem 4 is the source of all productivity and all problems of autonomy in this tradition. This was an application that took place, precisely, in order to solve the problem for Kantianism that it *cannot* account for the beauty of art, other than by abstracting from, or negating, the artefactual, art-status of the art work. It is here, historically, in Schiller's early (1793) *Kallias Letters* (his letters to Gottfried Körner, 'Concerning Beauty') that 'autonomy' first became philosophically associated with the work of art. The autonomy of the art work is thus, in this German tradition, philosophically mortgaged to Kant's *practical*, as opposed to his aesthetic, philosophy. This genealogy poses a political problem for nearly all accounts of autonomous art, Adorno's included; as it does also (albeit in a more subterranean, disavowed manner) for supposedly quite different accounts of the autonomy of *politics* – the supposedly Spinozist politics of Autonomia, in particular. (Where is the *theorization* of autonomy in Autonomia?) For this genealogy rests upon the myth of a *purely rational* determination of the will, the *in*applicability of which was to be mitigated by Schiller via the aesthetic mediations of the play and form drives. The residue of this history appears within the Autonomia tradition of political autonomy in its dependence on a Kantian *negative freedom* of autonomy *from* . . . *autonomy from* economics, capital, the state, the party, and ultimately, perhaps, the social

itself. Refusal – exodus – escape.

But what, then, of the aesthetic tradition: the historical manifestation of the Schillerian 'aesthetic regime of art'? Two things may be said about this. First, there *is*, certainly, historically, a Kantian *self-understanding* of the Schillerian 'aesthetic regime of art' – an 'aesthetic ideology' as it has been called. In its conventional form, it runs from 'art for art's sake' (in early nineteenth-century France), through aestheticism (in late nineteenth-century England), formalism (in late nineteenth-century Germany and early twentieth-century England and Russia) and formalist modernism (in mid-twentieth-century USA). Second, however, insofar as this 'aesthetic regime' exists as the practical enactment of a philosophical misunderstanding, it is *not the same thing as* the 'regime of autonomous modern art', or indeed, even the basis of the autonomy of the particular 'aesthetic' art that it theorizes. For once 'purposiveness without a purpose' becomes *the* purpose of art, as it did in 'art for art's sake' (as proposed by Benjamin Constant as early as 1804), such art's beauty is *no longer* 'free', on Kant's own terms – no longer actually 'without a purpose'. This is its dialectical dilemma.

Conceptualization of art's autonomy, or of autonomous art, must be sought elsewhere. The second most widespread misconception concerns self-referentiality.

2. Self-Referentiality

The autonomy of art is not – as it is often thought to be – the autonomy of self-reference. The idea of an autonomy of self-reference is the product of the transposition of the concept of aesthetic autonomy into a linguistic register, in literary modernism (T.S. Elliot influenced Greenberg here): a new way of conceiving of being 'without purpose'. This in turn became the basis for a reinterpretation of aesthetic autonomy in the visual arts, in Greenberg's transformation of the concept of self-referentiality into that of medium-specificity ('medium-specificity' *means* medium self-referentiality): aesthetic autonomy was thereby transformed into the *task* of *medium self-definition through purification.* Historically, this did achieve a (ideological) 'regime' of autonomy, for practices recognized as medium-based – not 'autonomous art', that is, but autonomous art*s* – but it arbitrarily denies autonomy to other art practices, ungrounded in the history of a medium. The institutional history of art practices, since at least the 1960s, embodies the widespread rejection of this foreclosure, as it does of the earlier, generalized 'aesthetic' variant.

Third common misconception (this one is more tricky, and also more 'living'): freedom of the artist.

3. The Freedom of the Artist

The autonomy of art cannot – as has often been thought – be reduced to the expression of the autonomy of the artist, although it is conditioned by whatever *elements* of autonomy (in the sense of rationally subjectively willed components) are involved in art practices. This is the difficult bit: theorizing those 'elements', other than by purely retrospective attribution to an artist-subject of the action of the structure articulating the process of which he or she is a part; that is, other than by retroactively confusing the 'artist-function' with the individual human being(s) inhabiting its place in the structure. (In fact, this confusion *is* 'the subjective process' – in its distinction from 'subjectivation' – to use the terms of Alain Badiou's *Theory of the Subject*).[1] Yet the whole point of the idea of autonomous art (it's metaphysical distinctiveness and experiential and political productivity) is that of the ontological primacy of the work of art, sedimenting the process of its production, as a whole, into an immanent structure, with its own, *apparently* independent productivity (*Schein*: actuality of the illusion of autonomy). As an organizing principle and component of the production process, the artist (and his or her intentions and intentionalities) drops out; his/her/their creativity is literally consumed by the work. The artist cannot be treated as the ground of the action of the work, which *appears* as the only relevant 'subject' at stake.

However, finally, this does not mean that art is free from social determinations.

1. Alain Badiou, *Theory of the Subject* (1982), trans. Bruno Bosteels (London/ New York: Continuum, 2009), Part V.

4. Freedom from Social Determinations

The autonomy of art is not – as it is often thought to be – a freedom of art from social determination. Historically (so the familiar story goes, and Bourdieu tells it quite well in *The Rules of Art*), the autonomous work required the production of a special social space in which it can be received as autonomous, from the standpoint of its art-character. This requires, of course, famously, first, the development of a market in art (the commodification of the art work), and second, the transformation of art-institutional spaces into spaces of exhibition for autonomous art. The social history is familiar. From the standpoint of the concept of autonomous art, however, the by-now-well-established dialectical point is that autonomous art requires (ideally) the social determination of a space *free from social determinations of meaning based on non-artistic functions.* Separation. Artistic autonomy is thus – in part – a social form, an institutional form, as Bürger famously argued, taking his cue from Adorno.

So, if the autonomy of art is not best conceived as any of these four things – *aesthetic autonomy, self-referentially, mere expression of the autonomy of the artist,* or *freedom from social determination –* how is it best conceived?

A Better Account (or, a More Dialectical Adorno)

A better account starts out from the notion of a socially determined autonomy: not viewed in a 'causal' sociological manner (although there *is* social determination/conditioning of that kind), as some kind of explanatory external determination, but rather, viewed as immanently construed, as art's taking up of its social conditions into itself, as part of its constitution as art, (historico-)ontologically speaking. Otherwise, social determination simply negates any 'actual' or 'effective' autonomy (which is the problem with so much of Bourdieu's work, of course.) Adorno famously writes, in a conjoint Dostoevskyian-Marxian vein, of art's 'double character' (*Doppelcharakter*) as autonomy and social fact (*fait social –* alluding to Durkheim's sociological notion, as one element), in order to express the *contradiction* at its core.[2] This contradictory double character is best expressed dialectically, in the

2. Adorno, *Aesthetic Theory* (1970), trans. Robert Hullot-Kentor (London: Athlone Press, 1997), 225.

idea of the work of art as being internally structured by dialectical relations between its autonomous and dependent elements. On this conception, rendered more formally dialectically explicit than it is in *Aesthetic Theory* (oddly, it is more so in *Dialectic of Enlightenment*, generally a less dialectical text), and adopting the language of a dialectic in which contradictions are 'structured in dominance': autonomous art is an art in which autonomous or immanent determinations of meaning 'dominate' heteronomous or dependent ones; dependent or heteronomous art is art in which heteronomous or dependent determinations 'dominate' autonomous ones. (These are 'determinations' in the logical/conceptual – not causal – sense.) There is dependence in autonomous art, and there is autonomy in dependent art – of course! The history of autonomous art is the history of the development and increasing complication of this dialectic. *Adorno subjects the social concept of autonomous art to the history of capitalism.* The history of modern art thus becomes for him, in large part, the history of art's relationship to/struggle with the commodity form – a dimension as absent from Rancière's account of the aesthetic *regime* of art, as it is from much Autonomia and post-Autonomia writing on art activism.

But what are the 'autonomous determinations', enabled by this social form? At this point, we need to refer back to Schiller's taking up of Kant's philosophy of practical reason into his attempt to supplement Kant's aesthetic with an 'objective' concept of beauty.

The first half of 'Theorem 4' of Kant's *Critique of Practical Reason* reads as follows: '*Autonomy* of the will is the sole principle of all moral laws and of duties in keeping with them; *heteronomy* of choice, on the other hand . . . is instead opposed to the principle of obligation and to the morality of the will [that is, to all universality, PO] . . . the sole principle of morality consists in independence from all matter of the law (namely from a desired object) and at the same time in the determination of choice through the mere form of giving universal law that a maxim must be capable of. That independence, however, is freedom in the *negative* sense, whereas this *lawgiving of its own* on the part of pure and, as such, practical reason is freedom in the *positive* sense. Thus, the moral law expresses nothing other than the *autonomy* of pure practical reason, that is, freedom.'[3]

This is not the autonomy of 'the subject', but the autonomy of 'pure practical reason' itself, or the autonomy of pure reason in its practical deployment, as Kant describes it, transcendentally. The subject's relation to the causality of this freedom, whose act it *is*, is problematic.

In the *Kallias Letters*, Schiller transposes this problematic from the domain of practice to the domain of the *appearance* of objects, viewing objects from the standpoint of pure practical reason – what he calls the 'adaption' or imitation' of 'the *form* of practical reason'. 'The analogy of an appearance with the form of pure will or freedom', he writes 'is *beauty* (in its most general sense). Beauty is thus nothing less than freedom in appearance', or 'autonomy in appearance'.[4] (Freedom and

3. Immanuel Kant, *Critique of the Aesthetic Power of Judgment* (1790), trans. Paul Guyer and Eric Mathews, edited by Paul Guyer (Cambridge/New York: Cambridge University Press, 2000).

4. Friedrich Schiller, 'Kallias or Concerning Beauty: Letters to Gottfried Körner', in J.M. Bernstein (ed.), *Classical and Romantic German Aesthetics* (Cambridge: Cambridge University Press, 2003), 145-183; 151-152.

autonomy are synonymous in this tradition.) Beauty, then, for Schiller is the *appearance* of the free or 'autonomous' *determination of form.* Autonomous art – which gets its first philosophical definition here – is an art that so *appears*. This is what Adorno is repeating when he refers to the autonomous work of art as *exhibiting* a *self-legislating* 'law of form'. It does not mean that the art work actually *is* 'autonomous', in some positive ontological sense, but that it *appears* to be so: it has the capacity to produce this illusion. Or, to put it another way, *the work of art is autonomous to the extent to which it can generate the appearance or illusion of autonomy.* As Peter Bürger argued, 40 years ago now, autonomy operates at two discrete levels: both as a set of institutional conditions; and as the achievement of an individual work, in each individual instance (this involves, but is not reducible to, the individuating moment of the aesthetic *aspect*). Certain social conditions (the market and art institutions) help make this possible, and can also hinder or negate it, but they can only *facilitate* what *appears as* a self-legislation immanent to the work.

Adorno's argument is that the appearance of self-legislating form positions the work critically in relation to the demand for social functionality – including its own functional aspects, which it must somehow internally 'resist' or counter, in order to achieve autonomy (meaning the illusion of autonomy); thereby allowing it to *figure* freedom. This is the 'truth' of art, in this tradition: the figuring of freedom, or what Adorno refers to as a free praxis. In this respect, *autonomous art is not part of an 'aesthetic regime of art', it is part of a 'supra-aesthetic artistic regime of truth'* (of which 'aesthetic art' is one restricted and historically passing variant). From this point of view, the historical development of modern art is a development in the social forms and dynamics of the dialectics of autonomy and dependence that constitute this *supra-aesthetic artistic regime of truth*. Politics is inscribed within the structure of this dialectic in three main ways.

First, as I have said, the political meaning of autonomous art resides in its *image* of freedom: the pre-figuration of a free praxis, or praxis in a free society. As such, it is taken to be a criticism of the existing state of unfreedom: hence, the work of art, *any* work of art, 'criticizes society by merely existing', Adorno somewhat hyperbolically claimed (or at least, a work that has achieved autonomy).[5] This is a politics of form – an affirmation of freedom as self-legislating form; not a 'distribution of the sensible'.

5. Adorno, *Aesthetic Theory*, op. cit. (note 2), 226.

Second, the political meaning of the dialectical unity of autonomy and dependence within the work is as a model of reconciliation. The unity of the work functions as a 'promise of happiness' by offering a model of reconciliation, a non-coercive identity, via the 'belonging together' of the one and the many. In both cases, the political meaning inherent in art is pre-figurative, and hence 'imaginary'. Yet it is also, thereby, in danger of being affirmative, in the bad, Marcusean sense – affirmative of the society in which such pre-figuration is possible – and hence socially functional. This complicates the critical criteria for the achievement of autonomy.[6] Furthermore, subsequent to the recognition of the socially affirmative function of autonomous art (in the early twentieth century) and the subsequent so-called failure of both the historical avant-garde's and institutional critique's assault upon the institution of autonomy, there is an additional critical requirement for the achievement of autonomy. Under these conditions, autonomous art critically requires an element of anti-art – the contradictory incorporation of an un-integrated, dependent element, for which collage and the readymade are the historical models – but 'politics' is another way – in order to mark (that is, to render self-conscious) the illusory character of the autonomy of the work of art by staging its connection, indexically, to the world.

This points to a third way in which politics appears within the dialectic of autonomy and heteronomy within the work: namely, as the major mode of heteronomy as external determination, necessity or constraint: politics is *one*

6. Herbert Marcuse, 'The Affirmative Character of Culture' (1937) in: *Negations: Essays in Critical Theory* (Boston: Beacon Press, 1968), 88-133. For Adorno's critically modified adoption of this position ('its thesis requires the investigation of the individual artwork'), see *Aesthetic Theory*, op. cit. (note 2), 252.

form of dependence – either *within* autonomous art (as a subordinate aspect) or as a type of dependent art, political art, which itself still has a (subordinate) autonomous aspect. However, when a political art (a dependent, non-autonomous art) is taken out of its practical political context, by historical change or geographical displacement, and ceases to function politically, autonomous (formal) aspects come to the fore, and the character of the work changes. This is what happens when, for example, classically, works of Soviet Constructivism and Productivism are displayed within Western art institutions as part of the history of the artistic avant-garde. Here, politics appears as an external condition that is nonetheless incorporated into the work as one of its conditions, remaining partly heteronomous, but nonetheless *thereby*, in its very anti-formalism, becoming form-determining in a new way, and hence 'autonomous', at a structural level.

As a paradigm of a dependent element, politics is thus one paradigmatic, if paradoxical, way of rendered art critically *autonomous*, that is, of *maintaining* its autonomy in a political sense. (This is one way of reading Thomas Hirschhorn's or Andrea Fraser's work.) However, this critical function, internal to autonomous art, only operates so long as the anti-art (dependent) element in question resists incorporation into the art institution's conception of art. Once it is incorporated, the originally anti-art element will itself become affirmative of 'art' – and hence art's affirmative function – contradicting its initial critical function. (This is another way of reading Thomas Hirschhorn's or Andrea Fraser's work.)

In this regard, autonomous and dependent elements of the work of art do indeed turn into their opposites: dependent becomes autonomous; autonomous becomes dependent. This is why a dialectical thought is still needed to grasp these dynamics. This is a great strength of Adorno's position: despite his personal artistic preferences, his position refuses the red herring of having simply to choose between monolithically conceived blocs of 'autonomous art' and anti-institutional 'avant-garde activism'. First, because the relationship is structurally dialectical; and second, because *the institution changes* in response to this dialectic. Contra Bürger, the issue is thus not anti-art-institutionalism, as such, but *socially alternative modes* of the institutionalization of art (which was the problematic of the productive phase of the Soviet experience, for example, in the first place).

This leads me to the limits of this conception of autonomous art: namely, its basis in the analogical application of Kant's concept of autonomy: autonomy of the will in its 'positive' guise as *self-determining universal form.*

The Limits of Adorno and Art Activism, Alike

The conceptual and political limits of Adorno's conception of autonomous art derive from the individualistic assumptions behind Kant's application of the concept of pure rational will. Adorno's notion of autonomy continues to pertain to *individual subjects*; autonomous art thus provides no more than an *immanent criticism of liberal capitalist societies*, through which it figures the possibility of a free *individual* praxis.

Now, Adorno's is not a 'straight' Kantianism, to be sure, but a certain kind of Marxian one. He is a Marxian Kantian. He thinks that the development of capitalism has destroyed/ demobilized collective subject formation, leaving a retreat to individual freedom the sole remaining progressive option. But this does not get around the conceptual issue that for him *the work of art images the political freedom of the ideal liberal individual*: this is its 'enigmatic', subject-like, singular object status. Despite the historical argument, the political limitation remains the result of a conceptual limitation. The question is: *Is this a limitation of Adorno's thought,* or, *an inherent limitation on the critical functioning of autonomous art in capitalist societies?* On the Schillerian argument that both Adorno and Rancière appear to accept, autonomy appears most adequately, albeit only *analogically*, in the art work, because it *cannot appear in the world*, directly, in practice itself – since freedom in the form of *pure* practical reason is *alienated from life*. Those who believe the contrary, however, that freedom does appear directly politically in a movement (Autonomia and post-Autonomia political movements, for example), believe that it can do so only through *withdrawal* ('exodus') from the existing form of the capitalistic form of the social. And they think this relationship, politically, primarily negatively (although they rarely acknowledge this fact): freedom as negative freedom – *autonomy from* . . . economic determinations, capital, the state, the party, etcetera – as the social condition of positive freedom; despite the latter's usually *ontological* construal. Yet, in an ironic mimesis of the autonomous work of art, such *autonomy from* – or separation from – prevailing forms of social practice makes the exercise of any such positive freedom *impotent*; impotence famously being the price of autonomous art's criticality. Political autonomy, in the Autonomia tradition, is thus not so much the negation of the autonomy of the work of art as its ironic political mimesis. It is thus *critically* redeemable primarily only as art – an art more strictly *autonomous* than the *political* art the *heteronomy* of which it aims to radicalize. Such is the dialectics of activism and art in the politics of Autonomia.

To put it more formally: Theorem 4, Kant's concept of autonomy, cannot be true of art (analogically) and politics (directly) at the same time. It is in the historical contradiction between art and politics that the truth of autonomy lies.

Presupposition of the Equality of Intelligences and Love of the Infinitude of Thought

A Discussion between Jacques Rancière and Thomas Hirschhorn

Between December 2009 and February 2010, French philosopher Jacques Rancière and Swiss artist Thomas Hirschhorn exchanged thoughts in a series of e-mails.[1] Using Hirschhorn's art project Bijlmer Spinoza Festival from 2009 in Amsterdam as an example, the two of them investigate the essence of a work of art in this day and age. Hirschhorn tries to analyse his work with terms like 'presence' and 'production', to which Rancière reacts and stimulates further reflection.

1. This e-mail exchange was previously published by Les Presses du Réel in collaboration with Les Ateliers de Rennes in 2010 and appeared in French and English as part 4 of *Le Catalogue. Cinq Opuscules pour un catalogue*, Opuscule 4/4.

Dear Jacques Rancière,

I am happy to have the opportunity to write you. I'd like to suggest that I begin our exchange by sharing with you some experiences I had during the *Bijlmer Spinoza Festival*, my latest work in public space, conceived for and with the inhabitants of an outlying neighbourhood of Amsterdam in 2009. I thought that sharing an experience, an experience I had thanks to my work, was a good starting point. The *Bijlmer Spinoza Festival* is a work of art conceived according to the 'Presence and Production' guideline: my presence and production as an artist, but also that of Vittoria Martini, as an ambassador, that of Marcus Steinweg, as a philosopher, and that of Alexandre Costanzo, as an editor. 'Presence and Production' is my own term, a guideline I created to define those of my works that require my presence and production during the entire duration of an exhibition. With this term 'Presence and Production', I want to put forward my own notions because I think I can assess what is involved in being responsible for 'Presence' and 'Production'. I can understand what it will require of me. However, I do not know what 'community art', 'participative art', 'educational art', and 'relational aesthetics art' mean. With the 'Presence and Production' guideline, my aim is to answer the following questions: can a work – through the notion of 'Presence', my own presence – create for others the conditions for being present? And can my work – through the notion of 'Production' – create the conditions for other productions to be established?

Over the three months of the *Bijlmer Spinoza Festival*, I noticed something that was new, unexpected and surprising to me: the first local inhabitants to come to the *Bijlmer Spinoza Festival* were inhabitants of the margins, the margins of the neighbourhood and undoubtedly of society. From the beginning, these inhabitants visited my work regularly and soon came every day. Of all the visitors, these were the ones who stayed the longest. As the first from the neighbourhood, they really involved themselves, yet they were all people on the margins.

Over time, they formed a kind of 'hard core' of the *Bijlmer Spinoza Festival*. Most of these people were isolated and did not know each other before the festival – or if so, barely. They often lived alone, had family issues, problems with work or were unemployed or disabled or had an awful lot of problems.

Their presence – which was lively and often funny –

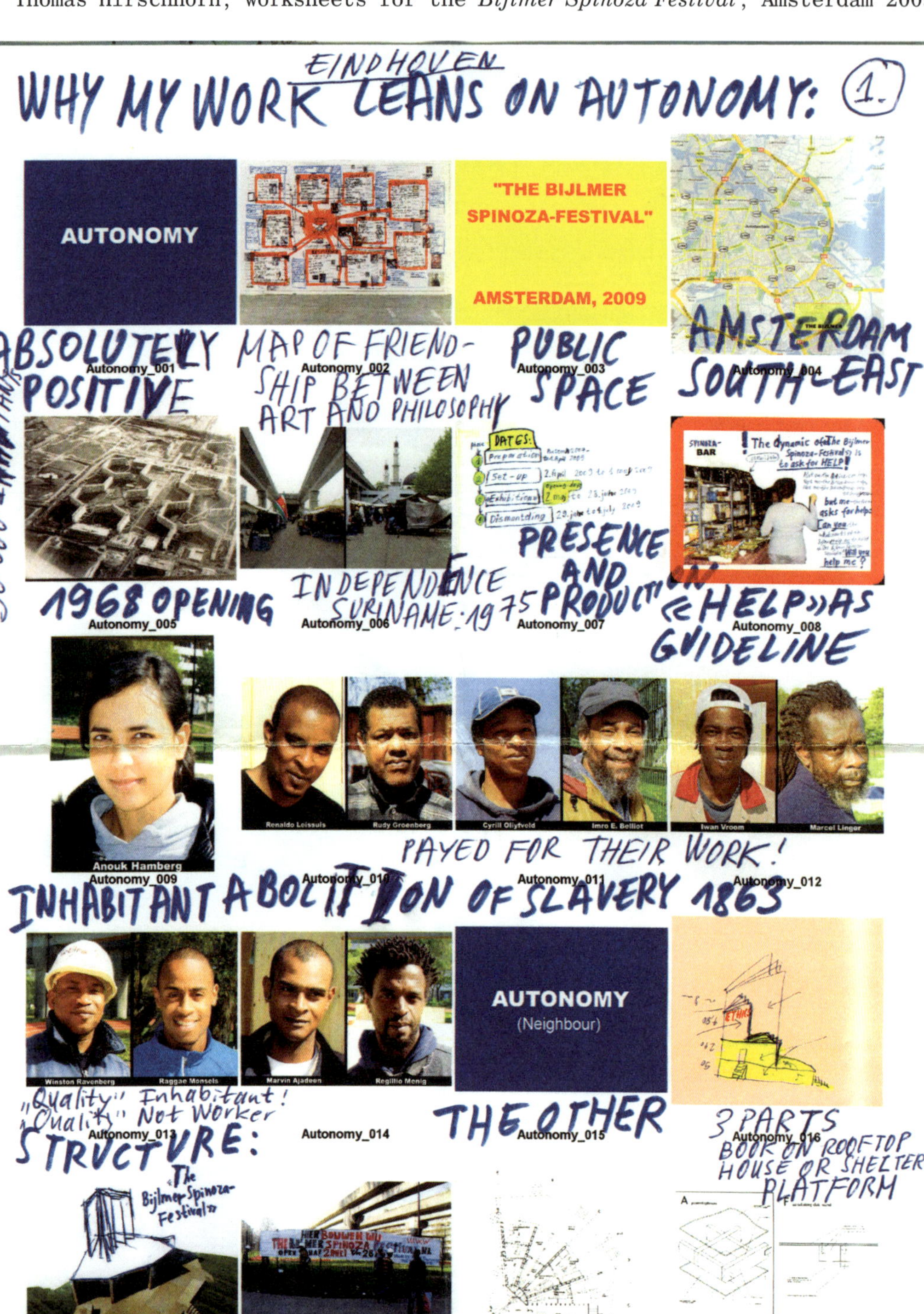
WHY MY WORK LEANS ON AUTONOMY: 1.
EINDHOVEN
AUTONOMY
"THE BIJLMER SPINOZA-FESTIVAL"
AMSTERDAM, 2009
ABSOLUTELY POSITIVE
Autonomy_001
MAP OF FRIENDSHIP BETWEEN ART AND PHILOSOPHY
Autonomy_002
PUBLIC SPACE
Autonomy_003
AMSTERDAM SOUTH-EAST
Autonomy_004
90'000 INHABITANTS
1968 OPENING
Autonomy_005
INDEPENDENCE SURINAME: 1975
Autonomy_006
PRESENCE AND PRODUCTION
Autonomy_007
«HELP» AS GUIDELINE
Autonomy_008
SPINOZA-BAR
The dynamic of the Bijlmer Spinoza-Festival is to ask for HELP!
but me asks for help
Can you help me?
Will you help me?
Anouk Hamberg
Autonomy_009
Renaldo Leissuls
Rudy Groenberg
Cyrill Oliyfveld
Imro E. Belliot
Iwan Vroom
Marcel Linger
Autonomy_010
PAYED FOR THEIR WORK!
Autonomy_011
Autonomy_012
INHABITANT ABOLITION OF SLAVERY 1865
Winston Ravenberg
Raggae Monsels
Marvin Ajadeen
Regillio Menig
AUTONOMY (Neighbour)
"Quality" Inhabitant!
"Quality" Not Worker
Autonomy_013
Autonomy_014
THE OTHER
Autonomy_015
Autonomy_016
3 PARTS
BOOK ON ROOFTOP
HOUSE OR SHELTER
PLATFORM
STRUCTURE:
"The Bijlmer Spinoza-Festival"
WHY
Autonomy_017
NAME
WHY FESTIVAL WHY BIJLMER WHY SPINOZA
Autonomy_018
Autonomy_019
PLANS
PRODUCER: STRAAT VAN SCULPTUREN
Autonomy_020

ONE MONTH CONSTRUCTION TOGETHER [2]
SELF-AUTHORIZATION (SELF-ERECTION)

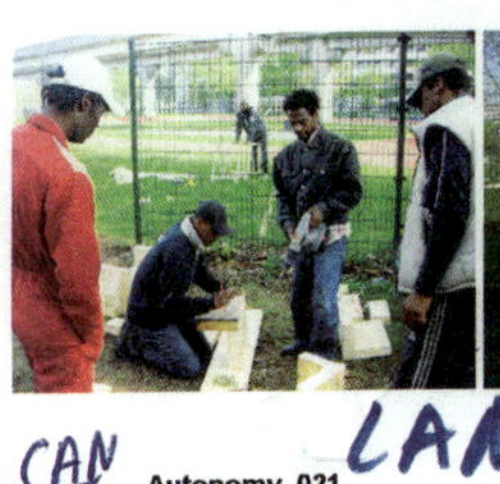

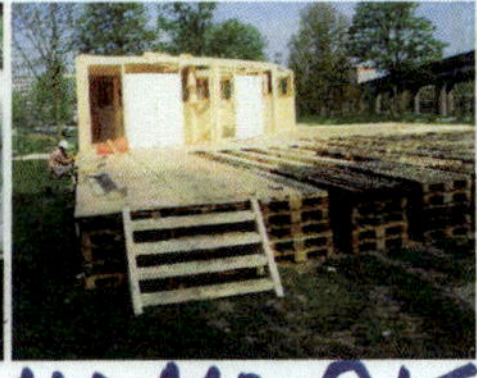

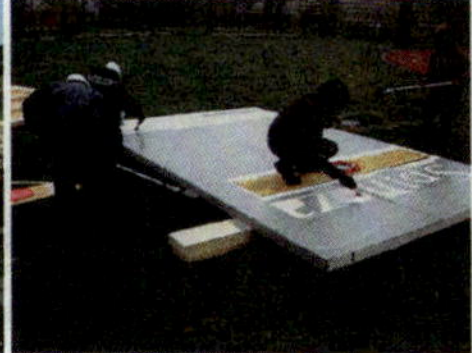

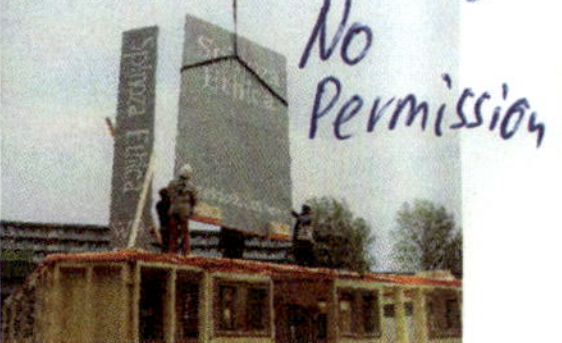

No Permission

CAN YOU DO WHAT I CAN DO!   LANDMARK

Autonomy_021

Autonomy_022

Spinoza's Relation to Amsterdam

Autonomy_023

No Obedience

Autonomy_024

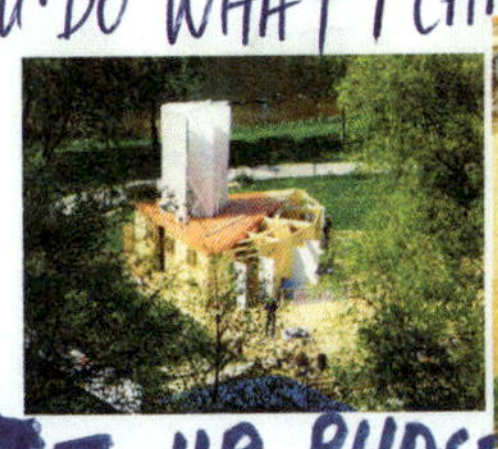

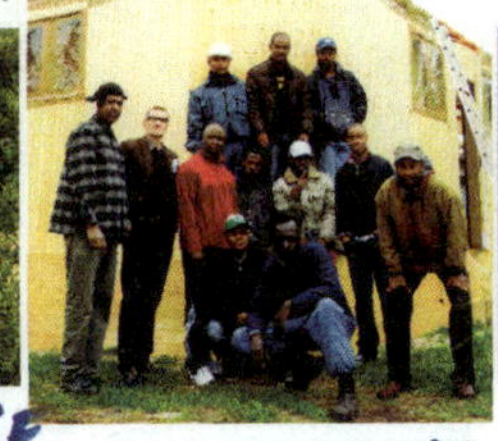

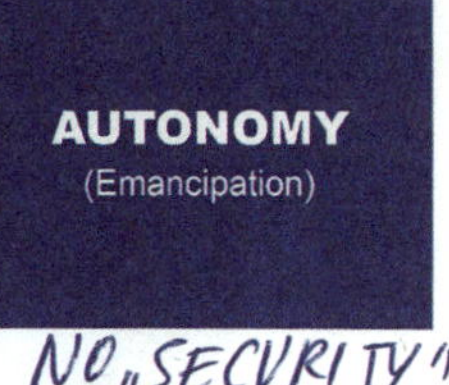

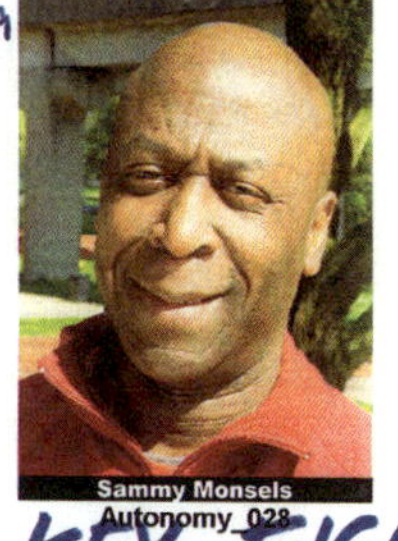

SET-UP-PHASE (72 Inhabitants)   EQUALITY

Autonomy_025

Autonomy_026

NO „SECURITY"
NO „SAFETY"

Autonomy_027

KEY-FIGURE S.M.

Autonomy_028

SPECIFIC

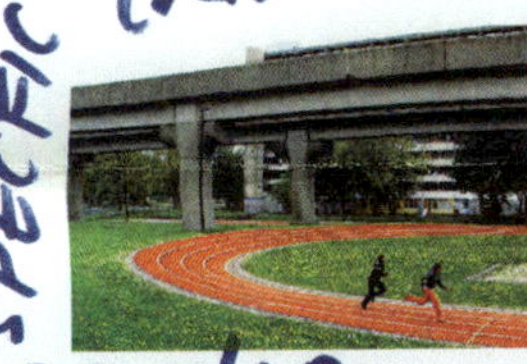

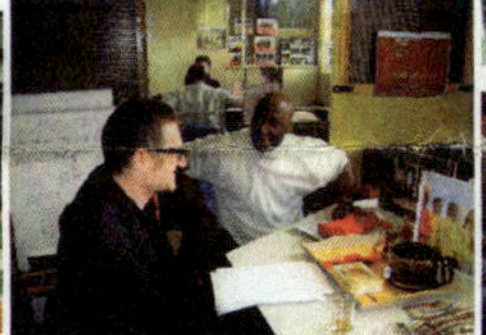

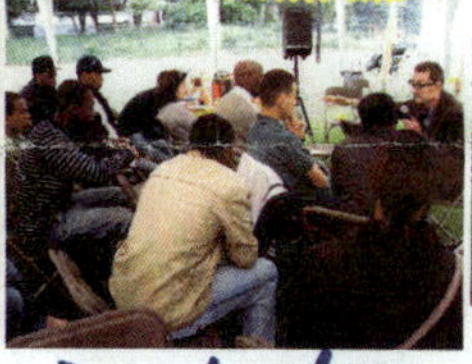

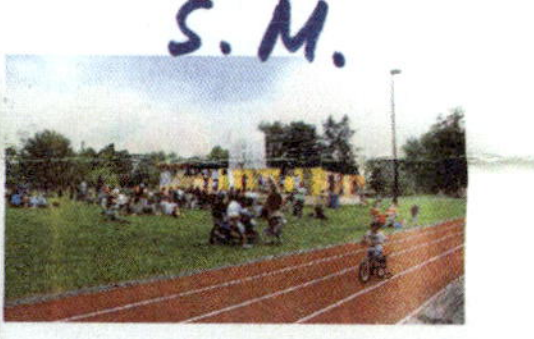

SPOT/LOCATION   9 Trips to Amsterdam   ATHLETIC-TRACK

AGREEMENT   Family, Friends and Athletes of Sammy   TRACTATUS

Autonomy_029

Autonomy_030

Autonomy_031

Autonomy_032

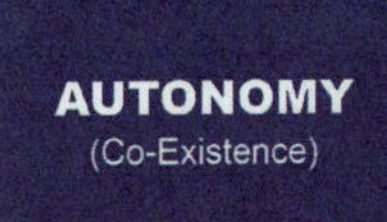

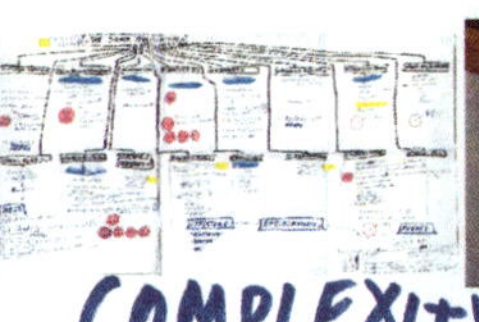

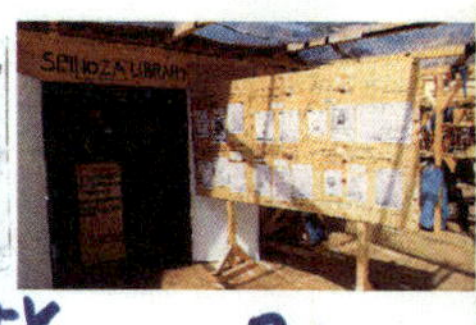

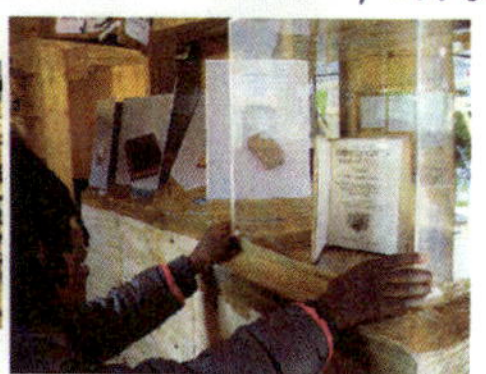

COMPLEXITY   BOOKS FROM AND ABOUT

Not Approving
Not Sentimentality

Autonomy_033

Autonomy_034

Autonomy_035

Autonomy_036

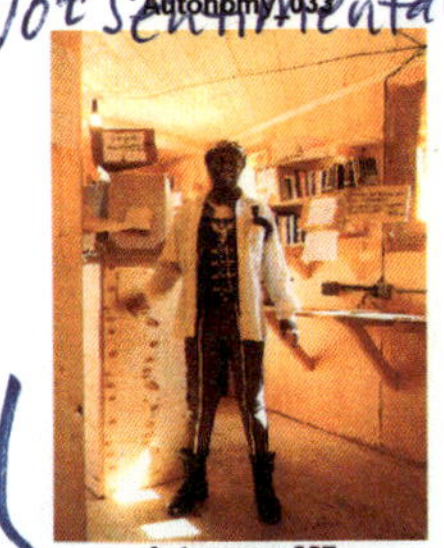

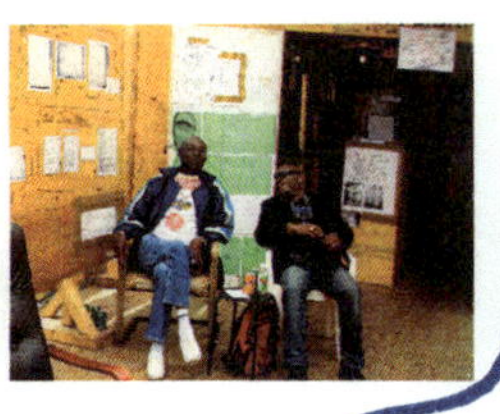

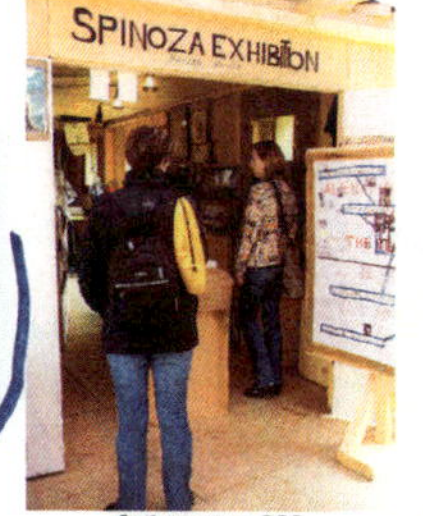

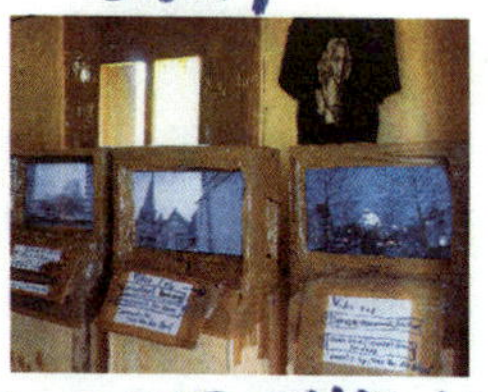

HARD-CORE of the Visitors   ABOUT THE LIFE SPINOZA: 1632–1677

Autonomy_037

Autonomy_038

Autonomy_039

Autonomy_040

made me happy at once. I was simply happy because there was 'Presence'. These first inhabitants to confront my work were not the family people, employees, workers and members of associations, those who are generally 'active'. On the contrary, they were those who are generally 'inactive'. I had hoped and worked for a few people in the Bijlmer neighbourhood to share their time with me, but I had not anticipated it would be these people!

With time, I understood why they were the first – the pioneers – to get involved with and in my work. They all had something: free time, 'too much time', and thus time to kill. I was moved by this realization – for I became aware that my 'Presence and Production' guideline had provoked something and that from here on out we would share this thing: time passing. These first inhabitants had time, lots of free time to come into contact with my work. And l, present all day throughout the exhibition, had time to come into contact with them. I asked myself the question: Could it be because I am also on the margins? Don't I have to be, as an artist? Will I ever have to stop being on the margins?

Being on the margins was what we had in common, what we could share, and also understand – understand thanks to art. I felt there was an equality between these inhabitants with too much time and me and my precarious project. The fact that we were present on site was the thing to be shared, it was our 'common good'. With its 'Presence and Production' guideline, the *Bijlmer Spinoza Festival* offered a focus point. It was a powerful experience for me that those who first took hold of it were those who do not have moments and spaces to enjoy in their daily lives. Was the *Bijlmer Spinoza Festival* able to create a space, a time and a moment of public space thanks to the presence of the work itself but also that of all the participants – including me? A new space in which 'excess time' could crystallize and take shape?

The 'Presence and Production' guideline allowed me to understand the relationship to the margins as a common good constituting an exchange. And what if this connection with the margins and the precarious opening that results was the key to coming into contact with the other? Is this precarious relationship dense enough to create a real event?

The notion of 'Presence and Production', which I intended as a challenge, a 'warlike' affirmation but also a gift – an offensive and even aggressive gift – has taken on a new meaning for me. The formula 'Presence and Production' has taken on the

dimension of a different and specific power. I thought I had an
experience that means something to me, isn't that the experience
of art?

Thomas Hirschhorn

Dear Thomas Hirschhorn,

Sadly, I wasn't able to participate in the experience of the *Bijlmer
Spinoza Festival*. I am sorry for that. I will therefore try to answer
based on what you tell me, on what I know of your previous work
and on my own concerns. The first thing I hear in 'Presence and
Production' is the sign of equality represented by 'and'. Equality
between two modes of presence that are commonly opposed: the
presence of the work of art as a result of the artist's work, offered
to viewers, and the presence of the artist as bearer or initiator of
an action. Relational art has claimed to substitute the creation of
relationships implying an interaction for the presence of the work
of art before the viewer. Activist art claimed to demystify the myth
of the artist by advocating an art that has become action. For my
part, I've always argued that under the guise of demystification
these strategies merely radicalized the traditional figure of the
artist by relieving him of the task of relinquishing a product of
his work, of separating it from his relationship to himself, to give
it over to the examination but also to the temporality of others.
There is no art without a production, giving the viewer the means
to approach and appropriate within a temporality other than the
artist's. 'Presence and Production' would then mean two things at
once: that the artist exposes himself to being objectified as a producer whose productions are judged by all, but also that the artist
is there, not being the work of art himself, but answering for what
he has done and answering to those who react to his apparatus by
adopting their time.
     This means, I think, that the artist's presence is not
that of an entertainer. This point probably needs to be clarified.

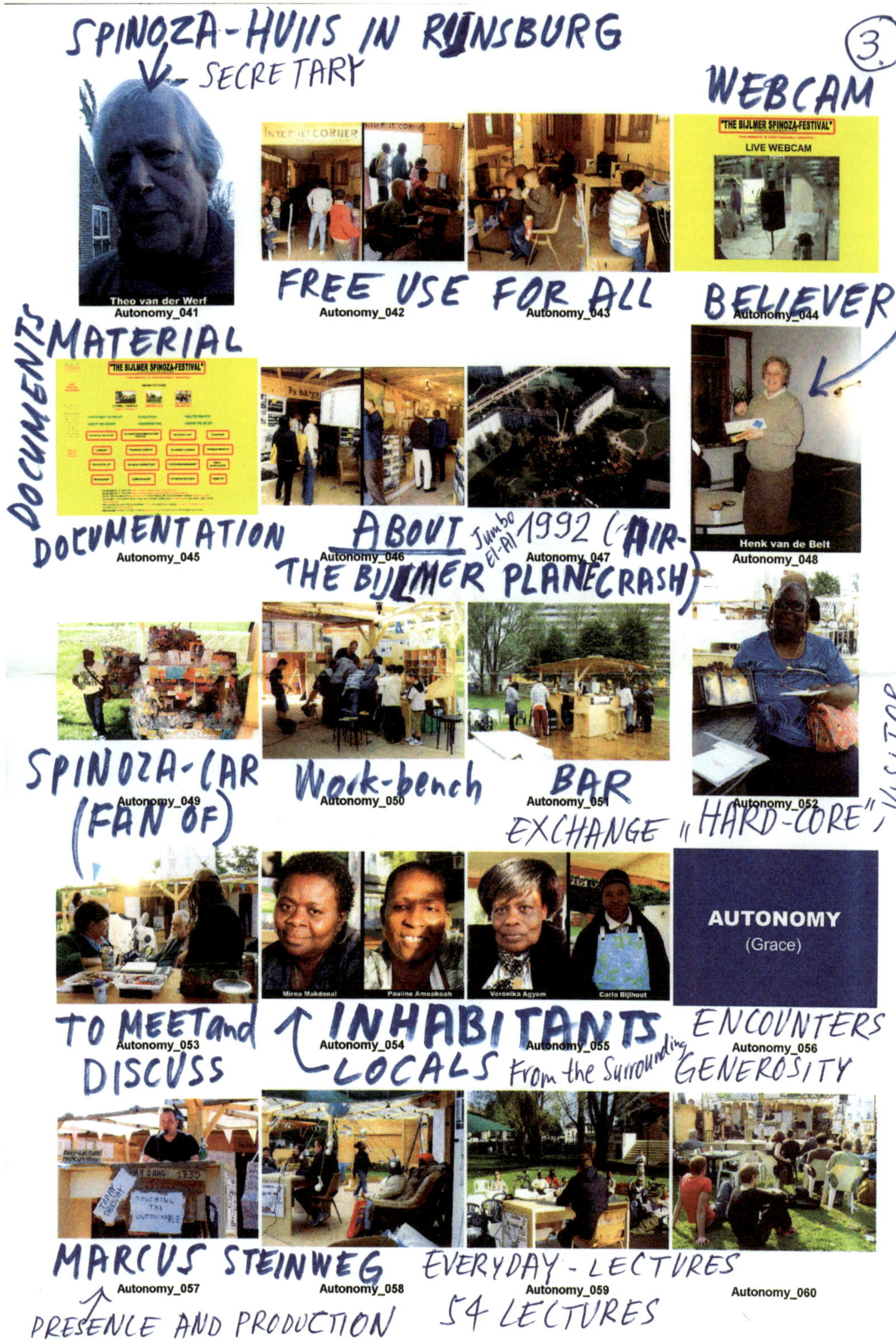

SPINOZA-HUIS IN RIJNSBURG
← SECRETARY
WEBCAM
3.
Theo van der Werf
Autonomy_041
INTERNET CORNER
Autonomy_042
FREE USE FOR ALL
Autonomy_043
"THE BIJLMER SPINOZA-FESTIVAL"
LIVE WEBCAM
Autonomy_044
BELIEVER
DOCUMENTS
MATERIAL
"THE BIJLMER SPINOZA-FESTIVAL"
Autonomy_045
DOCUMENTATION
Autonomy_046
ABOUT Jumbo El-Al 1992 ("AIR-
THE BIJLMER PLANECRASH)
Autonomy_047
Henk van de Belt
Autonomy_048
SPINOZA-CAR
(FAN OF)
Autonomy_049
Work-bench
Autonomy_050
BAR
Autonomy_051
Autonomy_052
"HARD-CORE" VISITOR
EXCHANGE
TO MEET and
Autonomy_053
DISCUSS
↑ INHABITANTS
Autonomy_054
LOCALS
Mirna Makdonal
Pauline Amoakoah
Autonomy_055
Veronika Agyom
Carlo Bijlhout
From the Surrounding
AUTONOMY
(Grace)
ENCOUNTERS
Autonomy_056
GENEROSITY
Autonomy_057
MARCUS STEINWEG
Autonomy_058
EVERYDAY-LECTURES
Autonomy_059
54 LECTURES
Autonomy_060
PRESENCE AND PRODUCTION

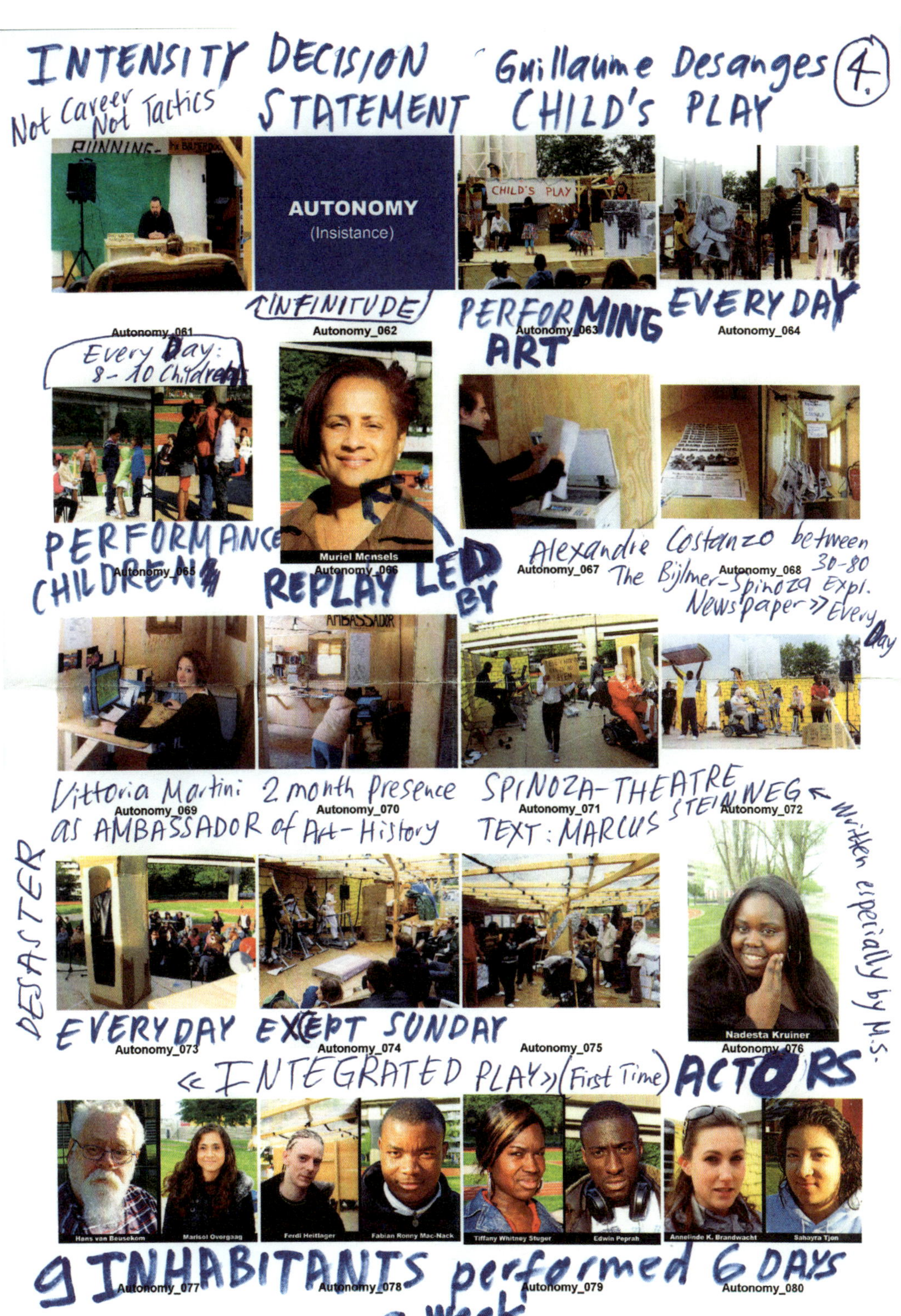

A Discussion between Jacques Rancière and Thomas Hirschhorn

If I understand correctly, this festival had in common with events you've organized in the past under other names (*Monument à Bataille, Musée précaire Albinet, 24h Foucault*) the joining of a work of visual art with a series of activities ranging from philosophy conferences and open reading areas to theatre and creative activities for local children. How exactly would you define the difference between this apparatus and those for debates, publications, workshops and various activities put in place by biennales and other events of the same type or even simply by museums for exhibitions? Is it the very fact that in your case there is not the usual separation between artistic production and a series of actions intended to make its meaning resonate or to create media impact among the general public? Is that also what 'Presence' means, given that what you do is something other than creating a public venue or organizing interactions?

The first element of an answer to this question of presence comes in terms of time: the equality 'Presence and Production' would also be a sign of equality placed between heterogeneous times. This has no direct relationship, but I'm reminded of what Pedro Costa says about his work as a filmmaker, shooting in *No Quarto da Vanda* (Vanda's Room) for over two years, going every day, the way you'd go to the office, to see these 'margin-dwellers' whose time is more than fluctuant. Many artists and various types of activists want to make people 'active' by identifying activity with mobility. They want to make them move off the seat they're sitting on, force them to talk when they feel like watching, listening or keeping quiet. This view of the meaning of activity is far too simple. Let's not forget that those we once referred to as 'active citizens' and 'men of leisure' were one and the same white 'passive' citizens were those whose time was occupied by manual activities. Privilege can be expressed by opposite qualities – activity or idleness – but its core is the disposal of time. The artist's approach to equality is thus the ability to adapt his time to the time of those who do not 'possess' time, those whose fate is always to have too much or not enough time.

'Too much' or 'not enough' time determines the politics of art. In the past, when we worked to bring art closer to the people, we wanted to bring it closer to those whose work did not leave them enough time: not enough time to live within art, not enough time to travel far enough to get to know it. This entailed a certain economy to concentrate the art-effect. With the Bijlmer experience, you point out an opposite phenomenon: those who were involved in the experience are those who have too much time, those whose time is not taken up by work.

Should we call them margin-dwellers and imagine a community between the artist and them as a shared position on the margins? I don't like this notion much, both because it threatens to raise certain stereotypes of the artist and to simplify the relationship of the work to its absence, of occupied time with idle time. The general phenomenon revealed by these kinds of experiences is the presence of powerful investments for knowledge, thought, art and any experience of this type in places where they aren't expected, among individuals whose business they aren't supposed to be. It has often been noted that the presence of time made available by force helps: prison provides more time to think and learn than the factory or the office: being in psychiatric institutions has provided a certain number of people with the time to explore their dramatic possibilities, etcetera.

But more generally, it is the porosity of the dividing line, the fact of circulating between occupied time and idle time that defines a type of experience that was largely present in yesterday's proletarian world but has been made more perceptible by all the current forms of precariousness and intermittence. The 'Presence' of the artist accompanying his 'production' would therefore be a manner of adopting this fluctuating temporality by confronting both his own work with other experiences of work and his available time with other available times. Making different times equal is in fact the condition for a public space, that is to say a space affirming anybody's ability to see, produce and think, to be created. The political power of art, rather than being in teaching, demonstrating, provoking or mobilizing, is in its ability to create public spaces thus conceived.

Jacques Rancière

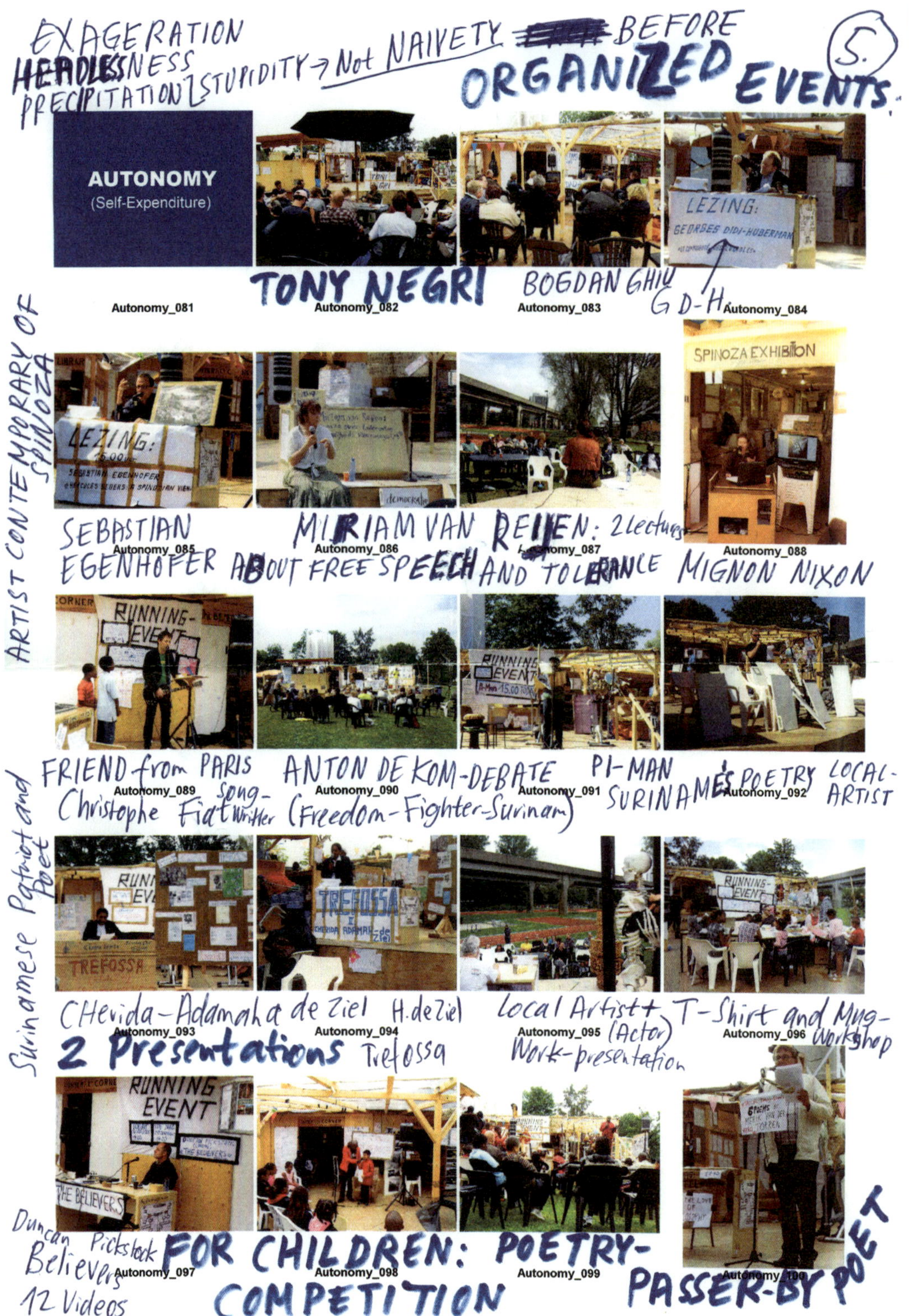
EXAGERATION
HEADLESSNESS
PRECIPITATION=STUPIDITY→Not NAIVETY ——BEFORE
ORGANIZED EVENTS. (5.)
AUTONOMY
(Self-Expenditure)
TONY NEGRI
BOGDAN GHIU
G D-H
LEZING:
GEORGES DIDI-HUBERMAN
Autonomy_081
Autonomy_082
Autonomy_083
Autonomy_084
ARTIST CONTEMPORARY OF SPINOZA
LEZING:
15.00
SEBASTIAN EGENHOFER
SPINOZA EXHIBITION
SEBASTIAN EGENHOFER
MIRIAM VAN REIJEN: 2 Lectures ABOUT FREE SPEECH AND TOLERANCE MIGNON NIXON
Autonomy_085
Autonomy_086
Autonomy_087
Autonomy_088
RUNNING-EVENT
RUNNING-EVENT
RUNNING-EVENT
FRIEND from PARIS ANTON DE KOM-DEBATE PI-MAN SURINAMESE POETRY LOCAL-ARTIST
Christophe Fiat song-writer (Freedom-Fighter-Surinam)
Autonomy_089
Autonomy_090
Autonomy_091
Autonomy_092
RUNNING EVENT
TREFOSSA CHEVIDA ADAMAH de Ziel
RUNNING-EVENT
CHevida-Adamaha de Ziel H.de Ziel Local Artist + T-Shirt and Mug-
2 Presentations Trefossa (Actor) Work-presentation Workshop
Autonomy_093
Autonomy_094
Autonomy_095
Autonomy_096
RUNNING EVENT
THE BELIEVERS
Duncan Pickstock
Believers FOR CHILDREN: POETRY- PASSER-BY POET
12 Videos COMPETITION
Surinamese Patriot and Poet
Autonomy_097
Autonomy_098
Autonomy_099
Autonomy_100

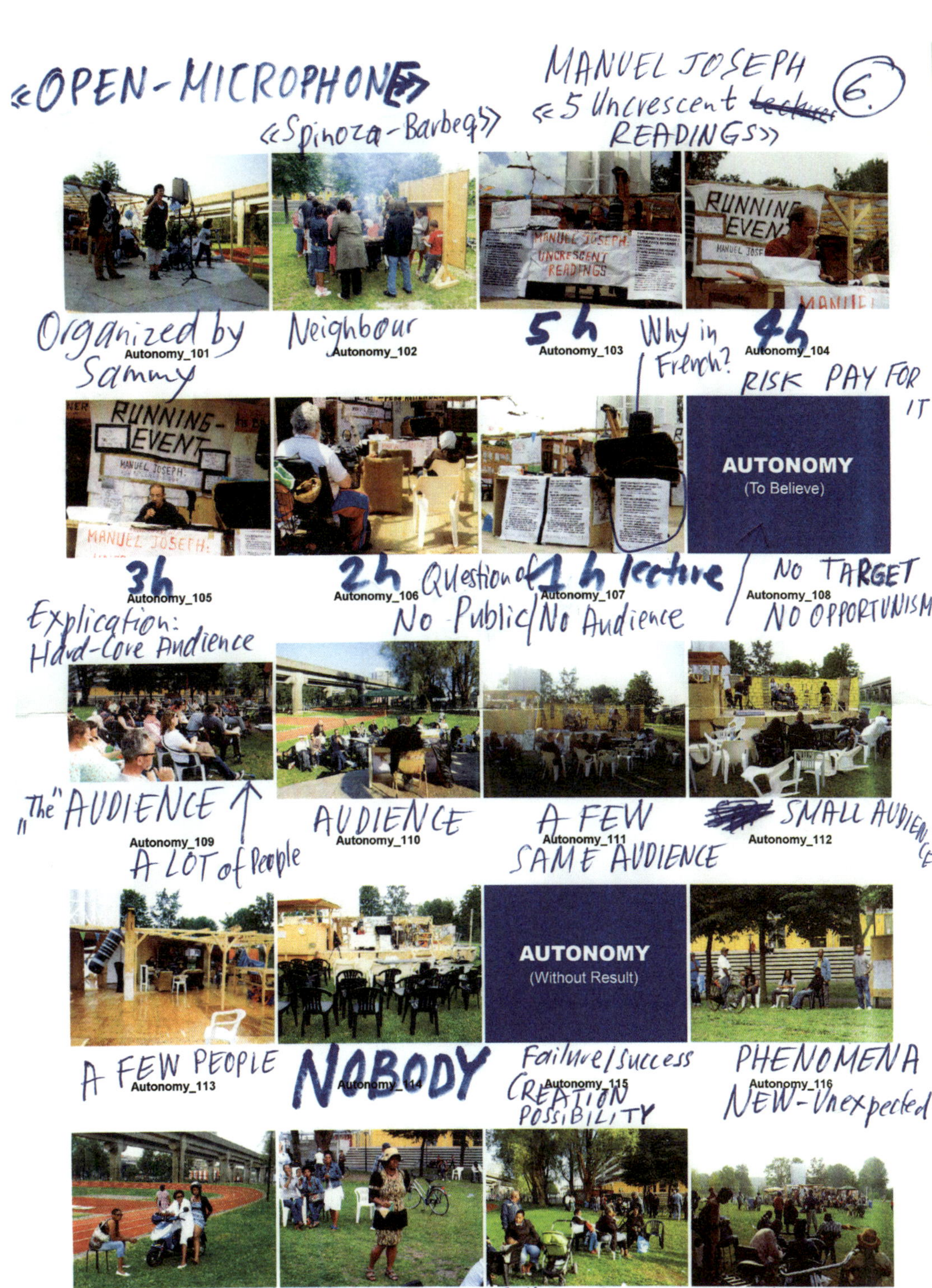

A Discussion between Jacques Rancière and Thomas Hirschhorn   139

Dear Jacques Rancière,

Thank you very much for your answer, which raises four points to which I'd like to respond: the question of the artist as an entertainer, the difference between my work and a cultural event, the question of 'participative art' in general and finally the question concerning the position of the margin and the stereotypes of the artist. Yes, the artist's presence cannot be that of an entertainer. The artist is not present because he is an artist (the creator of a body of work) – he is present because the most important thing is to be present. And he is present because he is responsible for everything, he is the concierge and the usher, the cleaning staff, the guarantor of his work: he is there to settle everything, to resolve everything. The artist is responsible for everything and even for what he cannot control or predict: this is why he must be present. I must be responsible for that for which I am not responsible. This is the noble task of my work and my presence. The artist is present to give of his time, the artist shares his time, the artist is present because there is nothing more important to do. The artist has nothing else – nothing more important – to do elsewhere. I was present beside my work for over three months in the Bijlmer neighbourhood, night and day without a break, because this was where the important thing for me was taking place, there was nothing more important to do anywhere else. That is the commitment and the sense of my presence. Presence is also an act of solitude, for I must be able to be alone, due to the complexity of my project, its irreducibility, its placement, its exaggeration, and its possible becoming. It is only by being alone that I can really be present and not make 'just another project': personally, I don't think in these terms – l couldn't – for a project like the *Bijlmer Spinoza Festival* requires such a high level of commitment, of open-mindedness, of strength, and energy, that it would never have come to fruition if I had considered it as 'just another project'.

The difference between a cultural event and the *Bijlmer Spinoza Festival* is not in production, the thing produced, whether it is a reading, a seminar or a workshop. The fundamental difference is the autonomy of the work that affirms itself and the audience it addresses. I'm interested in this exactness: the simultaneous affirmation of the Autonomy and the universality of the work and the 'non-exclusive' audience for which the production of the work is intended. It is not a production specifically adapted to a different audience, it is a production for a 'non-exclusive audience'. According to me, this means that the production must be able to address an uninterested audience. That the production is not there to satisfy a demand, that it is not trying to find 'its' audience and that it is not trying to be a success in terms of the size of the audience or a specific audience. The production – without any concessions – remains an affirmation and something autonomous. Insisting upon that is what makes the difference. The more I insist upon it, the more exact it is. For it must also be possible to make this production without an audience, which was the case during some days of the *Bijlmer Spinoza Festival* – nobody was there! This is possible when the production is based on love. The work is done with the inhabitants, in a gesture of love. Therefore, this gesture doesn't necessarily call for an answer – since it comes from me – this is both utopian and concrete. I want to create a new form, based on love for a 'non-exclusive audience'. And the form itself is the difference and the act that distinguishes it from a cultural event. My love for Spinoza is the love of philosophy, of things I don't understand, the love of the infinitude of thought. It is a question of sharing this, of affirming it, defending it, and giving it shape.

I agree with you that it is not a question of getting people to 'move'. I have never used the term 'participative art' in referring to my work – that is a meaningless term, because someone looking at an Ingres painting, for instance, is participating. He can participate without anyone noticing. Similarly, I never used the terms 'educational art' and 'community art'. And my work has never had anything to do with 'relational aesthetics'. Nor have I read the book about it. If certain superficial critics put me in this category of 'relational aesthetics', it is simply an inaccurate representation of what I do. Not a single one of my works in public space has been a project of 'relational aesthetics' for the simple reason that I want to create a relationship with the Other only if that Other has no specific relationship with aesthetics. This is – and has always been – my guideline: to create a form that involves the other, the unexpected, the uninterested, those who don't see any interest in it, that involves a neighbour, a stranger, an alien. I have always wanted to work for this 'non-exclusive' audience, it is one of my most important goals. To address a 'non-exclusive' audience means to face the real, failure, lack of success, the cruelty of disinterest, and the incommensurability of a complex

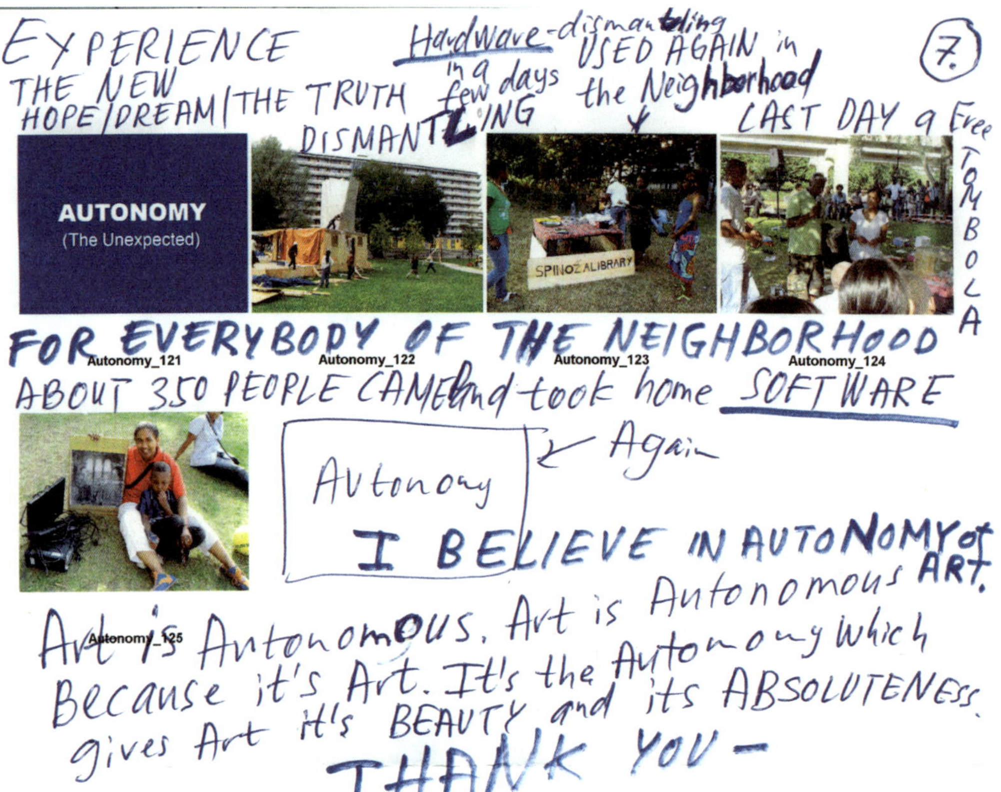
EXPERIENCE
THE NEW
HOPE/DREAM|THE TRUTH
Hardware-dismantling
in a few days
DISMANTLING
USED AGAIN in
the Neighborhood
LAST DAY a Free
TOMBOLA
7.
AUTONOMY
(The Unexpected)
SPINOZA LIBRARY
Autonomy_121
Autonomy_122
Autonomy_123
Autonomy_124
FOR EVERYBODY OF THE NEIGHBORHOOD
ABOUT 350 PEOPLE CAME and took home SOFTWARE
Autonomy
← Again
I BELIEVE IN AUTONOMY of
ART.
Autonomy_125
Art is Autonomous. Art is Autonomous
Because it's Art. It's the Autonomy which
gives Art it's BEAUTY and its ABSOLUTENESS.
— THANK YOU —

	Autonomy	POSITIV	Not self-enclosure
1	My Work LEANS on: Autonomy	SELF-INVENTION ASSERTION **FORM**	Not self-sufficience
2	Autonomy (Neighbour)	THE OTHER THE NON EXCLUSIVE AUDIENCE UNIVERSALITY THE ONE WORLD	Not Identity Not The Social Not The Context
3	Autonomy (Emancipation)	SELF-AUTHORIZATION SELF-WEAPON EQUALITY	Not Obedience Not seurity Not safety Not Fear
4	Autonomy (Co-Existence)	Agreement ✓ — The REAL — HAPPINESS	→ Not Approuving The Reality Not Cynicisme Not Sentimentality Not Phantasmes
5	Autonomy (Grace)	Engagement Generosity Love	Not Arrangements Not Circumstances
6	Autonomy (Insistance)	DECISION STATEMENT INTENSITY INFINITUDE	Not Career Not Tactics
7	Autonomy (Self Expenditure)	EXAGERATION HEADLESSNESS PRECIPITATION STUPIDITY	Not Harmony Not Naïvety
8	Autonomy (To Believe)	RISK STATEMENT READY TO PAY FOR IT	Not TARGET Not Opportunism
9	Autonomy (Without Result)	BEYOND FAILURE/SUCCESS CREATION POSSIBILITY	Not Satisfaction Not Function Not Justification Not Garantee
10	Autonomy (The Unexpected	THE NEW HOPE TRUTH DREAM	Not Analysez Not Criticism or Self criticism Not Control
11	Autonomy	Art is Autonomous because its Art. It's the Autonomy	which gives Art its Beauty and its Absolutness

situation. But it also includes those who love art, the specialists, and those for whom art is important. My work includes them as part of that 'non-exclusive' audience, without specifically targeting them. I know that as an artist I am always suspected (of making 'relational aesthetics', for instance). That's fine with me – I'm not complaining – for I must be the 'usual suspect', but that is precisely why what is truly 'suspect' must be clarified. What is 'suspect' is to reign supreme in my role as the 'usual suspect'. This is why I want to try to define my work with my own notions, like 'Presence and Production' and 'non-exclusive audience'. I am conscious that these notions are not perfect, ideal or even accurate, but how can you accurately define a work of art in a single word? These notions are not concepts, they are tools I invented for myself and that I built myself.

The notion 'marginal' is not accurate or exact either, I admit, and its use can be stereotyped and also sterile. Therefore I don't want to exploit it, manipulate it or turn it into politics. I want to be more precise and clearer. I hadn't found an appropriate term to explain my experience at the *Bijlmer Spinoza Festival* to you and it's true that we need to look more closely into this question and position regarding the margin. Moved by the experience I was having, I tried to give a name to something that I was thinking and grasping, and with which I was in agreement. But the difficulty for me is to give a name to an experience – if it is a real experience, something new – to understand it and speak of this thing that is new. This thing was coexistence. I want to be more rigorous in describing my experience. As rigorous as my work is – I hope. The difficulty is that as an artist, I must refuse to analyse my work before achieving it and experimenting with it. This is where the problem lies – and I'm not trying to avoid it – but you must understand that the artist must first do the work before he analyses it. This has always been my guideline: do first, analyse afterwards. I call it acting 'headless'. I'm conscious that with the *Bijlmer Spinoza Festival* or other projects acting 'headless' can be interpreted as a lack of rigour, but I think that it is the price to pay – as an artist – to do the work 'headless'. This is also why I believe my work deserves to be discussed in a critical manner, at a level that would include – for once – these questions in their paradoxical and problematic dimension. For I, who am neither theorist nor 'practitioner', must go beyond argumentation in order to be able to create a form, a form that comes from me and only from me.

I want to make my work in 'low control'. Acting in 'low control'
means to refuse to control, to put myself at a level of 'low control'
like someone on the ground, at the end of his rope, overwhelmed,
totally out of his depth yet not resigned, not reconciled and not
cynical.

Thomas Hirschhorn

Dear Thomas Hirschhorn,

Since we have limited space, I won't ask you any new questions,
which would remain unanswered. I just want to point out what
strikes me in your answer, in order to open the way to other
reflections. First of all, the term 'responsibility'. It seems to me that
this term was already at the heart of the experience of the *Musée
Précaire Albinet*. The Musée was placed under the responsibility – also day and night – of neighbourhood youths, who had to
fill every function, both practical and intellectual, required by
a museum. This amounted to scrambling the usual relationship
between activity and passivity, which is always conceived as the
reversal of symmetrical positions. And perhaps we have here a
more interesting interpretation of 'everyone is an artist' than that
which puts a paintbrush in the viewer's hand or tries to bring the
spectator on stage. Sharing, that is to say re-sharing, touching
upon the normal distribution of spaces and times is something
other than reversing. And of course the artist isn't a good soul,
he is first someone who produces, and this production does not
allow itself to be dissolved in the simple creation of a relationship
with others. I am struck by the fact that you insist so strongly
both on the autonomy of production and the taking into account
of an Other who goes beyond any system prepared to receive
him. It strikes me because it also leads me to think about my own
presuppositions. I have always adhered to Flaubert's requirement
that the author withdraw from his work. Where it was customary
to denounce an omniscient position and an aristocratic negation

of the other, I always saw, on the contrary, the condition for an emancipation of the reader and the spectator, to whom the author abandons his work, by giving him the freedom and the responsibility to appropriate in his own way a work that no longer belongs to the one who made it.

'Absence' then seemed the appropriate complement to 'production'. Your watchword calls this pattern into question. It links production with the risk of the presence that verifies the effects while these have never been the object of any calculation. It links production and presence beyond the usual figures of generosity that exiles itself from art venues to reach the 'non-audience' or beyond a sacrificial exposure to the cruelty of the one to whom we come, powerless. It may seem contradictory to create a form that involves an Other while affirming one's own production, without concession, without the need for a response. The answer might be that the two terms imply the presence of a third party that includes both of them and takes them beyond themselves. A *Bijlmer Spinoza Festival*, a *Deleuze Monument*, *Twenty-Four Hours for Foucault*: this means bringing into a contained time and space a power of thought, a power of community in which both the artist's absolutely determined, absolutely autonomous proposition and the unpredictable participation of a 'non exclusive audience', an audience without specificity, can be included. The autonomous and the non-exclusive then both appear as two forms of universality that are linked not in the dual relationship of the encounter but because the proposition itself is already permeated by this power of universality and otherness that I call 'presupposition of the equality of intelligences' and which you refer to as the 'love of the infinitude of thought'.

Jacques Rancière

book reviews

Jonas Staal
*Closed Architecture. A Project
by Jonas Staal Based on
a Concept by Fleur Agema*

Maaike Lauwaert

Art, Property of Politics III,
Onomatopee 63, 2011,
ISBN 978-90-78454-75-5
www.onomatopee.net

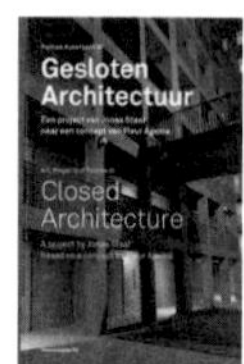

Closed Architecture by artist Jonas Staal (b. 1981) is the third book in a series titled 'Art, Property of Politics'. The first book, which was part of the exhibition *The People United Will Never Be Defeated* in TENT (2010, Rotterdam), brought together works from the art collections of political groups on the city council of Rotterdam. The second, *Freethinkers' Space*, was part of the exhibition *Tricksters Tricked* in the Van Abbe-museum (2010, Eindhoven) and presented works of art that had been shown in the Freethinkers' Space, a temporary exhibition space initiated by the People's Party for Freedom and Democracy (VVD) and the Freedom Party (PVV) that focused on Dutch artists contending with political or religious censorship.

And now we have the third in the series, a book that elaborates on and analyses the graduation project by PVV politician Fleur Agema done in 2004 in conclusion of her interior architecture studies. In this project, Agema (b. 1976) designed a prison model whereby the prisoner moves through a trajectory of four phases. She gave these the unambiguous names of

'The Bunker', 'The Habituation', 'The Wait' and 'The Light'. Good behaviour is awarded with the possibility of going on to the next phase and bad behaviour moves the prisoner back one phase. It is a cold and oppressive prison model, based on a mechanized concept of humanity, one of programming and conditioning. Not that Agema really believes in the possibility of 'improving the soul of the prisoner . . . but for the sake of the design it was more interesting to pretend that it's possible' (*De Pers*, 9 December 2011, 12).

Let me begin by saying – so that we have that out of the way – that giving a graduation project so much weight is slightly uncomfortable. Agema's texts, included in the book as a clarification of Staal's visualizations of the prison, are excruciating and awkward. One feels embarrassment for the ways in which she envisions and evokes her own model. For instance, she writes about phase two, 'The Habituation': 'The concrete is light-coloured. The spaces are separated by concrete and glass, the atmosphere is remarkably open, but very sober. I don't see any paintings or posters, for exam-

ple. There are no communal spaces and televisions here either.' (p. 60) This is truly a graduation project: naïve, with little reflection, lacking experience and depth.

In various interviews, Staal emphasizes that he is not primarily concerned with Agema's person. Nonetheless, he psychoanalyses Agema at length. Staal draws a connection between her disorder (posttraumatic dystrophy), her personal development (declared unable to work as an architect at the beginning of her career), and her view of society. In his introduction he writes: 'In a bizarre way, the moment that Agema becomes trapped in her own body coincides with the design of a building in which she intends to trap others. . . . She similarly liberates herself from the burden of her disease by increasing her power over others by means of her prison design and ultimately her political career.' (p. 27) This psychoanalysing is also uncomfortable, and in the indictment things too often wonderfully correspond to be truly believable. After all, there is a rule of thumb for conducting research that is comparable to the one for on-line shopping: 'If it seems too good to be true, it probably is.'

If the project is not so much about Agema as a person, then what is it about? Staal wants to use Agema and her graduation project in order to make a point about developments in our society that reflect the co-erciveness and authoritarianism of her prison model. 'As such, Agema's work needs to be considered as a case study within the debate about the repressive society and the society of control.' (p. 31) The repressive society, according to Staal, is 'oriented at discipline, efficiency, and productivity, in which all non-corresponding, i.e. unproductive elements need to be purged. . . . Agema's total prison architecture thus fully coincides with this type of society, in which all aspects of daily life are fully controlled, thus excluding any type of nuisance.' (p. 28) Those 'unproductive elements' are not only prisoners, explains Staal in an article in the *NRC Handelsblad* newspaper on 3 November 2011, but also the unemployed or artists.

An interview with Staal on the website of the art magazine *Metropolis M* reveals that Agema's design not only stands for a repressive and controlling society but also for a 'segregated society'. Her design 'shows the contours of a model that starts from the idea of classes – phases – that keep everybody imprisoned in their own social circumstances. The first phase would be so-called "problem" neighbourhoods like Rotterdam-South or the Bijlmer; the last, gated communities such as Lelystad or Dronten.' With her design, Agema shows us a 'society that no longer needs a prison, for it has become a prison itself. Agema is an architect disguised as a politician: her artwork is the world in which we have woken up today.' (http://metropolism.com/previews/blauw-druk-voor-de-gesloten-samen/ [in Dutch]). The interpretations and accusations pile up; Agema's design can hardly carry and support them. It's like a small body having to bear a large head.

That doesn't take away the fact that some of the developments Staal agitates against are worrisome. For example, the utilitarian mentality threatens to banish everything that is not profitable and not primarily market-oriented. In the Netherlands, we see this translated in the policy of the present coalition and the areas in which cutbacks are being made. The question is whether Staal needed to use Agema's graduation work in order to point this out. The multiplicity of interpretations, metaphors and accusations also obfuscates the whole. Agema's graduation project has become multi-utilizable, and suddenly seems to stand for everything that is wrong in today's society. The design, the focus on her person is distracting and bogs down the discussion in bickering. For instance, Agema reacted in the *NRC Handelsblad* on 5 December that it was 'terribly irritating' that Staal had 'stolen and raped' her design. 'That man is absurdly fixated on the PVV.' And: 'Staal only wants to say: look here, what a scary person.' Neither does Agema have to discuss content in free tabloids such as *De Pers*, for journalists are already happy enough with her open antipathy towards Staal. That, to put it mildly, is a missed opportunity.

The publication of the book was accompanied by a model of Agema's design and a film, which were shown at Extra City in Antwerp and in a two-day programme at Theater Frascati in Amsterdam.

Olga Goriunova
Art Platforms and Cultural Production on the Internet

Annet Dekker

London, Routledge 2011,
ISBN 978-0-415-89310-7,
112 p, £80

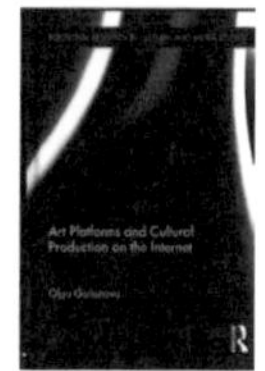

Olga Goriunova is well known for her involvement and contribution to the shaping of the field of software art, as co-organizer of the software art festivals Read_me, the set-up of Runme.org, an online software art repository, as well as curator of Funware, an international travelling exhibition that deals with the appreciation of fun as an inventive force in software (art) development. In her new publication *Art Platforms and Cultural Production* on the Internet she turns her attention to the organizational aesthetics of processes that produce digital culture.

A platform is an organizational concept with a long history. In times of political and social unrest, revolutions and avant-gardes, people form groups that are organized around a number of guidelines or specific issues. In 2005 Tim O'Reilly and John Battelle coined the phrase 'the web as platform' as the core principle of Web 2.0, thereby giving the notion of a platform renewed, albeit as Goriunova attests a flattened, meaning. Whereas the web as platform is foremost described as a conglomerate of technical development, Goriunova stresses the importance of art platforms as experiments in the aesthetics of organization. Rather than a set of objects, these experiments show a specific kind of cultural practice that is open-ended and emerges from grass-roots processes.

Groiunova clearly makes a difference between art platforms and earlier attempts to define online practices as networked. Although the art platform is a genre of networked organization in which it provides a 'conceptual device that allows for a differentiation and problematization of networks', by following the theoretical discourse around network theory, moving from Bruno Latour's sociologist Actor-Network Theory back to the concept of network theory. In the last decade, network theory was popularized by the publication *Linked* (2003) by physicist Albert-László Barabási, but Goriunova makes clear that that the coming together of the social sciences with the exact sciences was foremost based on a misunderstanding that can still be traced today. This, as Goriunova shows, doesn't mean that thinking about networks has stopped, several approaches can be named that have tried to imagine networks in heterogeneous and nonlinear ways, including 'bifurcation (Progogine and Deleuze/Guattari), networks as assemblages (Manuel DeLanda) and ecologies and media ecologies (Guattari, Bateson and Fuller)'. (p. 5) So what does the notion of art platforms add to this plethora?

An art platform would ideally be a concept that reflects upon its own media ecology. Whereas media ecology is a way of looking, seeing, doing and making, Goriunova describes an art platform as an entity, an activity and a process of development. 'Art platforms engage with living practices in their blurred and 'dirty' forms between a more broadly defined swathe of culture and art', they are to be found in the 'grey' zones of cultural production. Furthermore, she argues, art platforms make you think about the organizational forms of culture, thus an organizational aesthetics. Such an approach 'sheds light on the ways in which digital culture and aesthetics are constituted and advanced'. (p. 13) Goriunova defines organizational aesthetics as 'a process of emergence and a mode of enquiry that gives us a way to understand a digital object, process or body. It is not only a way of looking, but also a dynamic assembling and coming up with such a body.' (p. 17) Organizational aesthetics is grounded in the digital native and, while structuring and organizing creativity that traverses art platforms, it highlights the development of new forces to overcome repetition and strive for vitality. Moreover, it pays attention to the interplays of power and the kinds of structures and conduct these imply.

Goriunova makes these forces explicit in meticulous descriptions of several of these art practices. Perhaps not surprisingly, these examples move beyond the obvious Internet art practices that have gained recognition over the years. By affirming that the brilliant can be found in the grey and banal corners of the Internet, thereby moving away from the economically and socially deterministic post-Marxist critique of subordination as well as the liberal thinking on creative industries, Goriunova points to the first example, which few readers would consider art: Udaff.com. At first sight Udaff resembles a porn site and swearing pool inhabited by white male adults, on closer inspection it turns out to be especially interesting because of the writing of *kreativs*. As Goriunova explains, Udaff is a popular Russian language platform that hosts a variety of literary practices, of which the kreativs are the most vital. By analysing its structure, being innately digital and thus following digital structures of organization and aesthetic, its writing, 'DIY vocabulary; virtuoso and abundant swearing; and elegantly, purposefully wrong orthography' (p. 54) and its usage of commenting as well as the power of social figures that are being extended and transformed through the networks of production, Goriunova makes a strong argument that talks across social histories, networks, concepts and actors.

In a similar vein, Goriunova analyses the software art repository Runme.org, which she co-founded and was part of during its time of existence (2001 – present); although the site still functions, its prime importance lasted for five years. Runme.org was created as 'a format that would be something between an out-of-scale festival, a distributed salon, infinite exhibition, and open collection, sets of samizdat books, and sets of relationships – all in all, an art platform in the making'. (p. 71) Again, it is by closely tracing and analysing the structure and making various relations that the brilliance of the art platform happens and starts to shine. The quotes and snippets of conversations, of which the more interesting ones can also be found in the footnotes, exemplify the formation and functioning of the art platform. At times hilarious, funny and anecdotal it is always through thorough analysis that Goriunova makes her argument. Goriunova also tackles recent developments and practices on Second Life and phenomena like surf clubs and digital folklore. The breadth and reach of her observations, understanding and ability to decipher these practices is remarkable and not found in current writings about digital practices.

Goriunova is not someone to take her own writing, and analysis for that matter, for granted. This shows itself in the detailed explanations and elaborations of her reasoning by making connections to current and past (theoretical) debates. Nor is she afraid to tackle thorny issues, as for example the issue of the usefulness of open and free software, pointing her finger to the sore spots that are often neglected or (deliberately) ignored. For example she argues that a break 'from the fetishism of proprietary software may lead to the commodification of social processes that are layered into software production and operation'. (p. 23) The only drawback of the book is that it is too short, making it at times too dense. It would be great to elaborate on specifics to accommodate the reader who is not necessarily familiar with the various strands of thought that permeate the book. Nevertheless, this book is extremely important. From a theoretical point of view it shows how can we discuss and analyse new digital phenomenon from a material and aesthetical point of view. From a practical point of view, Goriunova provides us with a wonderful and thick description of the current usage of the web. Although she is leaving it open to where these new tendencies may lead, she provides users, audiences and theoreticians with workable tools and methods with which to analyse current movements. Or, as Goriunova has taught us, it is 'creating a means to speak about what is grey and banal on the Internet [that] allows for a recognition of the brilliant; and such a means of cautious differentiation may likely turn out to develop a sensibility for a set of interesting tendencies rather than dispensing with the developments in new media reign of banality at large'. (p. 45)

Julieta Aranda, Brian Kuan
Wood, Anton Vidokle (eds.)
*Are You Working Too Much?
Post-Fordism, Precarity,
and the Labor of Art*

New York/Berlin, e-flux journal/
Sternberg Press, 2011,
ISBN 978-1-934105-31-3,
216 p., € 12.-

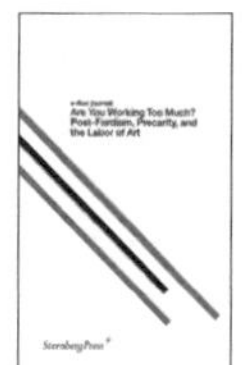

Ilse van Rijn

The notion that artists are often perfectly capable of functioning simultaneously in at least two or three professions, for which they moreover, in contrast to art, are well-paid and socially respected, is infuriating, is it not? And why would talented artists willingly limit themselves to one sector (art) in which so little compensation is offered for so much unpaid work? These questions form the introduction to e-flux's new volume, *Are You Working Too Much? Post-Fordism, Precarity, and the Labor of Art.* The book comprises a collection of essays that from various perspectives examine the current position of art professionals, one that is dominated by neo-capitalistic values and arguments. Dissatisfaction with the often precarious working relations determines the tone of the book. The professionals themselves are also to blame for this, according to e-flux editors Julieta Aranda, Brian Kuan Wood and Anton Vidokle. For after all, art professionals exploit themselves. The editors go on to ironically note that art is not a religion, however, or a charity where voluntary work provides added value. Nowadays, the only way in which you can maintain yourself financially in a world where you are held responsible for more and more costs is to work even longer in the field (not art) in which you meanwhile have been functioning as an expert.

Through the juxtapositon of the terms 'focus' and 'intensity', Diedrich Diederichsen describes the mentality and life-attitude of today's art professionals and the sphere in which they move. What is intense is today's 'networking economy', which is based on freedom and potential. In order to be able to profit from all of the possibilities within it, maximum dedication and an almost ecstatic enthusiasm are necessary. Whereas formerly a certain focus and purpose were required and work was geared to precise observations, in the present economy leisure prevails. Even wastefulness is currently ascribed value. You could translate the difference between focus and intensity as the difference between Fordism and post-Fordism. But this opposition is too theoretical for Diederichsen. In reality, he claims, one can indicate situations in which a bridge is erected between artificially separated worlds. He refers to the mixing of mentalities in a Berlin customs office where unidentifiable goods can be picked up. There you find people up to their ears in microcultural awareness, in a searching investigation of the economy, in self-marketing and speculation. Since the appearanc of novels like Bret Easton Ellis's *American Psycho* (1991), adds Diederichsen, we are familiar with the type of person who combines liberty and focus, purpose and wasteful extravagance. Doesn't the entrepreneurial attitude displayed by Patrick Bateman, the main character in *American Psycho*, combine a leftist, Nietzsian animosity towards the state and a vitalistic animosity towards bureaucracy? The fictitious pathological monster (Bateman overindulges in drink, sex, drugs and commits multiple murders) has become reality. In today's casino capitalism, the beast, in its baseless madness, returns and forms the heart of a well organized economic routine, says Diederichsen. Aren't characters like Bateman, who prefer to intensify their lives with work in which they develop themselves, in fact the ones who are in power?

Hito Steyerl also has doubts about all-too-artificially segregated expositions. Art and neoliberal post-Fordist speculation are inseparably connected with one another, after all. All over the world, biennials, museums and galleries are introduced in order to stimulate slow economies. Post-democratic oligarchies like 'Global Guggenheim' reign supreme. The actual work, however, is done by the 'nouveaux poor', according to Steyerl. These are the 'JPEG virtuosos' (the ones who polish up visual files in the wink of an eye) and the 'gallerinas' (who keep the galleries going), producing work for a pittance in an incredible tempo and with boundless enthusiasm. This loose-knit team of 'propertyless adventurers' is hardly capable of revolting against the system, however, seeing as they are part of it. Political art must not forget its function, exhorts Steyerl. Contemporary political art is a site of condensation of the contradictions of capital and of the sometimes devastating misunderstandings between global and local forces. Politics are present in the production, distribution and reception of art.

In *Are You Working Too Much?*, a diligent search is made for all sorts of images – musicological, literary (Diederichsen) and historical (Steyerl) – through which the present situation in art can be understood, described, compared and, as it turns out, possibly undermined. In his sociological analysis, Lars Bang Larsen uses the literary metaphor of the zombie, which stands for abjection and alienation. According to Larsen, 'zombification' can easily be applied to the Marxist notion that capital devours the body and soul of the worker, and that the living are exploited by 'dead work'. The current post-democratic society, which rests on immaterial work and which colonizes the brain and the nervous system, can be characterized as 'zombie-like'. The zombie can also function as an allegory to dramatize the oddity of what has become reality in the present 'experience economy', which is based on affect. After all, claims Larsen: 'The zombie isn't just any monster, but one with a pedigree of social critique.' Moreove, alienation, for which the zombie stands, can also be productive. Why don't we consider the zombie as a 'pre-being' (a child), instead of as a 'post-being, a no-longer-human', he suggests. For the zombie is a 'strange, tragicomic monster that displaces evil and its concept: the zombie isn't evil, nor has it been begot by evil; it is a monstrosity that deflects itself in order to show that our imagination cannot stop at the monster'. Thus, he concludes, through the figure of the zombie we can imagine the future anew.

Central to Franco Berardi Bifo's essay, 'Cognitarian Subjectivation', is the question of whether the process of making an autonomous, collective definition of the self is still possible in this day and age. Bifo's 'cognitarians' embody the concept of the 'general intellect'. Associated with the Italian post-operaismo of theorists like Paolo Virno and Maurizio Lazzarato, this concept emphasizes the interaction between work and language: social work is the endless recombination of fragments producing, distributing and decoding signs and symbols and other bearers of information. The network economy exploits the emotional energy of the cognitive class by supplying an overabundance of goods that demand attention. Today's cognitarians lack a body, a social and physical body, a social economic body, according to Bifo. Our political task thus consists of handing the conceptual instruments of psychotherapy and the language of poetry to the cognitarians. These can be used to undermine the universal language of the economy. Such assistance moreover restores a social body to the cognitarians, and thus the feeling of solidarity.

Their discomfort over the terms and conditions that determine today's cultural and aesthetic practice forces the authors in *Are You Working Too Much?* to base their argumentations by starting from the postcapitalist domain and at the same time going beyond it. Are there holes in the system? Are there stories that show the downside of postcapitalist tendencies which are now presented as a *fait accompli* (Marion von Osten, Keti Chukhrov)? Can possibilities be discerned and perhaps created in the present situation by tackling it from an interdisciplinary perspective (Tom Holert)? Frequent references are made to thinking in terms of coincidence, difference and nuance such as elaborated by the duo J.K. Gibson-Graham, first in *The End of Capitalism (As We Knew It)* (1996), later in *A Postcapitalist Politics* (2006) (Antke Engel bases her article on their 'politics of possibilities'). No ready-made answers to the inescapable neoliberal views that have made their entrance in the world of art are provided in *Are You Working Too Much? Post-Fordism, Precarity, and the Labor of Art*. The anthology reads as an evaluation, as a call to not let oneself be rendered powerless or lapse into an all-too-familiar pattern. Above all, the book presents a search for points of departure for radical change or for continuing a practice along other lines.

Serge Daney, *Volharden*

Solange de Boer (editor)
*Een ruimte om in te bewegen.
Serge Daney tussen cinema en
beeldcultuur*

Stoffel Debuysere

ISBN 978-94-90334-01-7,
160 p., € 13.50
ISBN 978-94-90334-04-8,
192 p., € 14.-
'Text & Context' series
Amsterdam, Octavo Publications

Set: ISBN 978-94-90334-06-2,
€ 20.-

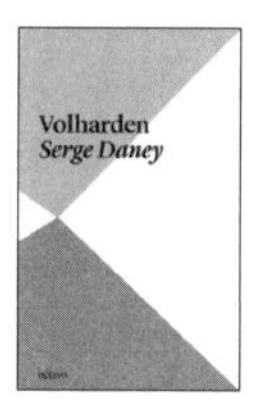
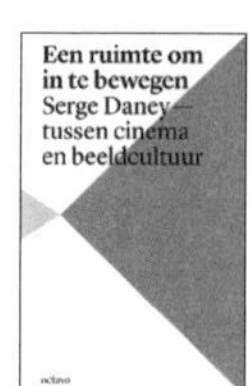

Two related books by and about the French film critic Serge Daney have been published for the first time in the Dutch language, as part of the series 'Text & Context'. The establishment of the consensus society, the development of the attention economy, the bankruptcy of cultural criticism: even for those who do not belong to Daney's generation, which is marked by the trauma of the Second World War, tried and tested by the spirit of May 1968, it is clear that over the past decades a gap has arisen in critical thinking on images and the world, a gap between the world of images and our image of the world. It is as if everything has been engulfed by an overwhelming wave of indifference and banality, in which there is no longer any room for dissensus.

During the last years of his life, Daney's greatest concern became the vanishing of his ultimate object of affection, cinema, into the vortex of the cult of television and information. The problem, according to Daney, is not that there are too many images, but too many images that we have seen over and over again; images that can be easily deciphered but no longer communicate anything at all. 'The shortage of images begins when the two related actions, seeing and showing, lose their self-evident quality and become deeds of protest, as it were,' he wrote in 1991 in 'Montage verplicht. De oorlog, de Golf en het kleine scherm' (Montage Required. The War, the Gulf and the Small Screen), included in the book *Een ruimte om in te bewegen* (A Space in Which to Move: Serge Daney between Cinema and Visual Culture). This was an answer to the reportage at the time on the Gulf War, a conflict that was not only decided on the battlefield but also on television.

For Daney, a self-declared *ciné-fils*, the world expressed in films could not be seen separately from the world surrounding them. Following time-honoured French cinephile tradition, he considered every film an expression of a standpoint, a vision of the world that simultaneously legitimizes and organizes a work. 'Film is an art of showing, presenting. And showing is a gesture, a gesture that forces one to see, to look. Without that gesture you only have pictures. But when something is presented, someone also has to sign for its receipt,' declared Daney in *Volharden*, the second part of this double publication. Criticism was a way of throwing back the ball for Daney; not as just any pass, but a cross pass, as a safeguard to new horizons.

Daney himself traces the arousing of his attitude to his reading of 'Over het abjecte' (On the Abject), an article by Jacques Rivette also included in the essay collection *Een ruimte om in te bewegen*. In this piece on the Holocaust drama *Kapo*, only a single scene is described: 'Look at the shot where Riva kills herself by throwing herself on an electric barbed-wire fence; the man who decides, at that moment, to have a dolly in to tilt up at the body, while taking care to precisely note the hand raised in the angle of its final framing: this man deserves nothing but the most profound contempt.' This condemnation – the ultimate focusing of Jean-Luc Godard's famous dictum, 'tracking shots are a question of morality' – determined the axioms of Daney's thinking and writing. In this article of Rivette's – about a film he never saw – Daney found everything that would continue to nourish his cinephile attitude: the discourse of the *Cahiers du Cinéma* family, which would also become his own; an aversion to filmic airs and graces; an emphasis on aesthetical and ethical justness; and above all, an awareness of the intimate relationship between cinema and history – his cinema, his history.

Volharden (Persevere) is the title of the second book in the 'Text & Context' series. This is Daney's posthumously published 'cine-biography', which besides 'De rijder uit Kapo' (The Tracking Shot in Kapo) originally written for the magazine *Trafic*, also contains a poignant interview with his crony Serge Toubiana. This book presents the scenario of his life: a history of cinema from 1944, the year of *Roma, città aperta* and the discovery of the concentration camps, to 1992, when the contours of a world 'without cinema' became visible; 'that is to say, without the feeling of being part of a people from a special country called cinema'. *Een ruimte om in te bewegen* is a thoughtfully compiled anthology of the pieces Daney wrote for *Cahiers du Cinéma* from 1960 to 1970 and for the daily paper *Libération* from the 1980s onward. The book also contains articles by his forebears (Rivette), his heirs (Olivier Assayas) and his comrades-in-arms (Godard). The last of these immortalized him in the pantheon of the greatest: 'To me Daney was also the end of criticism, as I had known it, which I think started with Diderot: from D to D, Diderot to Daney, only the French make real critics.'

'The question that arises in these loutish times,' wrote Daney in one of his last diary entries, 'is, "What can offer resistance? What can resist the market, the media, fear, cynicism, backwardness, unworthiness?"' (from 'Journal de l'an passé', in: *Trafic*, no. 1, 1991) These are the words of someone who has always reacted against consensus thinking: against the commercial spectacle of formula movies, the programme fillers on television, the retrocessive aestheticization of *Kapo*, the self-satisfied prefab of *Le Grand Bleu*, the cynical reasoning of the Benetton campaigns. Of those campaigns he wrote: 'In a period where contradiction is no longer the motor of anything, the compromise formation that Freudians know so well risks becoming the major trope of social communication.' (See: 'Kind zoekt badwater' [Baby Seeking Bathwater], 1991.) By the beginning of the 1990s, the idea of counterforce, so essential for Daney's generation, seemed to have evaporated, as it were, dispelled by a way of living that that had completely broken with 'those "thirty glorious years" after the war, when there was such a strong hunkering for emancipation and all sorts of "liberation".' (See: 'Montage verplicht' [Montage Required]) His thinking is rooted in a period of thirty years, from Rossellini to the death of Pasolini, which also formed the heart of modern cinema; the cinema of cruelty and compassion that taught him to continuously seek the 'other'. For Daney, cinema was a communal space for dissensus; for sharing and dividing, dreaming and awakening: an echo from another time, an impossible object of desire, an untenable promise of confidence.

Joost de Bloois is an assistant professor at the University of Amsterdam, department of Comparative Literature and Cultural Analysis. He has published extensively on the nexus between culture and the political. Currently, he is editing a special issue of *Rethinking Marxism* on post-autonomist thought (forthcoming in 2013).

Christoph Brunner works as a researcher at the Institute for Critical Theory at the Zurich University of the Arts. He is finishing a PhD thesis on research-creation and aesthetic politics at Concordia University, Montreal. He participates in the editorial collective Inflexions.org and is a member of the SenseLab.ca.

John Byrne is currently programme leader in Fine Art at the Liverpool School of Art and Design (John Moores University). He is also co-director of Static, an organization for creative production in Liverpool (statictrading.com). Byrne has published regularly on the relationships between contemporary art, media and popular culture.

Stoffel Debuysere is active in the field of media culture and media art as a curator, researcher and teacher. He has worked for various cultural organizations and institutions, including Argos, BAM, Impakt and Courtisane. As of 2012, he heads up the research project 'Figures of Dissent: Cinema of Politics, Politics of Cinema', within the auspices of the KASK/School of Arts (Ghent).

Annet Dekker is an independent curator and researcher. She is interested in the influence of new media, science and popular culture on art, and vice versa. Since 2008, she has been working on a PhD thesis on strategies for documenting net art at the Centre for Cultural Studies, Goldsmiths, University of London. See also: aaaan.net (in collaboration with Annet Wolfsberger).

Andrea Fraser is a performance artist. Her recent work includes an essay for the Whitney Biennial 2012 and the performance *Men on the Line: Men Committed to Feminism, KPFA, 1972*. She is a Professor of Art at the University of California, Los Angeles.

Johan Frederik Hartle teaches philosophy of art and culture at the University of Amsterdam (UvA). His research deals with institutional theories of art, the aesthetico-political and the heritage of Marxism. He is currently working on a book about the beauty of leftist politics.

Thomas Hirschhorn is an artist from Switzerland.

Maaike Lauwaert obtained her doctorate in cultural sciences and works as a visual art programmer for Stroom Den Haag. Over the last ten years she has published articles on visual art in magazines such as *Witte Raaf*, *Metropolis M*, *A Prior*, *Mister Motley* and *Tubelight*.

Sven Lütticken teaches art history at VU University Amsterdam. He is the author of *Secret Publicity: Essays on Contemporary Art* (2006) and *Idols of the Market: Modern Iconoclasm and the Fundamentalist Spectacle* (2009). Blog: svenlutticken.blogspot.com.

Roberto Nigro works at the Institute for Critical Theory of the Zurich University of the Arts (ZHDK) and is Program Director at the Collège international de Philosophie in Paris. Prior to that, he taught at various universities in Italy, France, Germany and the USA. His research mainly focuses on post-structuralist theories.

Peter Osborne is director of the Centre for Research in Modern European Philosophy (CRMEP), Kingston University London, and an editor of the UK journal *Radical Philosophy*. His new book, *Anywhere or Not at All: Philosophy of Contemporary Art*, will be published by Verso in early 2013.

Jacques Rancière is a French philosopher. He has written various books, including *Dissensus: On Politics and Aesthetics* (2010).

Gerald Raunig is a philosopher and art theoretician. He works at the Zurich University of the Arts (ZHDK) and is a coordinator for the eipcp (European Institute for Progressive Cultural Policies) of the international research projects *republicart*, see republicart.net, transform. eipcp.net and creatingworlds.eipcp. net. Among other things, he is also a member of the editorial board of *Open* and transversal.eipcp.net/. Recent books in English are *A Thousand Machines* (2010) and *Critique of Creativity* (edited in collaboration with Gene Ray and Ulf Wuggenig) (2011).

Ilse van Rijn is an art critic. She is working on her doctoral thesis, concerning autonomously published artists' texts.

Hito Steyerl works as a filmmaker and author in the area of essayist documentary films and videos, media art and video installations. Her works are located on the interface between cinema and fine arts, and between theory and practice. They centre on the question of media within globalization and the migration of sounds and images.

Steven ten Thije is a research curator affiliated with the Van Abbemuseum and the Universität Hildesheim. He is a coordinator of The Autonomy Project and co-organizer of the Autonomy Project Symposium. Recently, he co-curated Spirits of Internationalism, part of the European collaborative project l'Internationale.

Willem van Weelden is a teacher of media theory and an independent publicist with a background in sociology and visual art who is interested in the effects of new media on the tradition of visual art and art in public space.

CREDITS

Cover Rossella Biscotti, *Italy is a democratic republic founded on labour*, videostill, 2004.

Open Cahier on Art and the Public Domain
Volume 11 (2012) no. 23

Editors Jorinde Seijdel (editor in chief), Liesbeth Melis (final editing)
Contributing editor Sven Lütticken
Advisory council Nicolas Bourriaud, Brian Holmes, Sven Lütticken and Gerald Raunig
English copy editor D'Laine Camp

Dutch-English translations Jane Bemont (editorial and column by Jorinde Seijdel; texts by Johan Hartle, Steven ten Thije, book reviews by Ilse van Rijn, Maaike Lauwaert, Stoffel Debuysere; interview with Franco Berardi)
French-English Nicholas Elliot (discussion Rancière-Hirschhorn)

Graphic design Thomas Buxó and Klaartje van Eijk
Printing and lithography Die Keure, Brugge

Project coordinator Marieke van Giersbergen, NAi Publishers
Publisher Eelco van Welie, NAi Publishers

Open is published twice a year
Open 24 will be published in November

Editorial address
SKOR | Foundation for Art and the Public Domain
Ruysdaelkade 2
1072 AG Amsterdam
the Netherlands
Tel +31 (0)20 6722525
Fax +31 (0)20 3792809
open@skor.nl
www.opencahier.nl

SUBSCRIPTIONS

Abonnementenland
Postbus 20
1910 AA Uitgeest
the Netherlands
0900-2265263 – € 0,10 per minute)
Fax +31 (0)251 310405
www.aboland.nl.

Price per issue
€ 23.50

Subscription prices
(postage included)
the Netherlands: € 32.50
Within Europe: € 39.50
Outside Europe: € 45.00
Students: € 24.50

Subscription cancellation
Cancellations (in writing only) must be received by Abonnementen-land eight weeks prior to the end of the subscription period. Sub-scriptions not cancelled in time are automatically renewed for one year.

open

For a comprehen-
sive overview of
contents accor-
ding to author,
article and
theme, see:
opencahier.nl

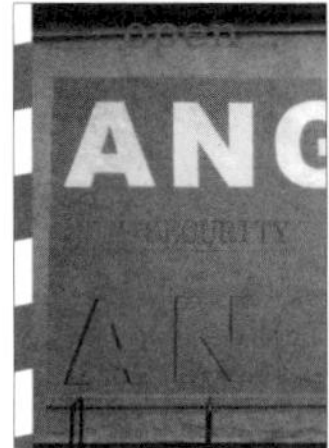

(IN)SECURITY

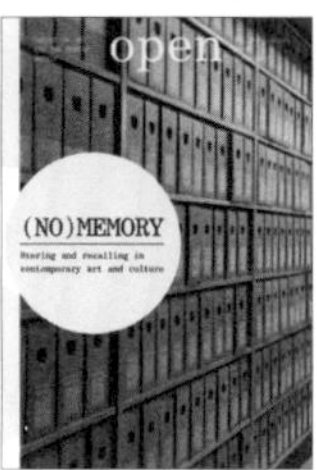

(NO) MEMORY

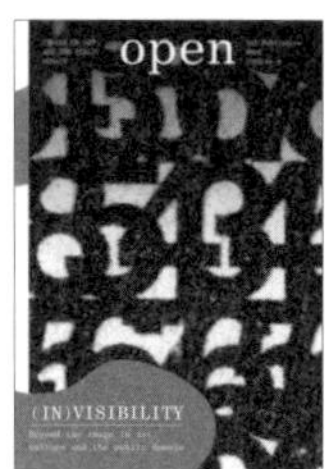

(IN)
VISIBILITY

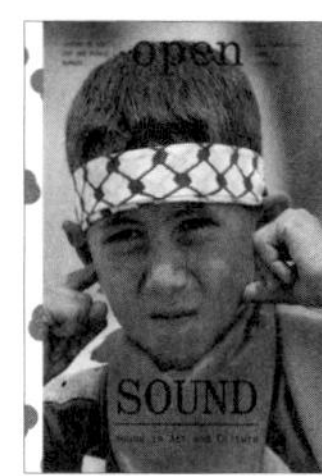

SOUND

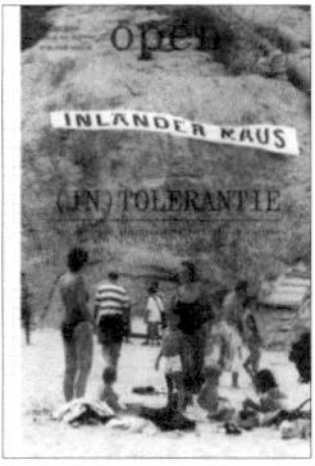

(IN)TOLERANCE

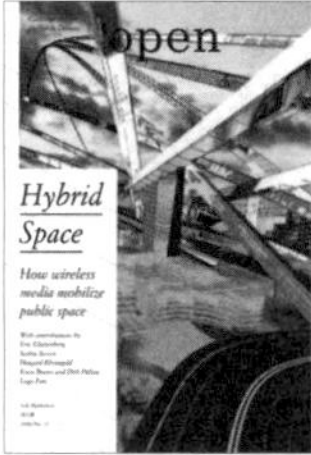

HYBRID SPACE

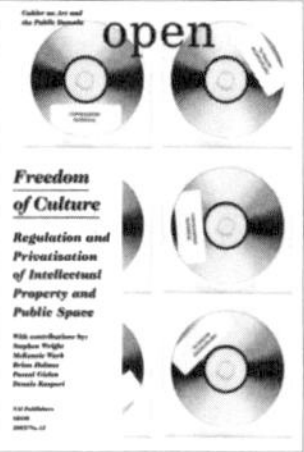

FREEDOM OF
CULTURE

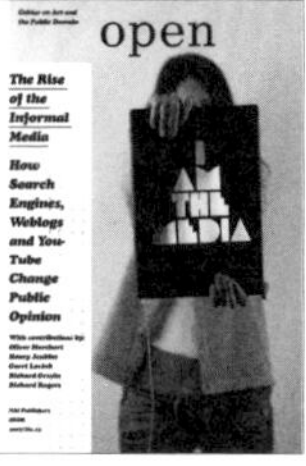

THE RISE OF
THE INFORMAL
MEDIA

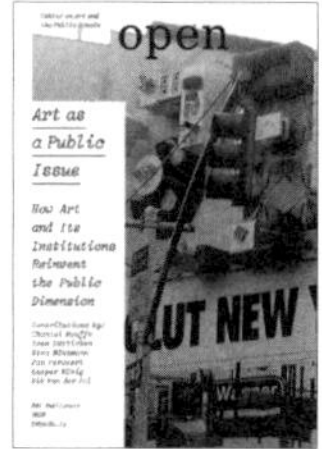

ART AS A
PUBLIC ISSUE

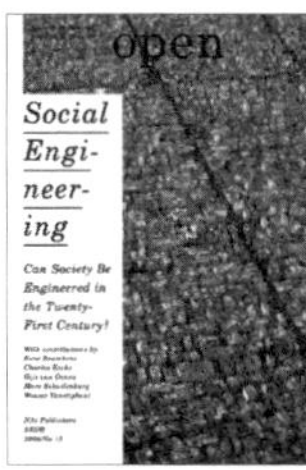

SOCIAL
ENGINEERING

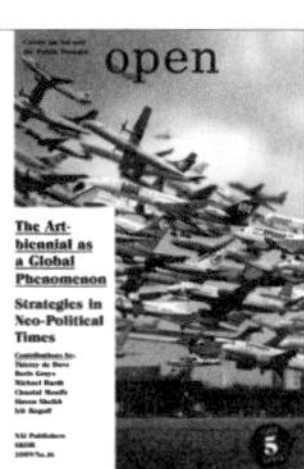

THE ART
BIENNIAL AS
GLOBAL
PHENOMENON

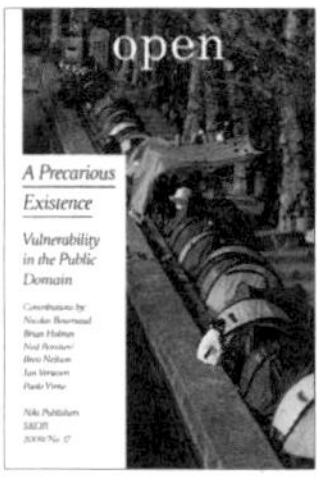

A PRECARIOUS
EXISTENCE

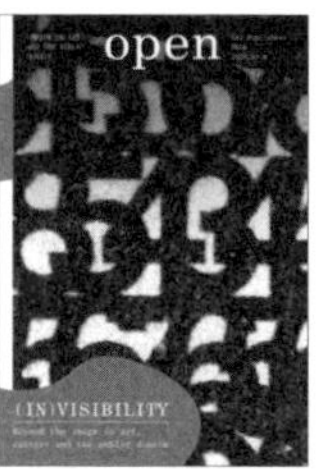

2030:
WAR ZONE

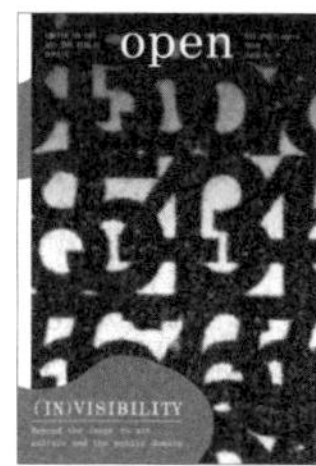

BEYOND
PRIVACY

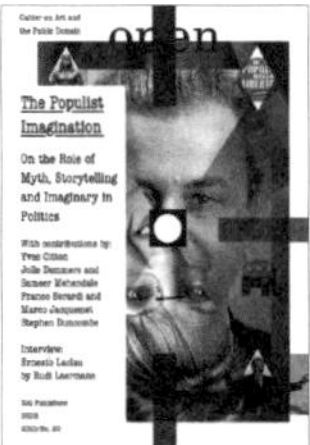

THE POPULIST
IMAGINATION

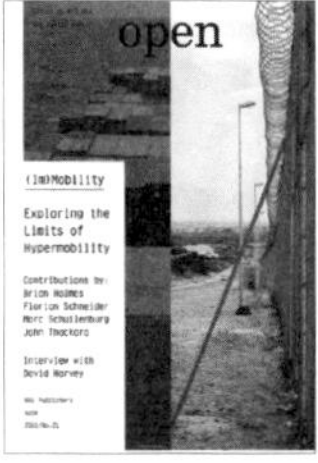

(IM)MOBILITY

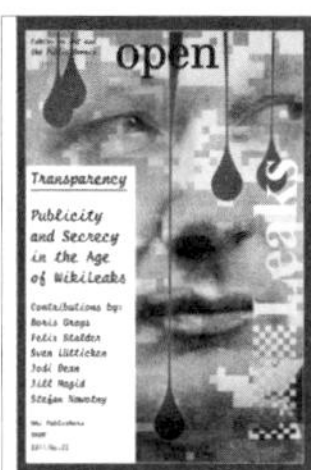

TRANS-
PARENCY

NAi Publishers is an internationally orientated
publisher specialized in developing, producing and
distributing books on architecture, visual arts and
related disciplines.
www.naipublishers.nl info@naipublishers.nl

It was not possible to find all the copyright holders
of the illustrations used. Interested parties are
requested to contact NAi Publishers, Mauritsweg 23,
3012 JR Rotterdam, The Netherlands.

Available in North, South and Central America through
D.A.P./Distributed Art Publishers Inc, 155 Sixth Ave-
nue 2nd Floor, New York, NY 10013-1507, Tel 212
6271999, Fax 212 6279484.

Available in the United Kingdom and Ireland through
Art Data, 12 Bell Industrial Estate, 50 Cunnington
Street, London W4 5HB, Tel 208 7471061, Fax 208
7422319.

SKOR | Foundation for Art and the Public Domain is an
organization whose objective is to realize special art
projects in public and semi-public settings
www.skor.nl info@skor.nl

Printed and bound in Belgium

ISSN 1570-4181
ISBN 978-90-5662-858-1